STUDIES IN
THE PROBLEM OF SOVEREIGNTY

STUDIES IN THE PROBLEM OF SOVEREIGNTY

By
HAROLD J. LASKI

NEW YORK
Howard Fertig
1968

First published in 1917 by Yale University Press

HOWARD FERTIG, INC. EDITION 1968
Published by arrangement with Mrs. Frida Laski

Library of Congress Catalog Card Number: 67-24584

PRINTED IN THE UNITED STATES OF AMERICA
BY NOBLE OFFSET PRINTERS, INC.

Your business as thinkers is to make plainer the way from something to the whole of things; to show the rational connection between your fact and the frame of the universe.

Speeches of Mr. Justice Holmes.

TO

H. A. L. FISHER AND ERNEST BARKER

FELLOWS OF NEW COLLEGE

WITH AFFECTIONATE GRATITUDE

FOREWORD TO THE 1968 EDITION

Studies in the Problem of Sovereignty was written during the First World War, and is reprinted here in an unaltered text.

At the time this book was written, it was Laski's intention to stress the fact that majority rule was not, in itself, the ultimate goal of a democratic state for, he contended, as long as political power was divorced from economic power, there would inevitably be conflict.

Today there is much talk of the one party state, majority rule, and the nature of the democratic process, and Laski would contend that admirable as the state's desire to secure the best life for all its members may be, the injustices of the modern world are largely rooted in the existence of economic privileges.

The degree of success that any state may achieve can only be measured by its ability to realize the equality of its subjects, and throughout his lifetime Laski maintained that the state as it exists today can only obtain a good life for certain of its members, not for the community as a whole.

In short, Laski argued that the accumulation of wealth is not an end in itself and is no longer compatible with democratic institutions. No country has yet been willing to surrender its sovereignty in order to aid in the conditions which alone can banish fear.

FRIDA LASKI
1967

PREFACE

This volume is the first of a series of studies in which I hope to discuss in various aspects the theory of the State. Its starting point is the belief that in such a theory, the problem of sovereignty is fundamental, and that only in the light of its conception can any satisfactory attitude be adopted. It is essentially a critical work, and it is only in the most tentative fashion that I have hinted at what seems to me the right avenue of approach. When I have finished similar studies in the political theory of the Catholic Reaction in France during the nineteenth century, and of the Conciliar Movement in the fifteenth, it may be that I shall be able to attempt a more constructive discussion. But it has not seemed to me entirely purposeless to point out the dangers of an attitude fraught with consequences so momentous to the character of our political institutions.

How much it owes to Maitland and Saleilles and Dr. Figgis, I dare not estimate; but if it sends anyone to their books (and particularly to Maitland's) I shall be well content. I owe much, too, to the work of my friend and colleague, Professor McIlwain, from whose 'High Court of Parliament' I have derived a whole fund of valuable ideas. Nor have I, as I hope, failed to learn the lesson to be learned from the constitutional opinions with which Mr. Justice Holmes has enriched this generation. I would add that it was from Mr. Fisher that I first learned to understand the value of individuality, as it was from Mr. Barker that I first learned the meaning of community.

I should like, too, to associate whatever there is of good in the thought of this book, with the name of my friend, Alec Rowan Herron, Scholar of New College and second-lieutenant in the King's Royal Rifles, who fell at Givenchy in the first year of war. What we have lost in him only those of us who had the rare privilege of his intimate friendship can tell; but I may be permitted to say that it was the opinion of those with the right to judge that a very brilliant career lay before him.

This book could never have been written were it not for the constant and splendid sympathy of my friend, Professor Frankfurter of the Harvard Law School. If I mention that, and the debt it of course owes to my wife, it is not in repayment, but in recognition. They, I know, will understand.

I have to thank the editors of the *American Political Science Review,* the *Canadian Law Times,* the *New Republic,* and the *Journal of Philosophy, Psychology and Scientific Methods* for leave to use material already printed in their pages.

H. J. L.

September 28, 1916.
Harvard University.

CONTENTS

		PAGE
Preface	. . . .	ix
Chapter I.	The Sovereignty of the State .	1
Chapter II.	The Political Theory of the Disruption	27
Chapter III.	The Political Theory of the Oxford Movement	69
Chapter IV.	The Political Theory of the Catholic Revival	121
Chapter V.	De Maistre and Bismarck . .	211
Appendix A.	Sovereignty and Federalism .	267
Appendix B.	Sovereignty and Centralisation .	277
Index	. . . .	289

CHAPTER I

THE SOVEREIGNTY OF THE STATE[1]

HEGELIANWISE, we can not avoid the temptation that bids us make our State a unity. It is to be all-absorptive. All groups within itself are to be but the ministrants to its life; their reality is the outcome of its sovereignty, since without it they could have no existence. Their goodness is gained only through the overshadowing power of its presence. It alone, so to speak, eternally is; while they exist but to the extent to which its being implies them. The All, America, includes, 'implicates' in James' phrase, its constituent states. They are one with it and of it—one and indivisible. Each has its assigned place and function in the great Whole which gives them life. This is essential; for otherwise we should have what Mr. Bradley calls 'a plurality of reals'; which is to destroy the predicated unity.

Of the exaltation of such unity a long history could be written. To speak only of medieval times, it would have to tell of Dante with his *maxime unum* as the *maxime bonum;* nor dare we

[1] Read at the Fourth Conference on Legal and Social Philosophy, at Columbia University, November 27, 1915.

repaint the picture he drew of that world state which is one because its law is one and its spirit also. State must be, Gregory VII will tell us, absorbed in Church; and so the eighth Boniface, perhaps with some lingering thought of Aquinas in his mind, will declare the heresy of dualism and straightway make claim to the lordship of the world. *Binarius numerus infamis*—so it was Aquinas wrote; and so it is that your pope must have the *plenitudo potestatis* and your emperor be *legibus solutus*. Thus will they embody all and transcend the shifting variety of an inconvenient multiplicity.

Your medieval thinker deals in worlds; with the Renaissance is born the national State. But only the perspective is altered. Still the problem is this monistic reduction. How to make of many one was surely the problem Henry VIII confronted when he declared the realm of England to be an empire; for if it is capable of such promotion then is its king imperial, and he may work his will with recalcitrant chancellors who look vainly Romewards. So, too, with the Stuart. He mistakes the popular basis of the Tudor throne, and thinks a sovereignty in practice theoretical also. It is his, he urges, by a right divine. Like another Richard II he feels that the laws are in his own breast; while non-juring Hickes will preach solemnly of the Stuart rectitude as he lays down the gospel of non-resistance.

It seems far off; yet in truth it is very near to us.

It would be no inapt definition of politics in our time to term it the search for social unity. Whatever political problems we may consider upon this fundamental question, we shall always ultimately be driven back. How far, and in what way, is our society one? How far is there an interest of the Whole, a monistic interest, which transcends the interests of the Many who compose that whole? It is a fundamental question; therefore—as the 'Parmenides' bears witness—it is amazingly subtle and difficult. We shall find, I think, that there is one best method of considering our problem. Suppose that on the one hand we adopt the monist solution, what concrete difference will that make to our political life? If we are pluralists, how does that affect our activities? What, in short, are the consequences of our attitude? It is from them we may deduce its truth.

And at the outset, let us note that we tend, in our political thinking, to adopt a sort of mystic monism as the true path of thought. We represent a State as a vast series of concentric circles, each one enveloping the other, as we move from individual to family, from family to village, from village to city, to county, thence to the all-embracing State. We talk of England, Greece, Rome, as single personal forces, transcending the men and women who compose them. We personalise, that is to say, the collective body. 'Rome,' writes Lord Bryce, 'sacrificed her domestic freedom that she might become the mistress of others.'

Here is a Rome beyond her citizens, a woman terrible in the asceticism of her supreme sacrifice.

Clearly the reality of the State's personality is a compulsion we may not resist. But the habit is common to other things also. To the American, New York has a personality no less real than that of the Republic. To the shipowner, Lloyds is not the mere sum of its individual underwriters. When we take any group of people leading a common life, to whom some kindred purpose may be ascribed, we seem to evolve from it a thing, a personality, that is beyond the personalities of its constituent parts. For us that personality is real. Slowly its reality has compelled the law, when dealing with associations, to abandon the theory of fiction. A man who looks at the battlefield of Europe will assuredly not deny that certain personalities, England, France, Germany, are real to the soldiers who die for them. A man who would remain cold to an appeal to stand by Englishmen waxes eloquent over the splendour of England; from all Englishmen he synthesises a thing greater than they. Think of the momentous consequences of such personalising and then ask if we dare attribute fiction to its nature. 'Our fellowship,' wrote Maitland, 'is no fiction, no symbol, no piece of the State's machinery, but a living organism and a real person, with body and members and will of its own.' If this be true, there are within the State enough of these monistic entities, club, trade-union, church, society, town, county, university, each with a group-life, a group-will, to enrich the imagination. Their significance assuredly we may not deny.

Yet, so we are told, the State itself, the society of which they form part, is mysteriously One above them. 'Everywhere the One comes before the Many. All Manyness has its origin in Oneness and to Oneness it returns. Therefore all order consists in the subordination of Plurality to Unity, and never and nowhere can a purpose that is common to Many be effectual unless the One rules over the Many and directs the Many to the goal. . . . Unity is the root of all, and therefore of all social existence.' Here is no mystic thought from the East, but a sober German jurist dealing with the essential political thought of the medieval world. Unity, it is clear, there finds laudation enough. And the State as the expression of that unity enjoys a similar benediction. It, too, must be one and indivisible. Trade-unionists and capitalists alike must surrender the interests of their smaller and antithetic group-persons to the larger demands of that all-embracing One, the State. Of that One it is first that you are part; only in secondary fashion do you belong to church or class or race. In the One differences become harmonised, disappear. There are no rich or poor, Protestants or Catholics, Republicans or Democrats, but all are members of the State. The greatest of ideas takes all others to itself. 'All

Manyness has its origin in Oneness, and to Oneness it returns.'

So may be described the monistic theory of the State. It is a theory of which the importance may not be minimised in our time. That this view—largely perhaps from its evident relation to the dominant philosophy of Hegel—has triumphed not only in modern Germany, but also, in some lesser degree, in modern Europe, is the merest platitude in a world where Treitschke furnishes the theme of drawing-room conversation. A time of crisis unifies everywhere what before bore the appearance of severalty. The exclusive State makes an easy triumph.[2]

We have to admit, so your monist philosopher tells us, that all parts of the State are woven together to make one harmonious whole. What the Absolute is to metaphysics, that is the State to political theory. The unity is logically necessary, for were there independence, one group, as Lotze argued, could never act upon another. Were there independence there would be impenetrability. Yet nothing is so evident as the supreme fact of mutual influence. Pluralism, in an ultimate sense, is therefore impossible; for it would make unintelligible any rational interpretation of society.

Certain implications of this doctrine are worth noting before we attempt any criticism of it. If it be conceded that the analogy of State and

2 On Bismarck and Hegel the reader can consult an admirable paper by Mr. William Clarke in the *Contemporary Review* for January, 1899.

Absolute be justified, clearly just as in metaphysics we can condemn the world as a whole, or praise it as a whole, so must the State be good or bad as a totality. It can not be good or bad in its separate parts. Pessimistic or optimistic, you may be in regard to it, but melioristic you have no right to feel so far as the State is concerned. For that which distinguishes your State must be implied in its parts, however various, *is* in its parts, could we but see it, and an evil part is evil, be it capitalist or labor agitator, only if the State as a totality is evil. We bridge over, in fact, the distinction between right and wrong, between good and bad. It is due only to the limitations of our finite political intelligence. It is not, so to speak, in the State-in-itself. It is only the appearance below which we must penetrate if we would grasp political reality. That is why Mr. Bradley can regard his Absolute—for us the State—as the richer for every disharmony; for that seeming pain is in truth but a minister to joy.

And here clearly enough Sovereignty emerges. The State must triumph and has need of some organ whereby its end may be attained. If we anywhere preach a gospel of non-resistance it is here. We go to war. We must fight with the State whether or no we feel the justice of its cause. When in 1870 the Vatican Council defined papal infallibility Mr. Gladstone was quick to observe that Roman Catholic loyalty was endangered. Did not Sir Robert Peel oppose Catholic emancipation because that sect could not in his view unify its allegiance? Was not the *Kulturkampf* but the expression of Bismarck's conviction that your sovereign must be one and know no fellow? When M. Combes aids in the separation of Church and State, on what other grounds does he base his attack than this,—that only State-rights are real? Corporations—wormlike Hobbes called them—cause but troublesome disease. Forthwith let them disappear that the sovereignty of the State may be unique.

What for us is here of deepest significance is the claim that what the State wills has therefore moral pre-eminence. We pass, if I may be old-fashioned and use Rousseau's terms, from the Will of All to the General Will, and assume their identity. So that force gains a moral sanction because the τό εὖ ζῆν is thereby to be achieved. What the State ordains begins to possess for you a special moral sanction superior in authority to the claim of group or individual. You must surrender your personality before its demands. You must fuse your will into its own. It is, may we not without paradox say, right whether it be right or wrong. It is lack of patriotism in a great war to venture criticism of it. It has the right, as in this sovereign view it has the power, to bind your will into its own. They who act as its organ of government and enforce its will can alone interpret its needs. They dictate; for the parts there is no function save silent acquiescence.

For practical politics there seems no moral rightness in such an attitude as this. We have, in fact, to deem acts right and wrong. We do point to groups within the State, or parallel to it, and urge that they are really harmful and really beneficent. We judge them in reference to themselves. We take what may be appearance as actually constituting reality. We credit, in short, human knowledge. We say that there is something in appearance. If we can not credit it, assuredly there is nothing in which belief is at all possible. Its finite character we freely admit. We can not know all things. We have to be content with a certain specialism, leaving omniscience to the Absolute.

If, as I urge, we know not all things, but some things, if we know not America and Germany, but England and France, nothing of Julius Caesar, but much of Napoleon, then we claim the right to make judgments upon them. They stand by themselves, can be known, that is to say, independently. I do not mean that Julius Caesar is not ultimately connected with Napoleon or that there is no relation between England and America, but simply that there is no necessary relevance between them. Applying this to politics, I mean that we do not proceed from the State to the parts of the State on the ground that the State is more fundamentally unified than its parts, but we, on the contrary, admit that the parts are as real and as self-sufficient as the whole. I do not know England before I know, say, Berkeley Square and London; from Berkeley Square and London I come to know England. But in James' phrase, 'everything you can think of, however vast or inclusive, has, on the pluralistic view, a genuinely "external" environment of some sort or amount. Things are "with" one another in many ways, but nothing includes everything or dominates everything. The word "and" trails along after every sentence. Something always escapes . . . the pluralistic world is thus more like a federal republic than an empire or a kingdom. However much may be collected, however much may report itself as present at any effective centre of consciousness something else is self-governed and absent and unreduced to unity.'

We are urging that because a group or an individual is related to some other group or individual it is not thereby forced to enter into relations with every other part of the body politic. When a trade-union ejects one of its members for refusing to pay a political levy it is not thereby bringing itself into relations with the Mormon Church. A trade-union as such has no connection with the Mormon Church; it stands self-sufficient on its own legs. It may work with the State, but it need not do so of necessity. It may be in relations with the State, but it is one with it and not of it. The State, to use James' terms once more, is 'distributive' and not 'collective.' There are no essential connections.

We are not taking up the position that the State has no relations with these groups. We are simply denying that the parts must be judged by the State,—the individual German, let us say, by the conduct of Germany. We have not to judge of all things in their State-context. Such a relation is a forced relation. It is charging to the account of your individual German things which are really accountable to Germany. We judge his conduct in life in reference to himself and not in reference to the State of which he is part. In the monistic theory of the State he derives his meaning from his relations; in the pluralistic theory, while his relations may be of the deepest significance, it is denied that they are the sole criterion by which a man ought to be judged. So in the pluralistic view of the State, there are, as James said of the pluralist world, 'real losses and real losers,' in the clashing of its parts; nor do these add mysteriously to the splendour of the whole.

How, then, it will be asked, is the will of the State to be made manifest? If the State is but one of the groups to which the individual belongs, there is no thought of unity in his allegiance. The answer to that is the sufficiently simple answer that our allegiance is not as a fact unified. In the event of a great war, for example, as a member of the State you may be called upon to fight; as a member of another group, the Quakers, you may be called upon to resist that demand. It seems clear that little is gained by talk of 'over-riding demands,' of saying, for instance, that the demands of the State are all-important. They are all-important only to the State. The history of societies fatally contradicts the view that in a crisis only the State will have power of compulsion. What of certain miners in South Wales? What of certain Unionists in Ulster? Of militant suffragists? Did not to them the wills of certain groups other than the State conflict with it and prove more intense in their demand? Such marginal cases will in all probability be rare, but there is no sort of guarantee that they will not occur.

Then, it will be protested, you will abolish what lawyers mean by sovereignty. You justify resistance to the State. You deny that each state must possess a legally determinate superior whose will is certain of acceptance. But it is surely evident that no such instrument does exist. We have nowhere the assurance that any rule of conduct can be enforced. For that rule will depend for its validity upon the opinion of the members of the State, and they belong to other groups to which such rule may be obnoxious. If, for example, Parliament chose to enact that no Englishman should be a Roman Catholic, it would certainly fail to carry the statute into effect. We have, therefore, to find the true meaning of sovereignty not in the coercive power possessed by its instrument, but in the fused good-will for which it stands. Men accept its dictates either because their own will finds part expression there or because, assuming the goodness of intention which lies behind it, they are content, usually, not to resist its imposition. But then law clearly is not a command. It is simply a rule of convenience. Its goodness consists in its consequences. It has to prove itself. It does not, therefore, seem wise to argue that Parliament, for example, is omnipotent in a special sense. The power Parliament exerts is situate in it not by law, but by consent, and that consent is, as certain famous instances have shown, liable to suspension. An omnipotence that Cardinal Wiseman can overthrow in 1851, that J. H. Newman can smilingly dissolve in 1875, that constitutes in the Judicial Committee of the Privy Council a tribunal for ecclesiastical causes which clergymen of repute will regard as of no authority, and, therefore, neglect, seems to represent an abstraction of the facts. Where sovereignty prevails, where the State acts, it acts by the consent of men.

What guarantee have we, then, in the pluralist view that the will of the State will prevail? It may seem that this view gives a handle to anarchy. It does not, I believe, give any more handle to anarchy than it at present possesses. If we become inductive-minded and make our principles grow out of the facts of social life we shall admit that the sanction for the will of the State is going to depend largely on the persons who interpret it. The monarchs of the *ancien régime* were legally the sovereign power in France, but their will was not the will of the State. It did not prevail because of the supreme unwisdom of the manner in which they chose to assume that their good was also the popular good. They confused what Rousseau would have called their 'private good' with the 'common good' and Louis XVI paid the penalty on the scaffold. The will of the State obtains pre-eminence over the wills of other groups exactly to the point where it is interpreted with sufficient wisdom to obtain general acceptance, and no further. It is a will to some extent competing with other wills, and, Darwin-wise, surviving only by its ability to cope with its environment. Should it venture into dangerous places it pays the penalty of its audacity. It finds its sovereignty by consent transformed into impotence by disagreement.

But, it may be objected, in such a view sovereignty means no more than the ability to secure assent. I can only reply to the objection by admitting it. There is no sanction for law other than the consent of the human mind. It is sheer illusion to imagine that the authority of the State has any other safeguard than the wills of its members. For the State, as I have tried to show, is simply what Mr. Graham Wallas calls a will-organisation, and the essential feature of such a thing is its ultimate dependence upon the constituent wills from which the group will is made. To argue that the State is degraded by such reduction in nowise alters, so far as I can see, the fact that this is its essential nature. We have only to look at the realities of social existence to see quite clearly that the State does not enjoy any necessary preeminence for its demands. That must depend entirely upon the nature of the demand it makes. I shall find again and again that my allegiance is divided between the different groups to which I belong. It is the nature of the particular difficulty which decides my action.

Nor is this view invalidated by the consideration that the purpose of the State is larger than that of any other conceivable group, does, in fact, comprehend it. I am not at all certain that this is the case. A State may in theory exist to secure the highest life for its members. But when we come to the analysis of hard facts it becomes painfully apparent that the good actually maintained is that of a certain section, not the community as a whole. I should be prepared to argue, for instance, that in the England before the war the ideal of the trade-unions was a wider ideal than that which the State had attained, one is tempted to say, desired to attain. It is possible, again, to say of the Roman Catholic Church that its purpose is wider than that even of a conceivable world-state in the future; for the State concerns itself with the lives of men on earth, while the Roman Catholic Church concerns itself also with their future existence. And, moreover, it is not so much greatness of purpose that seems important as the capacity to secure intensity of affection. This, as

I argued earlier, is surely the explanation of the attitude of those who resist the State. The purpose of their organisation is not more vast, but it comes nearer home to what the individual immediately desires; so it has for him a greater momentary validity. He subordinates the will of the State to the will of his group because the latter accords with his desire or his conscience. I think that any one who reflects on the history of opposition to the State will find that this is, psychologically, the most fruitful source of its understanding.

Now I admit quite freely that I have been discussing a sovereignty far wider than that which lawyers are accustomed to recognise. When a distinguished jurist thinks that 'sovereign power is that which within its own sphere is absolute and uncontrolled,' and when another equally distinguished legal thinker argues that law rests on sovereignty, I can only throw up my hands. For while, for example, in England, the sovereign power is Parliament, and, broadly speaking, only the rules laid down by it will be enforced by the courts, yet Parliamentary opinion, Parliamentary statute, are the result of a vast complex of forces towards which men and groups, within and without the State, make often enough valuable contributions. It seems to me that you can never find in a community any one will which is certain of obedience. That is why Korkunov is profoundly right when he urges that its phenomena can not be regarded as the manifestation of such unity. I can not too greatly emphasise the importance of a phrase used by John Chipman Gray. 'The real rulers of a society,' he says in a striking sentence, 'are undiscoverable.' But with the real rulers must go sovereignty; and if you can not find them it too must be beyond the reach of human insight. When you come to think of it, the sovereignty of legal theory is far too simple to admit of acceptance. The sovereign is the person in the State who can get his will accepted, who so dominates over his fellows as to blend their wills with his. Clearly there is nothing absolute and unqualified about it. It is a matter of degree and not of kind that the State should find for its decrees more usual acceptance than those of any other association. It is not because of the force that lies behind its will, but because men know that the group could not endure if every disagreement meant a secession, that they agree to accept its will as made manifest for the most part in its law. Here, at any rate, we clear the air of fictions. We do not bestow upon our State attributes it does not possess. We hold it entitled to ask from its members that which conduces to the achievement of its purpose not because it has the force to exact their consent, but because what it asks will in the event prove conducive to that end. Further than this we can not go.

There are, in this view, things the State can not demand from its members. It could not, for instance, demand from one of them that he assassinate a perfectly blameless man; for so to demand is to violate for both men the whole purpose for which the State exists. It would have, on the other hand, a clear right to ask from each member such contribution as he can afford to a system of national education, because the modern State has decided that the more educated are its members the more are they likely to fulfil its end. What I mean by 'right' is something the pragmatist will understand. It is something the individual ought to concede because experience has proved it to be good. So when the State demands from one of its members toleration for the religious belief of another as a right each should enjoy, it means that the consequences of toleration are more coincident with the end of the State than the consequences of religious persecution. Our rights are teleological. They have to prove themselves. That is why, I confess, one of the main comforts I derive from the study of Aristotle is the conviction that he attempted to delineate a pragmatist theory of the State. He gave to his rights the rich validation of experience; and surely a right that has no consequences is too empty to admit of worth.

The view of the State I am endeavouring to depict may perhaps be best understood by reference to a chemical analogy. The chemist draws a picture of his molecule—it is a number of atoms grouped together by certain links of attraction each possesses for the other. And when a molecule of, say, hydrogen meets a molecule of oxygen something new results. What is there may be merely hydrogen plus oxygen; but you must treat it as something different from either. So I would urge that you must place your individual at the centre of things. You must regard him as linked to a variety of associations to which his personality attracts him. You must on this view admit that the State is only one of the associations to which he happens to belong, and give it exactly that pre-eminence—and no more—to which on the particular occasion of conflict, its possibly superior moral claim will entitle it. In my view it does not attempt to take that pre-eminence by force; it wins it by consent. It proves to its members by what it performs that it possesses a claim inherently greater than, say, their Church or trade-union. It is no dry *a priori* justification which compels their allegiance, but the solidity of its moral achievement. So, I shall fight for England because I can genuinely accept the rightness of its cause; not because when the call comes I must unheedingly and, therefore, unintelligently obey it.

Surely, too, that State will be the stronger which thus binds to itself its members by the strength of a moral purpose validated. When, for example, your miners in South Wales go on strike, rather than attempt their compulsion by Munitions Acts to obey that for which they feel no sympathy, and thus produce that feeling of balked disposition of which Mr. Graham Wallas has written so wisely, you seek means of finding common ground between their group and yours, you will have done better. Is there not a tremendous danger in modern times that people will believe the legal sovereignty of a State to be identical with its moral sovereignty? Right is a dangerous word—for it is political no less than ethical, and in the hands of a skilful statesman the meaning may be insensibly fused. So it will be preached eventually that where a State, from this theoretic conception of Oneness, has a legal right, it has also a moral right which passes so easily into a moral obligation. Government, then, stands above the moral code applied to humbler individuals. It is almost unconsciously exalted into tyranny. It gains the power to crush out all that conflicts with its own will, no matter what the ethical implication of that will. I can then well understand why to an historian like Treitschke power can be the end of all things. For then power is moral and becomes more profoundly moral as it grows in extent. Is there the slightest historical justification for such a conclusion?

The thing of which I feel afraid, if the State be admitted limitless power, Professor Dewey has expressed felicitously in a single phrase, 'It has been instructed [he is speaking of the German State] by a long line of philosophers that it is the business of ideal right to gather might to itself in order that it may cease to be merely ideal.' Nor is what he urges true of Germany alone. When you hear in Great Britain of unamiable retired colonels on half-pay writing from the comfortable seclusion of a London club that the working-classes must be compelled to do certain things because the existence of the State is threatened, the voice may be the voice of an English colonel, but verily! the spirit of a certain retired German cavalry officer creeps into that voice. The State may ask the workers for their aid; but the condition must assuredly be, that when it fights, their good, no less than its own, is bound up with victory. It seems to me, frankly, that when many of us use the term 'State' at the present time we are performing a mental operation of which the content is essentially different. The State is not the same thing, for instance, to the Kaiser and to Herr Karl Liebknecht. When the former asks for the support of Germans that the State may not perish, he has in mind a thing almost antithetic to what it means for Herr Liebknecht. Is anything gained by ignoring this difference, and urging that this State, so fundamentally different to both men, is to have for both an equally valid claim? Assuredly, as the event proves, that can not be the case.

I have tried to show that the monistic theory of the State, making it sovereign and, therefore, absolute, runs counter to some of the deepest convictions we can possess. I have urged that it will ask from us sacrifices it is against our consciences to give. It may of course be said that such a sacrifice has in it a discipline it is well for men to undergo. But when men begin, at the cost of suffering, to surrender their convictions with a monotonous regularity they will end by surrendering them without a pang. May we not here apply that stinging aphorism of Coleridge—'He who loves Christianity better than truth, will love his sect or Church better than Christianity, and end by loving himself best of all'?

In the realm of philosophy, the last forty years have seen the consistent disruption of absolutisms. In the sphere of politics they are assuredly but the expression of what our rulers are fain to believe from half-instinctive desire. The history of recorded experience seems to show that this kind of dogma is the stumbling-block in the way of all progress. The State has sovereign rights; and those who manipulate it will too often cause it to be used for the protection of existing rights. The two get identified; the dead hand of effete ancestralism falls with a resounding thud on the living hopes of to-day. I said earlier that such absolutism bridges over the distinction between right and wrong. Is it not clearly so? Is it not claimed in Germany that an act is justified when State necessity compels it, and that without reference to the accepted criteria of moral action? In the South African War were there not statesmen who, because they condemned it, were adjudged morally degenerate? Is there not in the United States a tendency to approximate criticism of the constitution to original sin? Please observe that I am only asking questions.

How ever are we to get any worth out of historical experience if such absolutism is to be held valid? Every state then becomes exalted above the moral law. Spain was right in its attack on the Netherlands, and the Netherlands wrong in resisting the attack. Great Britain was right absolutely in the American War of Independence. Truly there is point in Mr. Chesterton's remark that only logic drives men mad.

Such difficulties as this the pluralistic theory of the State seems to me to remove. As a theory it is what Professor Dewey calls 'consistently experimentalist,' in form and content. It denies the rightness of force. It dissolves—what the facts themselves dissolve—the inherent claim of the State to obedience. It insists that the State, like every other association, shall prove itself by what it achieves. It sets group competing against group in a ceaseless striving of progressive expansion. What it is and what it becomes it then is and becomes by virtue only of its moral programme. It denies that the pursuit of evil can be made good by the character of the performer. It makes claim of the member of the State that he undertake ceaseless examination of its moral foundations. It does not try to work out with tedious elaboration the respective spheres of State or group or individual. It leaves that to the test of the event. It predicates no certainty because history, I think fortunately, does not repeat itself. It recognises the validity of all wills to exist, and argues no more than that in their conflict men should give their allegiance to that which is possessed of superior moral purpose. It is in fact an individualistic theory of the State—no pluralistic attitude can avoid that. But it is individualistic only in so far as it asks of man that he should be a social being. In the monist theory of the State there seems no guarantee that man will have any being at all. His personality, for him the most real of all things, is sacrificed to an idol which the merest knowledge of history would prove to have feet of clay.

I am well enough aware that in any such voluntarism as this room is left for a hint of anarchy. To discredit the State seems like enough to dethroning it. And when the voice of the State is viewed as the deliberate expression of public opinion it seems like the destruction of the one uniquely democratic basis we have thus far attained. But the objection, like the play queen in *Hamlet,* protests too much. It assumes the homogeneity of public opinion, and of that homogeneity not even the most stout-hearted of us could adduce the proof. Nor is its absence defect. On the contrary, it seems to me that it is essentially a sign that real thought is present. A community that can not agree is already a community capable of advance. And if public opinion is not homogeneous where and how is it constituted? How will it prevail? I have already raised these questions. I have urged that the proof is not general, but particular, lies in each special occasion as it arises. And that is to postulate a State far from uniquely sovereign, since on occasion it will not prevail as on occasion it may not be right.

I imagine the absolute Hobbes, who has seen internal dissension tear a great kingdom in pieces, hold up hands of horror at such division of power. Maybe I who write in a time when the State enjoys its beatification can sympathise but too little with that prince of monistic thinkers. And the reason is simple enough. It is from the selection of variations, not from the preservation of uniformities, that progress is born. We do not want to make our State a cattle-yard in which only the shepherd shall know one beast from another. Rather we may hope to bring from the souls of men and women their richest fruition. If they have intelligence we shall ask its application to our problems. If they have courage we shall ask the aid of its compelling will. We shall make the basis of our State consent to disagreement. Therein shall we ensure its deepest harmony.[3]

[3] On this whole subject see Mr. Barker's paper in the *Political Quarterly* for February, 1915.

CHAPTER II

THE POLITICAL THEORY OF THE DISRUPTION[1]

I

'OF political principles,' says a distinguished authority,[2] 'whether they be those of order or of freedom, we must seek in religious, and quasi-theological writings for the highest and most notable expressions.' No one, in truth, will deny the accuracy of this claim for those ages before the Reformation transferred the centre of political importance from Church to State. What is too rarely appreciated is the modernism of those writings in all save form. Just as the medieval State had to fight hard for relief from ecclesiastical trammels, so does its modern exclusiveness throw the burden of a kindred struggle upon its erstwhile rival. The Church, intelligibly enough, is compelled to seek the protection of its liberties lest it become no more than the religious depart-

[1] No adequate history of the secession of 1843 has yet been written. What exists is for the most part pietistic in form and content. Perhaps the least unsatisfactory work is that of R. Buchanan, *The Ten Years' Conflict*, Edinburgh, 1850. The Rev. W. Hanna's *Life of Chalmers*, Vol. IV, will be found to contain much material of value, though naturally of a biassed and edifying kind.

[2] J. N. Figgis, *From Gerson to Grotius*, p. 6.

ment of an otherwise secular organisation. The main problem, in fact, for the political theorist is still that which lies at the root of medieval conflict. What is the definition of sovereignty? Shall the nature and personality of those groups of which the State is so formidably one be regarded as in its gift to define? Can the State tolerate alongside itself churches which avow themselves *societates perfectae,* claiming exemption from its jurisdiction even when, as often enough, they traverse the field over which it ploughs? Is the State but one of many, or are those many but parts of itself, the One?

There has been no final answer to these questions; it is possible that there is no final answer. Yet the study of the problems they raise gives birth to certain thoughts which mould in vital fashion our theory of the State. They are old enough thoughts, have, indeed, not seldom been deemed dead and past praying for; yet, so one may urge, they speak with living tongues. At certain great crises in the history of the nineteenth century they have thundered with all the proud vigour of youth. A student of modern ultramontanism will not fail to find its basis in the stirring phrases of an eleventh century Pope; just as he will find set out the opposition to it in the stern words of a fifteenth century Chancellor of Paris University. Strikingly medieval, too, is the political theory no less of the Oxford Movement than of that *Kulturkampf* which sent a German prince a second time to Canossa. And in a piece of Scottish ecclesiastical history the familiar tones may without difficulty be detected.

II

On the eighteenth of May, 1843, Dr. Welsh, the Moderator of the General Assembly of the Established Church of Scotland, took a course unique in the history of his office. He made no formal address. Instead, there came the announcement that as a protest against an illegal usurpation of the rights of the Church, and in order to maintain that freedom of action essential to the Assembly, two hundred and three of its members were compelled to sever their connexion with it.[3] With a large number of lay and clerical followers he then withdrew to a hall that had been prepared near by. Prayer was offered up; the moderatorship of the seceding members was offered to, and accepted by, Dr. Chalmers; and the Assembly then proceeded to constitute itself the governing body of the Free Church of Scotland.[4]

To the adequate understanding of this striking event some brief survey of early Scottish ecclesiastical history from the time of Knox's invasion is necessary. Recognised as the State Church in 1567,[5] from the first a conflict of authority arose. The first General Assembly had approved the

[3] Buchanan, II, 594.

[4] Buchanan, II, 607.

[5] Calderwood, II, 388-389. Innes, *Law of Creeds in Scotland*, p. 14. I can not too fully acknowledge my debt to this admirable book.

Book of Discipline of the Church, but the Council from the outset was unwilling to sanction it.[6] As a result, the General Assembly proceeded to act as though this approval, having reference to an ecclesiastical matter, was unnecessary. The Book was made an essential part of the Church's doctrinal constitution; and from the first the conception of a *societas perfecta* was of decisive importance.[7] On the threshold, therefore, of ecclesiastical history in Reformation Scotland a problem arises. For while the State never accorded the desired recognition, it is at least equally clear that the Church was in nowise dismayed by that refusal. Jurisdiction, indeed, was awarded to it by the State in the same year;[8] but in terms ominous of future discord. To 'declaration' no objection could be raised; but the insertion of a power to 'grant' clearly cut away the ground from under the feet of Knox's contention that the power of jurisdiction was inherent without parliamentary enactment.[9] Yet, in a sense, the Church's desire for the recognition of its complete spiritual powers may be said to have received its fulfilment in 1592, when it was declared that an Act of Supremacy over Estates Spiritual and Temporal[10] 'shall nowise be prejudical nor derogate anything

[6] Innes, *op. cit.*, p. 20.

[7] As is apparent in Melville's famous sermon before James I. Cf. Innes, p. 21.

[8] Acts of Parliament of Scotland, III, 24.

[9] Knox, *History of Reformation*, p. 257, and cf. McCrie's *History of the Scottish Church*, p. 44.

[10] 1584, c. 129. The so-called 'Black Acts,' Calderwood, IV, 62-73.

to the privilege that God has given to the spiritual office-bearers in the kirk, concerning the heads of religion . . . or any such like essential censures specially grounded and having warrant of the word of God."[11] Here, at any rate, was the clear admission that in the ecclesiastical sphere the Church possessed powers no less than divine; and it may not unjustly be assumed that when the State affixed civil punishment to ecclesiastical censure, it stamped those powers with its approval.[12]

What pain the Church had to endure in the next century of its history it lies outside our province to discuss; for our purpose its relation to the Revolution Settlement is the next halting place. An Act of 1669 had asserted the royal supremacy over the Church;[13] this was rescinded,[14] and another statute, passed simultaneously, adopted the Westminster Confession as part of the law.[15] At the same time the abuse of lay patronage—complained of from the outset—was abolished, and the right of ministerial appointment was practically vested in the full congregation.[16]

Clearly, there was much of gain in this settle-

[11] 1592, c. 116. Acts Par. Scot., III, 541. Calderwood, V, 162.
[12] 1593, c. 164.
[13] Acts Par. Scot., VII, 554.
[14] 1690, c. 1.
[15] 1690, c. 5.
[16] McCrie, *op. cit.*, p. 418.

ment, though about its nature there has been strenuous debate. To Lord President Hope, for instance, the Act of 1690 was the imposition of doctrine on the Church by the State, and so the recognition of the latter's supremacy.[17] But it is surely clear that what actually was done was to recognise the Church practice without any discussion of the difficult principles involved;[18] and even that silent negligence did not pass uncriticised by the General Assembly.[19] Yet, whatever the attitude of the State, it is certain that the Church did not conceive itself either by this Act, or in the four years' struggle over subscription to its formularies, to have surrendered any part of its independence.[20]

The next great epoch in the history of the Scottish Church was, naturally, its connexion with the Act of Union in 1707. So securely was it deemed to be settled that the Commissioners appointed in 1705 to treat with the English Parliament were expressly excluded from dealing with the Scottish Church;[21] and the Act of Security was deemed fundamental to the Union. The Act pledged the Crown to the maintenance of the Acts

17 See his judgment in the Auchterarder case. Robertson's Report, II, 13.

18 This is well brought out by Mr. Innes, *op. cit.*, p. 45.

19 Innes, p. 46.

20 Buchanan, I, 136. Cf. Hetherington's *Hist. of Ch. of Scotland*, p. 555; and for some strenuous criticism of William's attitude, Mr. McCormick's *Life of Carstares*, pp. 43-44.

21 McCrie, *op. cit.*, 440.

of 1690 and 1693 in terms as solemn as well may be;[22] and it may reasonably be argued that Parliament conceived itself as then laying down something very like a fundamental and irrevocable law.[23] These may, indeed, have been no more than the recognition of a specially solemn occasion, for it is certainly difficult otherwise to understand why in 1712 Parliament should have restored that lay patronage which the Act of 1690 abolished.[24] The measure was carried through with indecent haste by the Jacobite party, and a spirit of revenge seems to have been its chief motive.[25] From this time until almost the close of the eighteenth century the General Assembly protested against the measure; but Parliament could not be moved.[26]

That such a course was a violation of the Act of Security is, of course, evident without argument; but the chief significance of the repeal lay rather in the future than in the past. 'The British legislature,' Macaulay told the House of Commons,[27] 'violated the Articles of Union and made a change in the constitution of the Church of Scotland. From that change has flowed almost all the dissent now existing in Scotland. . . . year after year the General Assembly protested against

22 Mathieson, *Scotland and the Union*, p. 183. Innes, *op. cit.*, p. 58.

23 See Sir H. W. Moncrieff, *Churches and Creeds*, p. 19.

24 10 Anne, c. 12.

25 Woodrow's *Correspon.*, 1, 77, 84. Carstares' *State Papers*, 82. Burnet, VI, 106-107.

26 Innes, *op. cit.*, p. 60.

27 Speeches, II, 180.

the violation, but in vain; and from the Act of 1712 undoubtedly flowed every secession and schism that has taken place in the Church of Scotland.' This is not the exaggeration of rhetoric, but the moderation of sober truth. For what the Act of 1712 did, in the eyes at least of the Church, was essentially to deal with a right fundamentally ecclesiastical in its nature, and so to invade the Church's own province. It became clear to the leaders of the Church that so to be controlled was in fact to sacrifice the Divine Supremacy to which they laid claim. Christ could no longer be the Supreme Head of the Presbyterian Church of Scotland if that Church allowed lay authority to contravene His commands. So that when it came, as they deemed, to a choice between His Headship and freedom on the one hand, and endowment and State control on the other, they could not hesitate in their duty.

III

The Disruption takes its immediate rise in an Act of the General Assembly in 1834.[28] There had long been signs in the Church of a deep dissatisfaction with the Establishment. It meant, so, at least, the voluntarists urged, enslavement to the civil power; and to the answer that the Church had spiritual freedom, the existence of civil

[28] Buchanan, I, 280 ff.

patronage was everywhere deemed a sufficient response.[29] If voluntaryism was to be combated, some measures against intrusion must be taken; and it was upon the motion of Lord Moncrieff, himself a distinguished lawyer, that it was declared, 'a fundamental law of the Church that no pastor shall be intruded on any congregation contrary to the will of the people.'[30] Patronage, in fact, was not abolished; but, clearly, the need for congregational approval deprived it of its sting. It is important to note that not even among the opposition to the measure was any sort of objection urged against the competency of the General Assembly to enact it.[31]

The challenge, however, was not long coming. Within six months of the decision of the General Assembly, a vacancy occurred in the parish of Auchterarder in Perthshire. Lord Kinnoull, the patron, made his presentation to a Mr. Robert Young, and the congregation promptly rejected him by an overwhelming majority.[32] The Presbytery then took steps to carry out the Veto Law.[33]

Lord Kinnoull was not long in deciding to contest his rights in the Courts. Into the history of the struggle it is unnecessary to go in any detail; the merest outline of its history must here

29 *Ibid.*, I, 282.

30 *Ibid.*, I, 293. The motion was carried by 184 votes to 138. *Ibid.*, p. 307.

31 *Ibid.*, I, p. 325.

32 Buchanan, I, 399.

33 *Ibid.*, I, 408.

suffice.[34] The Court of Session refused to accept the defence of the Presbytery that the rejection of a presentee for unfitness concerned only the ecclesiastical authorities, and laid it down that the Church was dependent upon the State.[35] To this the General Assembly replied almost immediately in a resolution which bound the Church 'to assert, and, at all hazards, to defend' not only the freedom of the Church from outside interference but also its determination to exact obedience to the Veto Law.[36] The consequence of this defiance was the Strathbogie cases. A Presbytery, following the decision of the Court of Session, neglected the Veto Act of 1834 and was suspended by the General Assembly.[37] The Court of Session at once protected it,[38] and ordained that the vetoed minister should be received.[39] The Presbytery of Auchterarder was condemned in damages to Lord Kinnoull and Mr. Robert Young;[40] a minority of the Presbytery opposed to the Veto Act was declared to be capable of acting as the Presbytery proper and the majority was inhibited from any interference.[41] The rejected presentee was forced upon

[34] The reader will find full details in Buchanan and the cases noted below.

[35] The First Auchterarder case. Robertson's report.

[36] Buchanan, II, 479.

[37] *Ibid.*, II, 284.

[38] 1840, 2 Dunlop, p. 585.

[39] 1840, 3 Dunlop, p. 282.

[40] 1841, 3 Dunlop, p. 778. This is the second Auchterarder case.

[41] 1843, 5 Dunlop, p. 1010. This is the third Auchterarder case. I

the Presbytery;[42] and the condemnation of the Presbytery by the General Assembly for disregard of the Veto Act was put on one side.[43] Truly the outcome of Knox's nationalism had been different from the conception of its founder.[44]

Attempted interference by statesmen proved of no avail. Upon so fundamental a problem the Church could not compromise, since it was her independence as a society that was at stake. Parliament would not surrender the position taken up by the Court of Session and the House of Lords. 'No government would recommend,' Mr. Bruce told the House of Commons,[45] 'and no Parliament would ever sanction the pretensions of the Church of Scotland, because if those claims were granted, they would establish a spiritual tyranny worse and more intolerable than that of the Church of Rome from which they had been delivered.' If it was less outspoken, the government, in the persons of Sir James Graham and Sir Robert Peel, was equally emphatic.[46] The Assembly took the only step that lay in its power. It presented a formal Claim of Right in 1842[47] which set out the theory of its position. This refused, the adherents to that

have not discussed the judgments of Brougham and Cottenham L. C. in the Lords, as they add nothing to the Scottish opinions.

42 1840, 3, D. 283.

43 1843, 5 Dunlop, p. 909.

44 Buchanan, II, 194.

45 Hansard, 3d Series, Vol. LXVII, p. 442, March 8, 1843.

46 Hansard, 3d Series, Vol. LXVII, pp. 382, 502. See also below.

47 Buchanan, II, 633.

Claim presented their Protest[48] in the following year, and withdrew from the Assembly to form the Free Church of Scotland.

IV

The party of which Dr. Chalmers was the distinguished leader had, whatever its deficiences, the merit of maintaining a consistent and logical position. The Church to them was a society itself no less perfect in form and constitution than that of the State. To the latter, indeed, they acknowledged deference in civil matters, 'a submission,' Chalmers himself said, which was 'unexcepted and entire.'[49] That to which they took so grave an objection was the claim laid down by the authorities of the State, to an absolute jurisdiction over every department of civilised life. They admitted, in brief, her sovereignty over her own domain; it was when she entered a field they held to be without her control that the challenge was flung down. 'The free jurisdiction of the Church in things spiritual, the Headship of Christ, the authority of His Bible as the great statute book not to be lorded over by any authority on earth, a deference to our own standards in all that is ecclesiastical . . . these are our principles.'[50] To them, therefore, the hand which was laid upon the Church was an un-

48 Innes, Appendix K.
49 *Life of Chalmers,* Vol. IV, p. 199.
50 *Life of Chalmers,* loc. cit.

hallowed hand; for when it thus struck at the foundation of her life it insulted the word of God.

The position of the Free Church is not different from that advocated by all who have accepted the principles of the Presbyterian system. It is a State of which the sovereignty is vested in the General Assembly. It acknowledges no superior in the field with which it deals. That sovereignty is sanctioned by a right which even in high prerogative times would have seemed to its adherents a thousand times more sacred than its kingly analogue.[51] The sovereignty of the State over its own concerns is not denied; but its universality would never have been admitted. The distinction between the societies must be maintained, otherwise the grossest absurdities would follow.[52] So Chalmers can make his striking claim. 'In things ecclesiastical,' he told a London audience in 1838,[53] 'we decide all. Some of these things may be done wrong, but still they are our majorities which do it. They are not, they can not, be forced upon us from without. We own no head of the Church but the Lord Jesus Christ. Whatever is done ecclesiastically is done by our ministers as acting in his name and in perfect submission to his authority . . . even the law of patronage, right or wrong, is in force not by the power of the State, but by the permission of the Church, and, with all

[51] Cf. Figgis, *Divine Right of Kings,* ed. 2, p. 267.

[52] *Jus Divinum,* p. 42, quoted in Figgis, *op. cit.,* p. 275.

[53] *Life of Chalmers,* Vol. IV, p. 54. Mr. Gladstone was present at and deeply impressed by these lectures. Morley (Pop. ed.), I, 127.

its fancied omnipotence, has no other basis than that of our majorities to rest upon. It should never be forgotten that in things ecclesiastical, the highest power of our Church is amenable to no higher power on earth for its decisions. It can exclude; it can deprive; it can depose at pleasure. External force might make an obnoxious individual the holder of a benefice; it could never make him a minister of the Church of Scotland. There is not one thing which the State can do to our independent and indestructible Church but strip her of her temporalities. *Nec tamen consumebatur*—she would remain a Church notwithstanding, as strong as ever in the props of her own moral and inherent greatness; and although shrivelled in all her dimensions by the moral injury inflicted on many thousands of her families, she would be at least as strong as ever in the reverence of her country's population. She was as much a Church in her days of suffering, as in her days of outward security and triumph; when a wandering outcast with naught but the mountain breezes to play around her, and naught but the caves of the earth to shelter her, as when now admitted to the bowers of an Establishment. The magistrate might withdraw his protection and she cease to be an establishment any longer; but in all the high matters of sacred and spiritual jurisdiction she would be the same as before. With or without an establishment, she in these is the unfettered mistress of her doings. The king by himself or by his representative might be the spectator of our proceedings; but what Lord Chatham said of the poor man's house is true in all its parts of the Church to which I have the honour to belong; "in England every man's house is his castle; not that it is surrounded with walls and battlements; it may be a straw-built shed; every wind of heaven may whistle round it; every element of heaven may enter it; but the king can not—the king dare not." '

A more thoroughgoing rejection of the royal supremacy on the one hand, and the legal theory of parliamentary sovereignty on the other, could hardly be desired. It is clear that an invasion of the Church's rights is not contemplated as possible. The provinces of State and Church are so different that Parliament could only interfere if the rights it touched originated with itself. Such a general theory of origin the adherents of Presbyterianism strenuously repudiated. 'Our right,' Professor McGill told the General Assembly of 1826,[54] 'flows not from Acts of Parliament. . . . I maintain the powers and rights of the Church of Scotland . . . to determine the qualifications of its members; that their right in this matter did not originate with Parliament; that Parliament left this right untouched and entire to the courts of this Church—nay, that of this right it is not in the power of Parliament to deprive them. . . . The religion of Scotland was previously embraced by the people on the authority of the word of God, before it was

[54] Quoted in Moncrieff, *The Free Church Principle* (1883), p. 35.

sanctioned by Parliament.' It is obvious that the relation of State to Church is, in this view, that of one power to another. Nor did Professor McGill stand alone in his opinion. When, in 1834, Lord Moncrieff considered the competency of the General Assembly to enact the Veto Law, he expressly repudiated the contention that any part of the ecclesiastical constitution except its establishment was derived from the civil power.[55] The establishment, indeed, they regarded as no more than a fortunate accident.[56] They were even accustomed to point to the distinction between their own position, and that of the Church of England. 'The Scottish Establishment,' said Chalmers in 1830,[57] 'has one great advantage over that of England. It acknowledges no temporal head, and admits of no civil or parliamentary interference with its doctrine and discipline. The State helps to support it, but has nothing to do with its ministrations.' Nor did he shrink from the obvious conclusion to such a situation. 'They may call it an imperium in imperio,' he said, thirteen years later,[58] 'they may say that we intrude upon the legitimate power of the civil courts or the civil law. It is no more an intrusion on the civil law than Christianity is an intrusion on the world.' He resented the suggestion that the Church was

[55] See Moncrieff, *The Free Church,* p. 37.

[56] Buchanan, I, 367.

[57] *Life,* III, 270.

[58] March 16, 1843. Moncrieff, *op. cit.,* p. 111. The remark is all the more significant since it is made on the eve of the Disruption.

dependent on the State. 'We are not,' he told the General Assembly of 1842,[59] 'eating the bread of the State. When the State took us into connexion with itself, which it did at the time of the Union, it found us eating our own bread, and they solemnly pledged themselves to the guarantees, or the conditions, on which we should be permitted to eat their bread in all time coming.' To the Church, clearly, the Act of Security was the conclusion of an alliance into which Church and State entered upon equal terms. It was an alliance, as Lord Balfour of Burleigh pointed out,[60] 'with the State as a State in its corporate capacity,' the union for certain purposes of one body with another. But it certainly was not conceived by the Church that its acceptance of an Establishment was the recognition of civil supremacy. Otherwise, assuredly, it could not have been argued, as in the resolution of the General Assembly of 1838,[61] that 'her judicatories possess an exclusive jurisdiction founded on the word of God,' which power ecclesiastical 'flows immediately from God and the Mediator Jesus Christ.'

Such, in essence, is the basis, as well of the Claim of Right in 1842, as of the final Protest in the following year. The one is a statement of the minimum the Church can accept; the other is the explanation of how acceptance of that minimum

59 Moncrieff, *op. cit.*, p. 102.

60 Hansard, 5th Series, Vol. XIII, February 12, 1913, p. 119.

61 Innes, *op. cit.*, p. 73.

has been denied. In ecclesiastical matters, the function of the civil courts was neither to adjudicate nor to enquire, but to assist and protect the liberties guaranteed to the Church.[62] The maintenance of those liberties is essential to its existence, since without them, it cannot remain a true Church. Were it to admit any greater power in the civil courts, it would be virtually admitting the supremacy of the sovereign; but this is impossible since only Jesus Christ can be its head. Not only, so the Claim holds, can the admission not be made, but the State itself has admitted the rightness of the Church's argument.[63] Already in 1842 the Claim foreshadows the willingness of the Church to suffer loss of her temporalities rather than admit the legality of the Courts' aggression.[64] The protest of the following year does no more than draw the obvious conclusion from this claim. An inherent superiority of the civil courts, an inhibition of the ordinances of the General Assembly, the suspension or reduction of its censures, the determination of its membership, the supersession of a Presbyterian majority, all of these decisions of the Court of Session, 'inconsistent with the freedom essential to the right constitution of a Church of Christ, and incompatible with the government which He, as the

62 Buchanan, II, 633.

63 Buchanan, II, 634, 'the above-mentioned essential doctrine and fundamental principle . . . have been by diverse and repeated Acts of Parliament, recognised, ratified and confirmed.'

64 Buchanan, II, 647.

Head of his Church, hath therein appointed distinct from the civil magistrate,"[65] must be repudiated. So that rightly to maintain their faith, they must withdraw from a corrupted Church that they may reject 'interference with conscience, the dishonour done to Christ's crown, and the rejection of his sole and supreme authority as king in his Church."[66]

It is worthy of remark that this is the position taken up by counsel for the Church in the Auchterarder case. 'If the Call be shown to be a part of the law of the Church,' Mr. Rutherford argued before the Court of Session,[67] it is necessarily a part of the law of the land,—because the law of the Church is recognised by the State: and if the Veto Act, in regulating that call, has not exceeded the limits within which the legislature of the Church is circumscribed, it is impossible, in a civil court, to deny the lawfulness of its enactments.' From the standpoint of the Church it is clear that this is theoretically unassailable. If the Church has the right to regulate her own concerns, she must have the right to regulate appointment of ministers. If, as a Rutherford of two centuries earlier argued,[68] 'the Church be a perfect, visible society, house, city and kingdom, Jesus Christ in *esse et operari;* then the Magistrate, when he cometh to be Christian, to help and nourish the Church, as

65 *Ibid.*, II, 649.

66 Buchanan, *loc. cit.*, 650.

67 Robertson's Report, I, 356.

68 Quoted in Figgis, *Divine Right of Kings*, p. 278.

a father he can not take away and pull the keys out of the hands of the stewards.' The State admitted her law to be its law in the Act of Security. The only question, therefore, that called for decision was the problem of whether the principle of non-intrusion was ecclesiastical or not. If it was, then clearly it was not *ultra vires* the General Assembly, and, unless the Act of Security were to be rendered nugatory, the civil court must uphold the Church's plea. In that event, to remedy the wrongs of the Church does not lie with the civil court. 'The question is,' so Mr. Rutherford urged,[69] 'whether an abuse by the Church of her legislative powers will justify the interposition of this court. It has been maintained on the other side that it will in all cases. I maintain the reverse of the proposition, that however competent it may be for the State, by the power of the legislature, to withdraw their recognition of a jurisdiction which is no longer exercised so as to warrant the continuance of the confidence originally imposed, it is not within your province.' 'In matters ecclesiastical,' he said again,[70] 'even if the Church acts unjustly, illegally, *ultra vires,* still the remedy does not lie with this court—nor can your lordships give redress by controlling the exercise of ecclesiastical functions when in the course of completing the pastoral relation.' Mr. Bell, the junior counsel, even went as far as to

[69] Robertson, I, 382.
[70] *Loc. cit.,* I, 383.

urge the Court not to hazard its dignity 'by pronouncing a judgment you can not enforce.'[71]

It is to be observed that the Presbyterian theory is not the assertion of a unique supremacy. It did not claim a sovereignty superior to that of the State. Rather, indeed, did they take especial care to explain the precise limitations of their demand. 'He was ready to admit,' Sir George Clerk told the House of Commons in 1842,[72] 'the Church of Scotland is ready to admit, that in all civil matters connected with that Church, the legislature had a right to interfere. The Church of Scotland did not refuse to render unto Caesar the things that were Caesar's, but it would not allow of an interference with its spiritual and ecclesiastical rights.' Mr. Buchanan, the historian of the Disruption, and one of its leading figures, explained at length the difference between the two organisations. 'It is,' he wrote of the Church,[73] 'no rival power to that of the State—its field is conscience; that of the State is person and property. The one deals with spiritual, the other with temporal things, and there is therefore not only no need, but no possibility of collision between the two, unless the one intrude into the other's domain.' Mr. Fox Maule, who was the authorised spokesman of the General Assembly in Parliament,[74] went so far as to say that even a claim to mark out the boundaries

[71] *Loc. cit.*, I, 124.

[72] Hansard, 3d Series, Vol. XXXV, pp. 575-581.

[73] Buchanan, II, 25.

[74] *Ibid.*, II, 572.

between the civil and the ecclesiastical provinces he would repudiate 'because it was fraught with danger to the religious as well as the civil liberties of the country.'[75] 'He was aware,' he remarked,[76] 'that it was difficult at all times to reconcile conflicting jurisdictions; but for one he would never admit that when two Courts, equal by law and by the constitution, independent of each other, came into conflict upon matters however trifling or however important, so that one assumed to itself the right to say that the other was wrong, there was no means of settling the dispute. As he read the constitution, it became Parliament, which was the supreme power, to interfere and decide between them.'[77] The separation of the two powers is, finally, distinctly set forth by the Claim of Right in 1842. 'And whereas,' it states,[78] 'this jurisdiction and government, since it regards only spiritual condition, rights and privileges, doth not interfere with the jurisdiction of secular tribunals, whose determinations as to all temporalities conferred by the State upon the Church, and as to all civil consequences attached by law to the decisions of Church Courts in matters spiritual, this Church hath ever admitted, and doth admit, to be exclusive and ultimate as she hath ever given and inculcated

[75] Hansard, 3d Series, Vol. LXVII, p. 356, March 7, 1843.

[76] *Ibid.*, p. 367.

[77] Yet a doubt must be permitted whether the Free Church party would have accepted an hostile decision even of Parliament. Chalmers, certainly, had not such doubts of his position as to think of mediation.

[78] Buchanan, II, 634.

implicit obedience thereto.' Than this no statement could well be more plain.

Mr. Figgis, indeed, has doubts of this conclusion. 'Presbyterianism,' he has written,[79] 'as exhibited in Geneva or Scotland, veritably claims, as did the Papacy, to control the State in the interests of an ecclesiastical corporation.' Certainly this fairly represents the attitude of Knox;[80] and it is the basis of the able attack on that system by Leslie and Bramhall in the seventeenth century.[81] Yet the vital conception of the two kingdoms, separate and distinct, was put forward in the first epoch of Scottish Presbyterian history by Andrew Melville;[82] and it is safe to say that the attempt thus to define the limits of authorities basically conceived as distinct is the special contribution of Presbyterianism to the theory of political freedom. The difference is of importance since it constitutes the point of divergence between ultramontanism and the Scottish system. The one teaches the supremacy of the ecclesiastical power, the other its co-ordination with the civil. Cardinal Manning, indeed, in the course of those controversies arising out of the definition of papal infallibility in which he played so striking a part,[83]

79 *Divine Right of Kings,* p. 186. But in the preface to his second edition Mr. Figgis considerably modifies his conclusion.

80 Cf. Works, IV, 539.

81 Cf. Leslie, *The New Association* and Bramhall's *A Warning to the Church of England.*

82 As Mr. Figgis notes, *Divine Right of Kings,* p. 286.

83 See his *Caesarism and Ultramontanism,* 1874.

went so far as to claim that every Christian Church makes the same demand of the State as the communion to which he belonged, and urged that the theories of Presbyterian writers are in substance papalist.[84] But Mr. Innes, in a very brilliant essay, was able most conclusively to dispose of this claim.[85] A theory of mutual independence is as far as possible removed from papalism.[86] The conscience of the State and that of the Church are kept as separate in Presbyterian theory as they have been combined in that of Hildebrand and his successors. Cardinal Manning, indeed, was (probably unconsciously), a fervent upholder of the Austinian theory of sovereignty; and he found his sovereign in the will of the Universal Church as expressed by its pontiff. But not even the boldest opponent of Presbyterianism can accuse it, outside its own communion,[87] of an Austinian bias. It is the antithesis of what Mr. Innes well terms the 'centralised infallibility' of the Roman system.[88]

Not, indeed, that contemporaries were wrong

[84] See his article in the *Contemporary Review* for April, 1874.

[85] See his paper 'Ultramontanism and the Free Kirk' in the *Contemporary Review* for June, 1874.

[86] Though the Encyclical *Immortale Dei* of 1885 in Denziger's *Enchiridion,* pp. 501-508, and Newman's *Letter to the Duke of Norfolk* are, as I hope to show in a later paper, very akin to the Presbyterian theory; and the Jesuits of the seventeenth century worked out a similar claim.

[87] I say outside because the General Assembly claims a control that is very like that of an Austinian.

[88] *Contemporary Review,* Vol. 24, p. 267.

who judged that, equally in 1843 as in 1870, the implicitly Austinian doctrines of Erastianism were at stake. 'We can not,' said the Catholic *Tablet,*[89] 'avoid seeing that on this question they have taken their stand on the only principles which, as Catholics, we can respect . . . their cry is down with Erastianism, and so is ours.' 'When the Civil Courts,' said the *North British Review,*[90] 'assumed the power of determining the whole matter, . . . the controversy was forced to assume its true character as in reality involving the very essence of the spiritual independence of the Church.' And Macaulay, who fought Edinburgh in the election of 1841, regretted that he could not teach the anti-Erastians some straightforward whig doctrine.[91]

V

Not less firm than that of Chalmers and his party was the stand taken by the opponents of the Scottish Church. It is, indeed, possible to find two, and perhaps three, different theories of the relations between Church and State in the various judicial opinions upon the Auchterarder and its connected cases; but all of them, with a single exception,[92] are traceable to a single basic principle. The judges found a conflict between two

89 Quoted in *Fraser's Magazine* for July, 1843.
90 *North British Review,* 1849, p. 447.
91 Trevelyan's *Life* (Nelson ed.), II, 57.
92 That of Lord Medwyn, see below.

societies—the Church and the State. Which was to prevail? Was the State to be deemed inferior to the Church, since the latter was grounded upon divine authority? 'Such an argument,' said Lord MacKenzie,[93] 'can never be listened to here.' In general, the attitude of the Courts seemed to imply an acceptance of the argument used by the Dean of Faculty in his speech against the Presbytery of Auchterarder. 'What rights,' he asked,[94] 'or claims had any religious persuasion against the State before its establishment. . . . When he (Mr. Whigham) described the establishment of the National Church as a compact . . . he took too favourable a view of the matter for the defenders. For any such compact implies the existence of two independent bodies, with previous independent authority and rights. But what rights had the Church of Scotland before its establishment by Act of Parliament to assert or surrender or concede?' He put forward, in fact, the concession theory of corporate personality.[95] There were no rights save those which the State chose to confer; and the Church of Scotland was merely a tolerated association until the Act of Security legalised its existence. This seems to have been the judicial attitude. Lord Gillies emphatically denied the possibility of looking upon

93 Middleton v. Anderson, 4 D. 1010.

94 Robertson, I, 185.

95 See my paper on 'The Personality of Associations' in the *Harvard Law Review* for February, 1916.

the Act of Security as a compact. 'I observe,' he said,[96] '. . . that it is an improper term. There can be no compact, properly speaking, between the legislature and any other body in the State. Parliament, the king, and the three Estates of the Realm are omnipotent, and incapable of making a compact, because they cannot be bound by it.' Even Lord Cockburn, in his dissenting judgment, based his decision rather on the supposed historic basis for the Veto Law than on the co-equality of Church and State.[97] The Lord President went even further in his unqualified approval of Erastian principles. The Church, he held, has no 'liberties which are acknowledged . . . *suo jure,* or by any inherent or divine right, but as given and granted by the king or any of his predecessors. . . . The Parliament is the temporal head of the Church, from whose acts and from whose acts alone, it exists as the national Church, and from which alone it derives all its powers.'[98] He would not for a moment admit that a conflict of jurisdiction between Church and State might occur, for, 'an Establishment can never possess an independent jurisdiction which can give rise to a conflict . . . it is wholly the creation of Statute.'[99] The General Assembly possessed no powers, but

96 Robertson, II, 32.

97 Robertson, II, 359.

98 Robertson, II, pp. 2, 4, 5, 10.

99 Cuninghame v. Lainshawe, Clark's report of the Stewarton case, 1843, p. 53.

only privileges.[100] It could not be a supreme legislature, for there could only be one such body in a State. Any other situation 'would be irreconcilable with the existence of any judicial power in the country."[101]

To Lord Meadowbank the Church of Scotland seemed comparable to a corporation to which as an 'inferior and subordinate department' of itself the State had given the right to make bye-laws. But its power was limited. It was a statutory creation which could exercise only the powers of its founding Act. 'The civil magistrate,' he said,[102] 'must have authority to interpose the arm of the law against what then becomes an act of usurpation on the part of the ecclesiastical power. Were it otherwise, anarchy, confusion and disaster would inevitably follow.' So, too, did Lord MacKenzie urge the final supremacy of the legislature, though, very significantly, he admitted that a churchman might think differently. 'The subjection of the Assembly,' he said,[103] to the State, 'is not owing to any contract between Church and State, but simply to the supreme power of the legislature, which every subject of this country must obey. . . . I repeat therefore that when the question is whether anything is illegal as being contrary to Act of Parliament, it is utterly vain to cite any act of the Assembly as supporting it in any degree.'

100 Robertson, II, 23.

101 *Loc. cit.*

102 Robertson, II, 88.

103 Robertson, II, 121.

Here, of a certainty, was the material for ecclesiastical tragedy. The difficulty felt by the majority of the Court is one that lies at the root of all discussion on sovereignty. Anarchy, so the lawyer conceives, must follow unless it be clearly laid down at the outset that beyond the decision of Parliament as interpreted by the Courts there can be no question. It is not a question of spheres of respective jurisdiction. The legislature of the State, the king in Parliament, exercises an unlimited power.[104] If the legislature be sovereign, then comparison between its powers and those of any other body becomes impossible since it follows from the premise that what Parliament has ordained no other organisation can set aside. Clearly, therefore, to the jurist, the claim of the Presbyterian Church to be a *societas perfecta* was *ab initio* void; for that claim would involve the possession of a sovereignty which theory will admit to none save king in Parliament.[105] That was what the Lord President meant by his assertion that the Church possessed not rights but privileges; for rights it could hold only by virtue of an unique supremacy, whereas privilege emphasised the essential inferiority of its position. The Courts, in fact, were denying the doctrine of the

104 This is of course the simple doctrine of parliamentary sovereignty discussed by Professor Dicey in the first chapter of his *Law of the Constitution*. It is very effectively criticised in the last chapter of Professor McIlwain's *High Court of Parliament*.

105 Cf. 'The Sovereignty of the State,' *supra*.

two kingdoms. Where the Presbyterian saw two States within society one of which happened to be his Church, the lawyer saw no distinction between society and the State and held the Church to be but an arm of the latter. By grace of Parliament the Church might legislate on matters purely ecclesiastical and a certain comity would give respect to its decisions. But the power was of grace and the respect was merely courtesy; for the definition of ecclesiastical matters in no way lay with the Church's jurisdiction.[106] Clearly between such an attitude as this, and the theories of Dr. Chalmers there could be no compromise. The premises of the one denied the axioms of the other. The Church dare not admit what Lord Fullerton called 'the supposed infallibility of the Court of Session'[107] without destroying its own independence. Nor could there be grounds for such a course. 'No church,' the pious Buchanan told the General Assembly of 1838,[108] 'could ever be justified in obeying another master than Christ.' It was useless to contend that if state-endowed the Church must be unfree, for it was on the basis of freedom that endowment had been accepted. The demands of the Court of Session would make the oath of ministerial obedience a mockery.[109] So was the issue joined.

106 Robertson, II, 37. Per Lord Gillies.

107 Buchanan, I, 465.

108 *Ibid.*, I, 472.

109 *Ibid.*, I, 478.

VI

The attitude of the ministry was in an important way different from that of the Court of Session. It was, indeed, very akin to that of the Moderate Party in the Church itself, of which the able Dr. Cook was the leader.[110] To him the Church was not the creature of the State. It was independent. There were the two provinces, civil and ecclesiastical, but where a difference arose between the two powers the ultimate decision must rest with the Courts of Law. 'When any law,' he urged in 1838,[111] 'is declared by the competent (civil) authorities to affect civil right, the Church can not set aside such a law . . . so to do would be to declare ourselves superior to the law of the land.' To him the claim of the Church seemed little less than an attempt at the erection of a new popery, and he refused from the outset to identify it with liberty of conscience.[112] The acceptance of an establishment made, in his view, a vital difference. It meant that the Church accepted the secular definition of its powers, and that resistance to such definition was tantamount to rebellion.[113] He did not deny the Headship of Christ. But he did believe, 'that there may be ground for diversity of

[110] The reader of Mr. Buchanan's work should be warned that the writer's prejudices lead him consistently to misrepresent Dr. Cook's attitude.

[111] Buchanan, I, 481. II, 21.

[112] *Ibid.*, II, 24.

[113] *Ibid.*, II, 261.

opinion as to what is comprehended under that Headship in all cases,' and the decision, in an ambiguous case where conflict arose between Church and State, seemed to him to belong to the State.[114] He was impressed, as the Court of Session was impressed, with the impossibility of arriving at a decision if the co-ordination of powers be admitted, and it was clearly upon their grounds that he urged the Church to give way. It was this difference between established and voluntary churches which finally weighed with Sir Robert Peel. The right of the Roman Catholics or the Protestant Dissenters absolutely to control those who choose to submit to their jurisdiction was unquestionable. The State would attempt no interference with it. 'But if,' he pointed out,[115] 'a Church chooses to have the advantage of an establishment and to hold those privileges which the law confers—that Church, whether it be the Church of Rome, or the Church of England, or the Presbyterian Church of Scotland, must conform to the law.' To him the position taken up by the Church was inadmissible since it involved the right to determine the limits of its jurisdiction. That could be done only by 'the tribunal appointed by Parliament, which is the House of Lords.' Nor did Sir James Graham, upon whom the defence of the government's

[114] *Ibid.*, II, 516. Cf. this with Manning's view that the power to fix the limits of its own power was essentially the right of the Church. *The Vatican Decrees* (1875), p. 54.

[115] Hansard, 3d Series, Vol. LXVII, p. 502, March 8, 1843.

attitude mainly rested, offer any greater consolation to the Church. 'They declare,' he told the House of Commons,[116] 'that any Act of Parliament passed without the consent of the Church and nation shall be void and of none effect. . . . I think that to such a claim . . . no concession should be made.' Since the sphere of jurisdiction between Church and State had not been defined, to admit the Presbyterian claim would be to admit 'the caprice of a body independent of law,' with the result that no dispute could ever admit of settlement. The Church was established by the State and was spiritually bound by the terms of its establishment. If it was not the creature of the State, 'still the state employs the Church on certain terms as the religious instructor of the people of Scotland,' and the employé was virtually demanding the right to lay down the conditions of its employment. That demand could not be admitted; for those conditions were embodied in statutes of which the interpretation must rest with the supreme civil tribunal. The Church was definitely inferior, as a source of jurisdiction, to the House of Lords. 'These pretensions,' he said,[117] 'of the Church of Scotland as they now stand, to co-ordinate jurisdiction, and the demand that the government should by law recognise the right of the Church to determine in doubtful cases what is spiritual and what is civil,

[116] *Ibid.*, March 7, 1843, pp. 382 ff.
[117] *Ibid.*

and thereby to adjudicate on matters involving rights of property, appears to me to rest on expectations and views so unjust and unreasonable, that the sooner they are extinguished the better.'

Some points of importance deserve to be noted in this connexion. The Church, certainly, did not claim the right to decide the nature of its jurisdiction.[118] What in fact it claimed was the essentially historic grant of a right to control its own affairs. To itself, that right, admitted in 1690, and doubly confirmed in 1705, was wantonly violated in 1712; and the Church was compelled to regard that Act as a nullification of the fundamental law made but seven years previously. The real head and centre of the whole problem was thus the theory of parliamentary sovereignty. The Church could not conceive an inherent right in Parliament to disregard an obligation assumed with such solemnity. Nor, equally, was it within the competence of the courts to disregard an Act which the Church, wrongly or rightly, condemned. For them there was no such thing as a fundamental law. They could not, with the Act of 1712 before them, announce that patronage was an ecclesiastical question and therefore within the competence of the General Assembly for so to do would be not merely to question the sovereignty of Parliament, but also to admit that the General Assembly was a co-ordinate legislature with Par-

[118] See above the references at notes 60 and 61.

liament. A new theory of the State was required before they would admit so startling a proposition.

A second point is of interest. In the judgment of Lord Medwyn there is a theory of Church and State, which, impliedly at least, was also the theory of Sir Robert Peel.[119] A voluntary Church possesses the authority and the rights claimed by the Church of Scotland; but when the alliance with the State was made the rights must be regarded as surrendered. All that the Church can do is to break the agreement, should it feel dissatisfied with the results of the alliance. But, as a fact, it was not law in 1838, and it is not now law, that a voluntary association is independent of the State in the degree claimed by the Scottish Church. If our antagonism to such societies has not found such open expression as in France,[120]—if, in brief, we have had no *loi le Chapelier*[121]—that is rather because by implication the power of control is already to hand. For, in the view of the State, immediately a Church receives property upon condition of a trust the State is the interpreter of that trust, and will interfere even with an unestablished Church to secure its enforcement.[122] Lord Medwyn and Sir Robert Peel were claiming

119 Cf. Innes p. 74 and the interesting note on that page.

120 Cf. Combes, *Une Campagne taïque,* p. 20—the citation from the Duc de Broglie.

121 And article 29 of the *Code Pénale* forbids associations of more than twenty persons even for social purposes. Seilhac, *Syndicat Ouvriers* (1902), p. 64.

122 See my paper, 'Trusts in favour of Religious Bodies' in the *Canadian Law Times* for March-April, 1916.

for the State a sovereignty far less than that of orthodox legal doctrine.[123] For if the Church once take any step which involves property-relations, it brings itself within the scope of the civil law; and its own inherent rights can not be a ground of contest against the supremacy of Parliament.[124] Allegiance to the law is absolute, since the law does not admit degrees of acceptance. What Lord Justice Clerk Hope said as to the effect of statute remains as true in relation to a voluntary body as in relation to the Established Church of which he spoke. 'Their refusal to perform the ecclesiastical duty is a violation of a statute, therefore a civil wrong to the party injured, therefore cognisable by Courts of Law, therefore a wrong for which the ecclesiastical persons are amenable to law, because there is no exemption for them from the ordinary tribunals of this country if they do not perform the duties laid upon them by statute.'[125] Clearly, Disruption was the one outlet from this impasse.

VII

One last judicial theory deserves some consideration. In his brilliant dissenting judgment, Lord Jeffrey took a ground very different from that of his brethren.[126] His whole conception of

123 Sir F. Pollock has protested (10 L. Q. R., 99) that English lawyers do not accept this view; it is certainly the theory of the Courts.

124 Robertson, II, 121.

125 Kinnoull v. Ferguson, March 10, 1843, 5 D. 1010. Innes, p. 82.

126 See Robertson, II, 380 ff.

the problem was based on his belief that once Lord Kinnoull had presented Mr. Young to the living of Auchterarder, the proceedings became ecclesiastical in nature; and for the Court of Session to force Mr. Young upon the Presbytery was to intrude 'in the most flagrant manner almost that can be imagined on their sacred and peculiar province. It would be but a little greater profanation if we were asked to order a Church Court to admit a party to the Communion Table,[127] whom they had repelled from it on religious grounds, because he had satisfied us that he was prejudiced in the exercise of his civil rights by the exclusion."[128] Lord Jeffrey, in fact, argues that there is a method of discovering the right province of any action of which the exact nature is uncertain. The result of the action ought to be considered, and if that result be fundamentally ecclesiastical rather than civil, the Courts ought to treat the case as the concern of an independent and co-ordinate jurisdiction—the Church Court. He pointed out that practically every action has in some sort a civil result. 'When the General Assembly,' he said,[129] 'deposes a clergyman for heresy or gross immorality, his civil interests, and those of his family suffer to a pitiable extent. But is the act of deposition the less an ecclesiastical proceeding

127 But this has now been done in the Church of England. See Bannister v. Thompson [1908], pp. 362, and on the rule for Prohibition R. v. Dibden [1912], A. C., 533.

128 Robertson, II, 372.

129 Robertson, II, 362.

on that account?' He adopts, it is clear, a pragmatic test of the ownership of debatable ground. The limits of jurisdiction are not, as in Chalmers' view, so clearly defined at the outset as to make collision impossible. Rather is its possibility admitted and frankly faced. What Jeffrey then suggested as the true course was to balance the amount of civil loss Lord Kinnoull would suffer against the ecclesiastical loss of the Church; if that were done, he urged that the Church would have suffered more, and he therefore gave his decision in its favour. The argument is a valuable contribution to that pragmatic theory of law of which Professor Pound has emphasised the desirability.[130]

VIII

It was a dictum of Lord Acton's that from the study of political thought above all things we derive a conviction of the essential continuity of history. Assuredly he who set out to narrate the comparative history of the ideas which pervade the Disruption of 1843 would find himself studying the political controversies of half a thousand years. For than the questions the Disruption raised it is difficult to find more fundamental problems; nor has there been novelty in the

130 27 *Harvard Law Review*, 735. For a splendid example of the way in which the theory can be worked out see his paper in 29 *Harvard Law Review*, 640.

answers that then were made. The theory of those who opposed the Free Church has its roots far back in the Reformation. It can be paralleled from Luther and Whitgift, just as the theory of Chalmers and his adherents is historically connected with the principles with which Barclay confronted Ultramontanism, and the Jesuits a civil power that aimed at supremacy.[131]

The Presbyterians of 1843 were fighting the notion of a unitary state. To them it seemed obvious that the society to which they belonged was no mere cog-wheel in the machinery of the State, destined only to work in harmony with its motions. They felt the strength of a personality which, as they urged, was complete and self-sufficient, just as the medieval state asserted its right to independence when it was strong enough not merely to resent, but even to repudiate, the tutelage of the ecclesiastical power. They were fighting a State which had taken over bodily the principles and ideals of the medieval theocracy. They urged the essential federalism of society, the impossibility of confining sovereignty to any one of its constituent parts, just as Bellarmine had done in the seventeenth century and Palmieri and Tarquini in even later times.[132] If there seems something of irony in such a union, the Miltonic identification of priest and presbyter will stand

[131] Figgis, *From Gerson to Grotius,* p. 63.

[132] Cf. Figgis, *op. cit.,* p. 184.

as voucher for it.[133] The problem which Presbyterian and Jesuit confronted was, after all, at bottom fundamentally identical. We must not then marvel at the similarity of the response each made.

Nor was the attitude of the Court of Session less deeply rooted in the past. Historically, it goes back to that passionate Erastianism of Luther which was the only answer he could make to the Austinianism of Rome.[134] If, in the nineteenth century, the divinity he claimed for civil society has disappeared, the worship of a supposed logical necessity in unified governance—itself a medieval thing[135]—has more than taken its place. Lord President Hope seems to have been as horrified at the implicit federalism of the Free Church as was good Archbishop Whitgift at the federalism of Cartwright.[136] He does not understand the notion of the two kingdoms and so falls back on the stern logic of parliamentary sovereignty. The State, so it is conceived, can not admit limitations to its power; for from such limitation anarchy is eventually the product. Therefore the societies

133 It is a matter of great interest that the Presbyterians, like the Jesuits, should have had two quite distinct theories of the State. In the seventeenth century one has to distinguish sharply between that of men like Cartwright and that of the Presbyterians in the Parliaments of Charles I. The latter was definitely Erastian and it was against that theory that Milton intelligibly inveighed. Cf. Figgis, *Divine Right of Kings,* Chapter IX.

134 Works, Jena ed., 12, 339.

135 Cf. Maitland's *Gierke,* p. 102.

136 Shype, *Life of Whitgift,* II, 22 ff.

within the State can exist only on sufferance; and if the England of 1843 did not emulate the France of sixty years later, it was from no want of theorising about the rights of congregations.[137] It is one of the curiosities of political thought that just as in the medieval Church insistence on the unity of allegiance should ultimately have led to the Reformation, yet its consequence should have been the creation of an organism demanding no smaller rights than its predecessor. The State, like the Church of past days, is set over against the individual, and stout denial is given to the reality of other human fellowships.

Between two such antithetic ideals compromise was impossible. The assertion of the one involved the rejection of the other. If the State, theoretically, was in the event victorious, practically it suffered a moral defeat. And it may be suggested that its virtual admission in 1874 that the Church was right[138] is sufficient evidence that its earlier resistance to her claims had been mistaken. If its resistance was mistaken, the source of error is obvious. A state that demands the admission that its conscience is supreme goes beyond the due bounds of righteous claim. It will attain a theoretic unity only by the expulsion of those who doubt its rectitude. It seems hardly worth while

[137] Mr. Figgis, both in his *From Gerson to Grotius* and *Churches in the Modern State* attacks very bitterly the Austinianism of M. Combes as seen in his *Campagne Laïque* but I do not feel that he understands the provocations to which the Republic was subjected.

[138] Innes, p. 113.

to discuss so inadequate an outlook. The division of power may connote a pluralistic world. It may throw to the winds that omnicompetent State for which Hegel in Germany and Austin in England have long and firmly stood the sponsors. Yet insofar as that distinction is achieved will it the more firmly unite itself to reality.

CHAPTER III

THE POLITICAL THEORY OF THE OXFORD MOVEMENT[1]

I

IF, in its broader aspects, Tractarianism is no more than the English side of that reactionary romanticism which, on the Continent, drove men like Schlegel back to the ideals of the Roman Church,[2] in a more narrow sense, it is to certain great political causes that we must look for its origin.[3] The Church of England ceased to derive benefit from that indifference which, in an age of benevolent complacency, had shielded it from criticism. 'The Church of England,' Bentham remarked with a calm joy,[4] 'is ripe for dissolution.' The famous *Black Book* which John Wade flung

1 For the purposes of this paper I have regarded the movement as ending with the conversion of Manning rather than of Newman. There is, of course, a sense in which the movement has not yet ended. In that view Mr. Figgis' *Churches in the Modern State* might be read as the lineal successor to Pusey's tract on the royal supremacy.

2 Cf. V. F. Storr, *Development of English Theology During the Nineteenth Century*, pp. 126 ff.

3 Cf. Church, *The Oxford Movement*, p. 1, n. 1.

4 Church of Englandism, Works, II, 199. Cf. Stanley, *Life of Arnold*, I, 326. *Fraser's Magazine*, March, 1835, p. 247. *Quarterly Review* (1834), Vol. 50, p. 509.

in 1820 at an outraged aristocracy[5] did much to reveal a state of affairs with which not even the most comfortable could express contentment. There had been for some time signs of movement from within. The evangelism of Knox and Simeon, of Milner and of Wilberforce, had been essentially a protest of spiritual insight against political worldliness;[6] and if the movement was distinguished rather by its moral, than by its mental strength, there was good reason to see in men like Daubeny and Knox the hope of a great intellectual renaissance.[7]

Simultaneously with the hopes of this revival, the growth of liberal ideas in the second and third decades of the nineteenth century did much to destroy the privileged position of the English Church. The repeal, in 1828, of the Test and Corporation Acts placed the Dissenters on an equal political level with Anglicans. In the next year Roman Catholic emancipation followed; and when, in 1832, the Reform Bill was forced upon a reluctant House of Lords, it must have seemed to indignant Tories that the flood gates of democracy had been opened.[8] It was certainly possible

5 D. N. B., Vol. 58, p. 416.

6 Cf. Storr, *op. cit.*, p. 63 ff.

7 Mr. Storr, indeed, contends that Knox anticipated most of the characteristic ideas of the Tractarians, *op. cit.*, p. 85.

8 Sir John Walsh is an admirable index of this attitude. See his voluminous pamphlets especially *Popular Opinions on Parliamentary Reform Considered* (London, 1832), pp. 7, 12, 16, and Colonel Stewart's *Examination of the Principles and Tendencies of the Ministerial Plan of Reform* (Edinburgh, 1831). Scarlett, *Letter to Lord Milton* (London,

no longer to see Church and State as convertible terms. The State was accepting as its fully qualified members men who by no possible stretch of the imagination could be deemed Anglican in outlook. There were even thinkers of repute, like Arnold, to whom the peculiar identity of the Church of England counted as nothing,[9] but who simply desired a vague, generalised Christianity as the best of citizenship.[10]

It was scarcely remarkable that there should be deep apprehension for the future. 'The Church of England,' wrote the *Quarterly Review* in 1834,[11] 'is as a beleaguered city.' Even the placid Greville was convinced that its reform must be undertaken;[12] and an able writer in the next year went so far as to maintain that 'the only point worthy of consideration was how that reform may be effected so as at once to occasion the least amount of hazard to the party about to be reformed,"[13] while James Mill complacently speculated as to how best the Church might be transformed into a kind of gigantic mechanics institute.[14]

1831), p. 37, 'I hold it as a maxim that every government which tends to separate property from constitutional power must be liable to perpetual revolutions.'

9 Cf. Newman's question as to Arnold, *Apologia* (ed. Wilfrid Ward), p. 134.

10 Cf. Stanley, *Life of Arnold*, Vol. I, pp. 205, 207, 333. II, p. 133, and his consequent opposition to Jewish emancipation, II, p. 40, 44.

11 Vol. 50, p. 509.

12 Greville, III, 206.

13 *Fraser's Magazine*, March, 1835, p. 247.

14 *London Review*, July, 1835. Cf. L. Stephen, *English Utilitarians*, II, 57.

It was into such an atmosphere that the Ministry of Lord Grey flung their bombshell of Irish Church Reform. The English Church in Ireland had long been the object of fierce and bitter attack. The establishment of a small minority, it was supported by the tithes of an alien community. It had means that were, unquestionably, more than sufficient to its end. The collection of its revenues had long been one of the plagues of the Home Secretary. At last the ministry decided upon a drastic reform. If State support was continued, nevertheless ten of the bishoprics were suppressed;[15] and it was perhaps even more striking that in his admission of its abuses,[16] Lord John Russell went out of his way to state that where Church funds could be more profitably utilised they should be confiscated.[17] It was long since the Church had received so thoroughgoing a challenge.

Newman has told[18] us how bitter was his resentment against the Liberals when news of the event travelled out to Italy. It was not the Bill itself so much as the movement of which it was the striking manifestation that angered him. 'It was,' he wrote,[19] 'the success of the Liberal cause which

15 Brodrick and Fotheringham, *History of England from 1801-1837*, p. 322.

16 Greville (ed. of 1874), Vol. III, pp. 9, 267. Lord Grey had already warned the bishops to set their house in order. Storr, *op. cit.*, p. 250.

17 Walpole, *Life of Lord John Russell*, I, 197.

18 *Apologia* (Ward's ed.), p. 134.

19 *Loc. cit.*

fretted me inwardly. I became fierce against its instruments and its manifestations.' He hurried home to England with the perception clearly in his mind that a great work had been committed to his charge.[20] Five days later Keble, already famous as the author of the *Christian Year,* from his pulpit in the University Church, attacked the impious hands of the government in his famous sermon on 'National Apostasy.' From that utterance the Oxford Movement takes its rise.[21] It was a protest not merely against a particular measure. The Oxford group felt that 'the Government's real object was to gratify the priests by the abolition of the hierarchy of the Church of England as a first step to the entire destruction of the Church's status and property, and the formation of a Roman Catholic establishment; but they did not venture to avow this motive and pretended that the measure was for the purpose of reforming and strengthening the Church itself . . . the shock upon the introduction of this sacrilegious bill was electric. The bill called upon Newman and his friends to resist as one man the enactment of laws contrary to the first principles of the Church's discipline, divesting Christians of spiritual privileges not originally bestowed by the State, and which the State could not take away.'[22] It was

[20] *Op. cit.,* p. 135.

[21] *Loc. cit.,* p. 136.

[22] Palmer, *Narrative of Events,* p. 45. It is difficult to say how much truth there is in his story of a contemplated Roman Catholic establishment. Peel had certainly considered the idea. *Life,* Vol. I, p. 369.

obvious that some measure of protection must be taken. Palmer, Froude, Newman and Keble founded the *Association of Friends of the Church* of which the object was to preserve 'pure and inviolate' its identity.[23] In the *British Magazine,* then under the able guidance of Hugh James Rose, with whom at this time Newman became acquainted, they already had an organ for their opinions.[24] Newman himself, with the strong approval of Froude and Keble, had begun the publication of the famous *Tracts for the Times;* he was writing on Church reform in the religious journals.[25] Care was taken to secure their circulation among the clergy where they seem to have met with a large measure of approval.[26] In 1834 the important adhesion of Pusey—already Regius Professor—was gained.[27] The confidence of the Tractarians was high. 'It would be,' wrote Newman,[28] 'in fact a second Reformation:—a better reformation, for it would be a return not to the sixteenth but to the seventeenth century.'

But the movement was not to meet without opposition. From the outset it was bitterly anti-Erastian. 'With Froude,' Newman tells us,[28] and it must be remembered that by Froude, Newman was above all influenced, 'Erastianism was the

[23] *Ibid.,* p. 49.
[24] *Apologia,* p. 140.
[25] *Apologia,* p. 144.
[26] See Appendix A to Palmer's *Narrative.*
[27] Palmer, p. 60.
[28] *Apologia,* p. 141.

parent, or if not the parent, the serviceable and sufficient tool of Liberalism.' But anti-Erastianism was not likely to meet with approval among the political ecclesiastics of London. It drew its inspiration, at any rate, in its Tractarian expression, from the Middle Ages;[29] and to admire the medieval popes was already to conceive of a Church infinitely superior to the secular state. It was as passionately opposed to the latitudinarian spirit of the politicians; Sir Robert Inglis with his uncompromising orthodoxy was its political ideal. The Oxford Movement set its face firmly towards the past. It did not desire a charitable breadth of view. The truth was to be found in the writings of the fathers, and of the divines of the seventeenth century.[30] The Church was to purge itself of heresy and to build itself around the essential doctrine of the Apostolic succession.[31] The identity of the Church, in fact, was to be found not in its life but in its tradition.[32] It thus relied essentially upon authority, and for its source it went back to the ages when, as it deemed, the Church was untrammelled by a State-connexion. Clearly, it had thus no sympathy from the outset with the notion of a royal supremacy—'that blighting influence upon our Upas-tree' as

[29] *Apologia,* p. 154.

[30] Cf. Storr, *op. cit.,* p. 258.

[31] Cf. *Tract 4.*

[32] Hence, in *Tract 90,* Newman logically endeavours to read the Tridentine tradition, *i.e.,* to him the pre-Reformation tradition, into the Thirty-Nine Articles.

Hurrell Froude termed it[33]—and was naturally alien in spirit to those who, like Arnold, looked upon Christianity essentially as a spirit and not a body of doctrine. It was, in brief, a Catholic and not a Protestant conception,[34] and was thus bound to challenge dissent from its conclusions.

For to the majority of men, and certainly to the majority of influential men, the Church was not the Church, but the Establishment.[35] What it was, perhaps, even more, what it might become, was essentially a matter of parliamentary enactment. With Newman's keen sense of a separate clerical order,[36] and his challenging demand for independence, it was impossible for them to feel any sympathy. To men like Lord John Russell, for instance, the Church was no more than one among many national institutions, and, equally with James Mill, though unconsciously, he was prepared to apply to its revenues the criterion of social utility.[37] Sir James Graham did not hesitate to affirm that the State might re-distribute Church property in any manner it thought fit, 'as long as it was distributed for purposes strictly Protestant.'[38] 'The Church of England,' John

[33] Remains, I, 405.

[34] The reader may note how in Dr. Figgis' *Churches and the Modern State* this attitude is, perhaps a little vaguely, implied. Cf. especially pp. 43-47.

[35] Cf. Church, *The Oxford Movement,* p. 51.

[36] Cf. the startling commencement of the first tract—*Ad clerum.*

[37] Cf. Hansard, New Series, Vol. XXIV, p. 802, June 23, 1834.

[38] Hansard, New Series, Vol. XXVII, March 30, 1835, p. 423.

Cam Hobhouse told the House of Commons,[39] 'is emphatically the offspring and child of the law, and the parent may deal with the child.' Even Sir Robert Peel could only defend the right of the Church to the increment-value of its improved property by urging that no distinction should be introduced between its possessions and those of other corporations.[40] Clearly such an attitude was virtually antithetic to that of the Tractarians. It explains the appointment of Dr. Hampden to the Regius Professorship of Divinity; for Hampden was at least a Liberal and had shown no notions of high prerogative in regard to the Church. And it was precisely on the ground of his liberalism that his appointment provoked so vehement an opposition.[41]

From the moment of that conflict the story possesses a tragic inevitability. The Tractarians went to extremes in their effort at least to neutralise the appointment;[42] and Dr. Hampden did not forget the part they played when the opportunity for return arose.[43] The contest turned the inchoate band of sympathisers into a party; and its members began to understand their responsibilities not

39 *Loc. cit.*, p. 534, March 31, 1835.

40 Gladstone noted that Peel was wholly anti-Church and unclerical and largely undogmatic. Morley, I, 132. Hansard, New Series, Vol. XVII, April 16, 1833, p. 1002.

41 Cf. Church, *The Oxford Movement*, p. 168 ff.

42 Church, *op. cit.*, p. 170. Palmer, *Narrative*, p. 131. Mr. Palmer makes it clear that the Tractarians were only a small number of the opposition.

43 Church, *op. cit.*, p. 320.

less than the need for giving them expression.[44] Into the story of its growth it is not now possible to enter;[45] but it is permissible to point out that few movements have been so admirably served by their leaders. They were tireless with pen and with tongue. The Tracts flowed on without end. The four o'clock sermons at St. Mary's drew audiences which, if never very large, contained much of what was best in the University. There was endless thinking and endless investigation into the one fundamental question—What is the Church? Enquiry began to be made into that most fascinating and dangerous of questions its origins. Quite early in its history the necessity of defining the relation of the movement to the Church of Rome became apparent, and the consequent change of emphasis in the tone adopted to that organisation was the point of disruption between the Tractarians and the Evangelicals.[46] The arrival of Monsignor Wiseman on his mission served also to emphasise the need for a right understanding of Catholic doctrine.[47] The Tractarians were already astutely aware that they were working out a midway between two extremes; but they saw, too, that in certain decisive fundamentals Catholicism and Anglicanism were in essential

44 *Apologia*, p. 166.

45 It is needless, perhaps, to refer to Dean Church's incomparable *Oxford Movement*.

46 *Apologia*, p. 163.

47 *Op. cit.*, p. 164.

agreement.[48] Little by little they drew further along the road. Newman notes the first rumblings of the storm in 1838.[49] By 1841 it is clear that accusations against Rome had lost their former significance. Tract 90 was essentially an attempt to exclude Protestantism from the Thirty-Nine Articles—'they were tolerant,' he wrote,[50] 'not only of what I called "Catholic teaching," but of much that was Roman.' The authorities treated the Tract in the one way that was bound to create difficulties. It was met, writes Dean Church, 'not with argument, but with panic and wrath.'[51] The acrimony of the atmosphere was intensely aggravated; suspicion of Rome set in everywhere. Every question was made a theological question. The Tractarian candidate to the poetry chair was defeated; Dr. Hampden obtained an ignoble, if curious revenge; Pusey was suspended in absurd fashion by the Vice-Chancellor from preaching.[52] In the midst of difficulties a man born to intensify them plunged precipitately into the conflict. Mr. W. G. Ward seems to have had all the logical remorselessness of Hurrell Froude with a physical vigour of which the latter was deprived. His *Ideal of a Christian Church* was tantamount to an admission that Rome had always been right.[53]

48 *Op. cit.*, p. 169.
49 *Op. cit.*, p. 175.
50 *Op. cit.*, p. 182.
51 Church, *op. cit.*, p. 290.
52 Church, *op. cit.*, 312-335.
53 It is hardly needful for me to remark here how greatly I am

That would have been harmless enough at another time. As it was, the condemnation it invited only drove Newman steadily along the road upon which it was now, as it seemed, inevitable[54] he should travel. He gave up his college position and retired to Littlemore to work and to think. Of the mental struggle through which he vainly lived he has himself written matchlessly, nor dare another retell the story.[55] In October, 1845, there occurred that event of which Mr. Gladstone so rightly said that 'it had never yet been estimated at anything like the full amount of its calamitous importance.'[56]

For a time there was peace. If Newman and Ward had gone, Keble and Pusey remained and they devoted themselves with singular courage to the task of repairing the breach that had been made.[57] Yet the Church had by no means completed its time of travail. In 1847 Lord John Russell precipitated a further controversy by making Dr. Hampden a bishop—'an indication,' Lord Morley comments,[58] '. . . of a determination to substitute a sort of general religion for the doctrines of the Church.' Certainly, it was not the type of appointment which might reassure those whom the secession of Newman had caused

indebted to Mr. Wilfrid Ward's brilliant *W. G. Ward and the Oxford Movement.*

[54] Cf. Morley's *Gladstone,* I, 230. *Apologia,* p. 293.

[55] See especially Part VI of the *Apologia.*

[56] Morley, I, 234.

[57] Church, *op. cit.,* p. 406. Palmer, *op. cit.,* p. 240.

[58] *Life of Gladstone,* II, 280.

to waver. But worse was to follow. In the year 1850 Bishop Philpotts refused to institute to the living of Bampford Speke the Reverend George Gorham on the ground of uncertain doctrine in regard to baptism. Mr. Gorham sued the bishop in the Court of Arches; but the court decided against him. He thereupon took his case on appeal to the Judicial Committee of the Privy Council—a purely lay body in which the two archbishops and the bishop of London sat as assessors. This latter Court reversed the proceedings of the Court of Arches by a majority verdict and Mr. Gorham took the living. But the decision was a disastrous one.[59] Everyone knew that the Court had been instituted to satisfy the restless ambition of Lord Brougham;[60] and the latter himself testified in the House of Lords that it had not been intended that the Court should deal with such a class of cases.[61] It was urged that political causes had not been without their influence on the judgment;[62] certainly it asserted in a striking manner the inherent right of the Crown to settle matters of faith. Pusey and Keble no less than Gladstone and Manning were horrified. 'The case of the Church of England at this moment,' wrote Mr. Gladstone to Lord

59 See the special report by Moore. The facts of the case and Lord Langdale's judgment are given conveniently in Brooke's *Six Privy Council Judgments.* It is noteworthy that Bishop Blomfield, the most ecclesiastically minded of the three prelates, should have refused to concur in the judgment.

60 Greville, I, 18.

61 Hansard, 3d Series, Vol. III, p. 629.

62 Palmer, *Narrative,* p. 245. Purcell's *Manning,* I, p. 523.

Lyttleton,[63] 'is a very dismal one, and almost leaves men to choose between a broken heart and no heart at all. But at present it is all dark or only twilight which rests upon our future.' A declaration of protest was issued by all the leaders of the High Church movement.[64] It was clear to Manning that the parting of the ways had come. Mr. Gladstone tried to urge delay, but to him the implications of the judgment were irresistible.[65] He tried to stimulate the clergy to an attack on the extension, as he deemed it, of the royal supremacy to ecclesiastical affairs, but met with little or no response.[66] A letter to his bishop was equally unavailing. His friends, men like Dodsworth and Maskell,[67] could do nothing by their protests. The government seemed determined to stand by the judgment. In the end Manning felt himself compelled to give up the struggle. 'I gradually came to see,' he wrote,[68] 'that there was no intermediate position between the Catholic faith and an undogmatic pietism.' By September, 1850, it is clear that he was convinced,[69] and when he was called upon to protest against the Papal Aggression of 1851 he found it impossible to do so.[70] On the sixth of April, 1851, he was received into the Roman

63 Morley, I, 283.

64 The document in Purcell's *Manning,* I, 532.

65 Purcell, I, 539 ff.

66 *Op. cit.*, I, 543-545.

67 The great authority on liturgy.

68 Purcell, I, 558, n. 1.

69 See the letter of S. Wilberforce to Gladstone, Purcell, I, 568.

70 Purcell, I, 578.

Catholic Church. His conversion was the last of those which may be directly traced to the influence of the Oxford Movement.

II

No one can read the *Tracts for the Times* without realising how far removed is their atmosphere from one of contented acceptance of State interference. They do not, indeed, specifically reject the establishment;[71] but they point out with unhesitating directness the distinction between their position and that of the world at large. The Church does not depend upon the State. Its property is its own. It will not submit to the test of utility. The clergy must choose whether they will be for the Church or against it;[72] they must magnify their office. They must protest against what seems 'a most dangerous infringement on our rights on the part of the State.' They must not be content to be its creation. 'No one can say that the British legislature is in our communion, or that its members are necessarily even Christians. What pretence then has it for, not merely advising, but superseding the Ecclesiastical power?'[73] The Church must resist such encroachment on its rights. 'You may keep it before you as a desirable object that the Irish Church should

[71] The first tract actually points out 'how miserable is the state of religious bodies not supported by the State.'

[72] *Tract 1*, p. 4.

[73] *Tract 2*, p. 2.

at some future day meet in Synod, and protest herself against what has been done; and then proceed to establish or rescind the State injunction as may be thought expedient.'[74] Here, clearly, is a high sense of prerogative. Its origin is equally obvious. It is not from a secular legislature that change must derive. 'When corruptions,' says the fifth tract,[75] 'prevalent among the professedly Christian world render it necessary for her to state the substance of her faith in articles (as was done in A. D. 1562), or when circumstances appear to require any change or variation either in the Forms of her Liturgy, or in her general internal government, the king has the constitutional power of summoning the houses of convocation, a sort of ecclesiastical parliament composed of Bishop or clergy, from whom alone such changes can fitly or legally emanate.' But the king is only the temporal head of the Church. 'We are not thence to infer that she gave, or could give to an earthly monarch, or to his temporal legislature, the right to interfere with things spiritual.'[76] It was natural that a protest should in this sense be made against the re-arrangement of dioceses by a Royal Commission in 1836[77] 'without confirmation of their acts on the part of the Church.'[78]

[74] *Tract 2*, p. 4.

[75] P. 13.

[76] *Loc. cit.*, p. 13.

[77] The reference is apparently to the Ecclesiastical Commissioners' Act, 1836, 6 and 7 William IV, c. 77, but the protest is written in 1839.

[78] *Tract 33*, note on p. 7.

It is clearly against a presumed supremacy of the State over the Church that protest is made; and it is this which constitutes the key to the political theory of Tractarianism. Starting as it does in a movement against an invasion of what Keble deemed its prerogatival right to self-reformation, it was inevitable that this should be the case. Indeed seven years before the commencement of the Oxford Movement, Whately, in his *Letters on the Church,*[79] had emphasised the idea of the Church as a perfect and self-sufficing society of divine institution, and had argued from that conception first to its rights of jurisdiction over all who voluntarily become its members;[80] and next to the need for a complete separation of Church and State since the idea underlying each of the societies was essentially distinct.[81] Nor was he alone in this attitude. Almost at the end of the eighteenth century Bishop Horsley of St. David's had insisted that to think of the clergy as State-servants is self-excommunication.[82] The work of Whately, as we know, profoundly influenced Newman and Froude. 'What he did for me in point of religious opinion,' wrote the former,[83] 'was, first, to teach me the existence of the Church as a

[79] It is simply stated to be by 'an Episcopalian' and Whately, I believe, never acknowledged the authorship. But it is usually ascribed to him.

[80] In the third letter.

[81] See the fourth letter.

[82] Cf. Storr, *Development of English Theology*, p. 84.

[83] *Apologia*, p. 115.

substantive body or corporation; next to fix in me those anti-Erastian views of Church polity which were one of the most prominent features of the Tractarian movement.' For if once it was admitted that Church and State were distinct, and that the former possessed Apostolic succession, to admit the superiority of the latter would be intolerable. That had been the importance of Keble's sermon. The nation had apostatised itself; it was no longer the Church. 'This hateful circumstance it was,' Lord Morley has written,[84] 'that inevitably began in multitudes of devout and earnest minds to produce a revolution in their conception of a church, and a resurrection in curiously altered forms of that old ideal of Milton's austere and lofty school,—the ideal of a purely spiritual association that should leave each man's soul and conscience free from "secular chains" and "hireling wolves."' Once a new conception of the Church was needed it was inevitably upon dogma and orthodoxy that the Tractarians were driven back.[85] To find out what the Church was they were compelled to discover what it had been. They sought to know it in the days of its purity—in its Catholic time. Hence the necessity for a rigid exclusiveness; since it could not claim to be a branch of the Church Catholic

[84] *Life of Gladstone,* I, 115.

[85] In our own day an eloquent and brilliant defence has been made of this position by Dr. Figgis in his *Churches in the Modern State* from the Anglican standpoint and Dr. Forsyth in his *Theology in Church and State* from the Nonconformist.

and Apostolic unless that steady and decisive continuity of unimpaired doctrine had been maintained.

It is this notion of a Church as a *societas perfecta,* founded upon a definite and statutable creed, which so clearly lies at the basis of the Tractarian antagonism to the State. For the State had become non-Anglican, or, as they would have said, non-Christian, and they could not submit to a reform they knew to be inevitable at the hands of men whose doctrines they abhorred.[86] They had an uncomfortable suspicion that, as J. A. Froude remarked,[87] 'the laity would never allow the Church of England to get on stilts . . . the State would remain master, let Oxford say what it pleased.' Inevitably, therefore, the central point of their attack was the royal supremacy since in it, as they were to learn,[88] was involved the notion that the State was supreme no less in spiritual than in temporal affairs. Their object from the outset was, if not to free the Church from the trammels of an Establishment, at any rate to minimise its consequences in the direction of secular control. 'Churchmen,' said Dean Church many years later,[89] 'believe the Church to be a religious society

[86] Cf. Froude—*The Oxford Counter-Reformation* in *Short Studies* (ed. of 1883), Vol. IV, p. 154.

[87] *Op. cit.*, p. 164.

[88] I say 'were to learn' since it is clear from a variety of sources, *e.g.*, Purcell's *Life of Manning,* I, 541, that many of the clergy did not understand the royal supremacy in this broad sense.

[89] *Life and Letters of R. W. Church,* p. 289. He is speaking of the Church Boards Bill.

as much as a congregational body, as much so as the Roman Catholic body. It has also become in England an Established Church; but it has not therefore ceased to be a religious society with principles and laws of its own.' The claim is that of the Presbyterians in 1843[90] and, repudiated in both cases by the State, it led to the foundation of the Free Church of Scotland in one event as to the revival of Roman Catholicism in the other.

It was emphatically against Erastianism that the Tractarians were contending. 'Lord Grey,' Mr. Froude has reported,[91] 'had warned the bishops in England to set their houses in order, and was said to have declared in private that the Church was a mare's nest.' Bishop Wilberforce—assuredly no enemy to the Establishment—quoted in the House of Lords an extraordinary example of contemporary opinion. 'The Church of England,' so the *Globe* asserted,[92] 'as by law established, is emphatically a creature of this world. It is impossible to affix any intelligible character to her profession or practice unless we bear steadily in mind that she is essentially a machine for embodying the spiritual element in the changing public opinion of the day, and not a contrivance for transmitting sacraments, or defining creeds.' The doughty Mr. Faithfull was urging in the House of Commons that Church and nation were

[90] See my paper on *The Political Theory of the Disruption* printed in this volume.

[91] *The Oxford Counter-Reformation* in *Short Studies,* IV, 185.

[92] Hansard, 3d Series, Vol. CXVIII, p. 552.

synonymous terms, and that the nation might dispose freely of its property; he had no high conception of office-bearers in the Church who were merely 'the arbitrary choice of the Crown or of certain individuals who had the right of appointing them.'[93] To assert that the Church had any 'absolute and unalienable rights,' Lord Brougham told the House of Lords,[94] was a 'gross and monstrous anomaly' since it would make impossible the supremacy of Parliament. The argument of Dr. Arnold against the admission of 'Jews or any other avowed unbelievers in Christ' into Parliament was based on the fact that in such an event 'Parliament can not be the legislature of the Church, not being an assembly of Christians; and as there is no other Church legislature to be found under our actual constitution, the government of the Church will be *de jure* extinct,'[95]—an unqualified acceptance, even if on high grounds, of the fullest Erastianism. 'The House,' Joseph Hume complacently remarked in 1823,[96] '. . . must be well aware that there was no precise authority in the Scriptures for any particular

93 Hansard, New Series, Vol. XVIII, p. 185, April 16, 1833. One imagines how this would have been greeted by Newman and Hurrell Froude.

94 Hansard, New Series, Vol. XIX, p. 991, July 19, 1833.

95 Quoted in Wilfrid Ward, *W. G. Ward and the Oxford Movement*, p. 378.

96 Hansard, New Series, Vol. VIII, p. 368, March 4, 1823. He is speaking of the Irish church, but he would of course have applied the doctrine to that of England, and doubtless he was speaking with the support of the Utilitarians.

establishment; it was altogether a civil institution, the creature of the law; and by every rule of reason, the same authority that created could alter, nay! could even annul it altogether.' Nor was the purport of such doctrines mistaken by the more high-minded bishops of the time. 'The legislature, in fact,' wrote Lloyd of Oxford to his old pupil, Sir Robert Peel,[97] 'say to the Church of England: so long as we guarantee you your property, we will take for ourselves the right of controlling your discipline, and of preventing you from exercising any spiritual power over your own members.' It is a villainous argument, and as oppressive as it is mean.'

It is sufficiently clear that between such an attitude as this, and that of the Tractarians, there could be no compromise. If the Church of England was to fulfil the function assigned to it by the *Globe,* and do no more than mirror in itself the shifting gusts of popular opinion on religious questions the notion of a dogmatic basis must be abandoned. What to men like Newman were its very roots would have to be torn up. There would be room for the continuous exercise of private judgment and influence—to the Tractarians essentially a dangerous thing.[98] There would be 'fraternisation' with 'Protestants of all sorts' which, in the matter of the Jerusalem bishopric Newman

[97] *Memoirs of Sir Robert Peel,* Vol. I, p. 84.

[98] Cf. Newman's *Correspondence,* Vol. II, p. 310. The letter to a 'lady of excitable temperament.'

called 'a fearful business.'[99] It would have prejudiced what they deemed the essential thing in Anglicanism—the title to be a branch of the Apostolic Church.[100] State control to them was essentially a handle to novelty—itself among the most deadly of religious sins. 'If the English Church,' wrote Newman to the Bishop of Oxford,[101] 'is to enter upon a new course and assume a new aspect, it will be more pleasant to me hereafter to think that I did not suffer so grievous an event to happen without bearing witness against it.' They were anxious, moreover, to emphasise their complete dissociation from temporal concerns, even such as were concerned with the possessions of the Church.[102] Their only reason, indeed, for not 'dreading' alliance with the State was the fact that they simultaneously emphasised their determination to maintain 'the integrity of the Church's rights and privileges.'[103] Their relations were being continuously altered by the civil power and it was 'the duty of the Church to demand corresponding alterations' in favour of the prevention of any extra-ecclesiastical interference.[104] So eager are they for the rigid definition of doctrine that, as they urge,[105] 'the

99 *Correspondence,* II, 315, letter to J. W. Bowden.

100 Cf. *Correspondence,* II, 323, letter to the Bishop of Oxford.

101 *Loc. cit.*

102 *Correspondence,* II, 4.

103 *Ibid.,* II, 16.

104 *Op. cit.,* II, p. 23. The reference to Warburton's *Alliance between Church and State* in this letter is very significant.

105 *Op. cit.,* II, 77.

abandonment of State prosecutions for blasphemy, etc. . . . and the disordered state of the Christian Knowledge Society, where books are taken cognisance of and condemned, render it desirable that there should be some really working Court of heresy and false doctrine . . . the chief advantage of this would be its practical curb upon the exercise of the king's power . . . the whole Church would be kept in order . . . the theological law of the Church must be revived, and ecclesiastical law, moreover.' They are anxious to take patronage out of the hands of the Crown, on the ground that it encroaches on the action of the Archbishops.[106] They expect the probable abandonment of Church by State and ask how it may best be builded in the hearts of the people;[107] for the Church is essentially a divine institution 'with nothing to hope or fear from Whig or Conservative governments, or from bishops, or from peers, or from courts, or from other visible power. We must trust our own ἦθος—that is, what is unseen, and its unseen Author."[108] Where people shrink from the Catholicity of their doctrine as 'implying want of affection for our National Church' they are bidden 'remind them that you take the National Church, but only you do not take it from the Reformation. In order to kindle love of the National Church and yet to inculcate a Catholic

106 *Loc. cit.*, II, 160, letter to Keble.
107 *Op. cit.*, II, 166.
108 *Op. cit.*, II, 216.

tone, nothing else is necessary but to take our Church in the Middle Ages"[109]—that is, to take the Church at a time when the Tractarians believed it to be pure from the corruption of the State control introduced by Henry VIII. They object to an effort after Church comprehension which does not include 'public revocation' by dissenters, 'of their wicked errors."[110] Even should the State Church remain there would be special and peculiar ground for its retention. It would be because a visible Church existed upon earth upon which all States should depend and by which they should be guided. Within her sphere the Church would retain her independence and the State would refuse to assist those who were hostile to her claims. It was an alliance of two kingdoms;[111] nor were there wanting those who were prepared to assert that the Church was far from being the inferior power.[112] So moderate a man as Dean Church thought that it might urge the deposition of kings, and in a choice between a weak church system and one with the pretensions of Gregory

109 *Op. cit.*, II, 308.

110 *Op. cit.*, II, 329.

111 So at least I would summarise Mr. Gladstone's *State in its Relations with the Church*—though, as Bagehot (*Collected Works*, III, 294) whimsically said, he defended it 'mistily.' I assume it more or less met with Tractarian approval. It was mainly influenced by James Hope and W. Palmer of Worcester; and Newman thought that it would do good. Morley, I, 135.

112 Cf. Ward, *Ideal of a Christian Church*, p. 49; and compare the remarkable letter to Manning written in 1844 by Dean Church. Purcell, I, 696.

VII and Innocent III, he approves of the latter's decision.[113]

It is a tremendous and brilliant plea for ecclesiastical freedom that is clearly born from the passionate sense of a corporate church. The Tractarians were anxious, so to speak, to delimit its boundaries that the exclusiveness of its character might become the more apparent. They insist on a rejection of all doctrine that encroaches upon its independence. They desire to proclaim definitely the character of its doctrine and to insist on the acceptance of that doctrine so that none save those who felt as they did might be its members. They were eager to control Church patronage and Church discipline[114] for the same reasons as those urged by Presbyterian theorists—because the Church only can deal effectually with ecclesiastical matters. Since they do not possess the safeguards which make possible such self-control, 'it may obviously be the duty of churchmen in mere self-defence to expose and protest against their destitute and oppressed condition."[115] They need these things because the Church must possess unity, and unity can not be obtained if they allow the play of private fancy about its dogmas.[116] Everywhere, too, the Tractarians magnify the clerical office and depreciate whatever in the liturgies or doctrine seems traceable

113 See the letter quoted in the last note.

114 Cf. *Tract 59.*

115 The closing words of *Tract 59.*

116 *Tract 60.*

to lay influence.[117] Nor do they admit the possibility of change save in the limited degree that expansion may take place 'only as to whatsoever is read in Holy Scripture, or may be proved thereby';[118] and it is rather to the declaration of old truth than the determination of new that they desire men's energies to be directed.

That such an unconscious theory of the State was at the bottom of much Tractarian speculation becomes the more obvious when one examines those times at which the leaders of the movement judged themselves to have special cause for resentment against the government of the day. Keble's sermon in 1833 was nothing so much as the casting off of a nation which by following false gods had been guilty of grave heresy.[119] Mr. Golightly, having urged Newman to arouse an indignant activity among the Irish clergy, goes on to beseech him not to be too moderate in what he says of the Establishment. 'One of your principles,' he wrote,[120] 'I own I do not like; you protest "against doing anything directly to separate Church and State." I would do the same, perhaps, in ordinary times; but, when the State takes upon herself to

117 Cf. for instance *Tract 71*, the discussion of the liturgy and the account of the quarrel between the Upper and Lower Houses of Convocation in 1689. It is perhaps significant that the stoutest Erastian of recent times, Sir William Harcourt, should have been the firm upholder of lay influence. See his *Lawlessness in the National Church* (1899).

118 See Pusey's *Letter to the Bishop of Oxford*, p. 19; though in Newman's *Essay on Development* this becomes capable of formidable modification.

119 The very title of his sermon seems to express this feeling.

120 Newman's *Correspondence*, Vol. I, p. 392.

decide, and that without consulting the Church, how many bishops are necessary for the superintendence of the clergy, and the clergy are cowardly or ignorant enough to submit to her decisions, it appears to me that the time for separation is come.' Though Newman is eager for the retention of the Establishment he writes to F. Rogers that 'the State has deserted us,' and that 'if the destructives go much further in their persecution of us—*e.g.*, if they made Arnold a bishop—I might consider it wrong to maintain that position longer, much as I should wish to do so."[121] 'They who are no Christians themselves,' wrote Mr. Rickards to Newman,[122] 'must not legislate on matters of religion for those who are Christians.' It was the events of these past few months, so he told Hurrell Froude,[123] which brought to Newman the realisation that with most Englishmen 'the Church is essentially a popular institution, and the past English union of it with the State has been a happy anomaly.' How passionate was the sense of resentment against the State the reader of Mr. Palmer's fascinating narrative will not fail to detect.[124] The Address to the Archbishop of Canterbury, for which he was responsible, was well understood to have no other significance than this.[125]

121 *Ibid.*, I, 396.

122 *Ibid.*, I, 399.

123 *Ibid.*, I, 403.

124 See his *Narrative of Events*, pp. 44-46.

125 In this connexion the letter quoted in Mr. Palmer's appendix at p. 217 is of deep interest.

Not less clearly does this vivid corporate sense appear on the two occasions when Dr. Hampden was made a protagonist in the drama. It has already been noted that his appointment it was which made the Tractarians from a scattered band of enthusiasts into a party.[126] For whatever merits Dr. Hampden may have possessed, he represented in the highest possible degree those latitudinarian principles against which the Oxford Movement was the incarnate protest. 'He had just reasserted,' wrote Church,[127] 'that he looked upon creeds, and all the documents which embodied the traditional doctrine, and collective thought of the Church, as invested by ignorance and prejudice with an authority which was without foundation.' He had, in fact, no sense whatever of its corporateness, and no respect for its history. He regarded its creeds and dogmas as matter not for belief but for speculation. He did not realise, as Dean Church so strikingly said,[128] 'that the Church is so committed to them that he can not enter on his destructive criticism without having to excuse, not one only, but all these beliefs, and without soon having to face the question whether the whole idea of the Church, as a real and divinely ordained society, with a definite doctrine and belief is not a delusion.' That Dr. Hampden did answer that question in the affirmative does not admit of

[126] Above, p. 6.
[127] *The Oxford Movement*, p. 158.
[128] *Op. cit.*, p. 163.

doubt; but he was suspect because, Scripture apart, all other authority was to him matter for human inference. The appointment, however well meant, was a mistaken one; but what was far more significant was the way in which, despite almost unanimous protest in Oxford, Dr. Hampden was forced upon the University.[129] 'Again,' said Newman,[130] 'the Ministry will be at open war with the Church.' The idea of a petition to the king—which frightened the Archbishop—called forth a protest from a nettled Prime Minister who unwarily betrayed the realities behind a legal fiction.[131] Convocation protested against the appointment, though the Proctors vetoed the proposal.[132] Almost immediately, and very significantly, Newman writes of the 'probability of the whole subject of Church authority, power, claims, etc., etc., being re-opened.'[133] 'It was,' said Dean Church of the appointment,[134] 'a palpable instance of what the Church had to expect' when her guardianship was taken from her own hands. Eleven years later Lord John Russell, neglecting the obvious warning of 1836, and, seemingly, with the thought of paying a tribute to the liberalism of Arnold in his mind,[135] appointed Hampden to the bishopric of Hereford.

129 Cf. Church, *op. cit.*, p. 169.
130 *Correspondence*, Vol. II, p. 150.
131 *Op. cit.*, 161 (letter of Archdeacon Froude).
132 *Letters of J. B. Mozley*, p. 54.
133 *Op. cit.*, I, 166.
134 *The Oxford Movement*, p. 177.
135 Liddon, *Life of Pusey*, Vol. II, p. 158.

To accept it, protested Pusey,[136] 'was to connive at heresy.' They attempted to open up the whole question of Dr. Hampden's orthodoxy but in vain. Yet they learned certain important lessons. 'It is certainly humbling enough,' Pusey wrote,[137] '. . . if there is no help whatever, if any person, however unfit, whether on moral or doctrinal grounds, be chosen by the Minister of the day for a Bishop, except in a resistance to the law.' 'The injury therefore to the Church of England,' said Mr. Baddeley in arguing for a mandamus in the Court of King's Bench,[138] 'if its pastors are thus to be forced upon it at the mere beck of the Prime Minister of the day, will be incalculable.' For the Church would lose its identity unless some means were taken to remove it from control by the chance turns of the political wheel. That, surely, was what Newman had meant in 1836 when he asked Pusey if it were not 'very clear that the English Church subsists in the State, and has no internal consistency (in matter of fact, I do not say in theory), to keep it together, is bound into one by the imposition of articles and the inducement of State protection, not by ἦθος and a common faith? If so, can we regret very much that a deceit should be detected.'[139]

Certain parliamentary legislation dealing with

[136] *Life*, II, 160.

[137] *Life*, II, 165.

[138] See Jelf, Report of R. v. Canterbury (Archbishop). The whole case is most instructive.

[139] *Life of Pusey*, Vol. I, p. 368.

the Church at this time called forth opinions of some importance. They protested against using the churches for the announcement of dissenters' marriages.[140] When, in 1836, it was proposed to abolish the ancient bishopric of Sodor and Man, they urged not merely that it was an unjustifiable interference with established ecclesiastical right, but also that the Commission was acting in tyrannical fashion[141]—the fact that the see did not carry with it membership in the House of Lords they regarded as a valuable precedent.[142] In 1838, Phillpotts of Exeter protested against the Church Discipline Bill of that year in significant fashion. He condemned it because ecclesiastical authority seemed to him independent of the sanction of the temporal laws 'which merely adds temporal consequences to the ecclesiastical censures, the infliction of which is part of the power of the Keys, vested in the Church by its divine founder, and exercised by it in the earliest ages. It follows that the State, though it may refuse to add a civil sanction to the exercise of the spiritual authority, can not either grant that authority, which does not spring from any human source, or take it away from any one in whom the divine constitution of the Church has vested it;"[143] and it is in a similar sense that the Bishop of London protested against the Church

140 Newman's *Correspondence,* II, 27, 78.

141 *Op. cit.,* II, 170-171.

142 *Op. cit.,* I, 169.

143 Hansard, 3d Series, Vol. XLVIII, June 4, 1839, p. 1338.

Discipline of 1850.[144] The consistency of these protests is beyond all question. They connect as closely with the ἦθος of the Oxford Movement as the Claim of Right in 1842 with the whole character of Presbyterian history.

But nowhere is the whole nature of that ἦθος so apparent as in the controversy which raged round the Gorham judgment. 'It is,' Mr. Gladstone wrote to Manning,[145] 'a stupendous issue.' Here was a definite declaration on the part of the State as to what must be taken to be the true doctrine of the Church of England. The judgment caused widespread consternation. It seemed to make the Church what an able writer later termed 'simply a religious body to which the State concedes certain rights, dignities and possessions not enjoyed by non-established churches, and over which the State, in return for this concession, exercises an authority from which non-established Churches are free.'[146] It was a denial of the Church's right to declare its own belief to which, so Pusey urged, Magna Charta was the pledge; 'if the State,' he told a great London audience,[147] 'will not, as Magna Charta pledges it, allow that "the Church should have liberties inviolate," we must ask that the State will set us free from itself.' A striking protest was drawn up against the right of the Privy Council 'practically to exercise in

144 Hansard, 3d Series, Vol. III, June 3, 1850, p. 600.

145 Morley, I, 280.

146 See an able essay in the *Guardian* for October 12, 1887.

147 *Life,* II, 249.

spiritual matters a jurisdiction for which they are utterly incompetent, and which never has been, nor even can be, confided to them by the Church."[148] Mr. Maskell, the well-known liturgical scholar, wrote a pamphlet urging that not even a bench of bishops could deal with the matter, so long as their authority was not derived from the Church.[149] 'It was now,' writes Pusey's biographer,[150], 'definitely asked whether the changes which had been assented to on the part of the Church of England three centuries ago were such as to forfeit her claim to be a part of the Church of Christ.' Pusey himself wrote a laborious tract to prove, as he hoped, that ecclesiastical authority alone could decide doctrine. A priest, so he urged, who appeals to a lay court from his bishop's decision is degrading his office. Manning, Robert Wilberforce and Mill of Cambridge, drew up a protest which repudiated all acceptance of the royal supremacy in any save a strictly temporal sense.[151] Gladstone repudiated all idea of a commission to decide doctrine which did not originate with, and depend upon, the Church.[152] Philpotts of Exeter actually renounced communion with the Archbishop of Canterbury for his share in the judgment.[153]

The reason for this indignation is perfectly

[148] *Life of Pusey,* II, 254.
[149] *Life of Pusey,* II, 256.
[150] *Loc. cit.*
[151] *Life of Manning,* I, 540.
[152] *Life of Manning,* I, 534.
[153] Morley's *Gladstone,* 1, 281.

clear. The Church of England would cease to be a separate society did she permit such invasions of her proper sphere. 'There can be no doubt,' wrote Mr. Henry Drummond,[154] 'that the Church of England is not organised as the Church and Kingdom of Christ ought to be; that she has ever been, and is now more than ever, trampled upon by the civil power; that having recognised fully only two sacraments, one of these has been pronounced by the civil power to be useless, in other words, no sacrament at all, and that consequently she is almost unchurched altogether.' 'Either the governing power in the State must allow the objectionable decision to be reviewed by proper authority and the usurpation to be abated for the future,' wrote the gentle Keble,[155] 'or the governing power in the Church must at all hazards demur to the State's interference and disregard its enactments.' 'To all calling themselves churchmen,' he urged again,[156] 'we may say, is there not a treasure of Sacred Truth, and a living Body entrusted with that treasure? And can it be right for any consideration to make over the trust to those who are not of the Body? Again, to all candid persons of every creed we may say, Is it not a part of Religious Liberty for a Religious Body to declare its own doctrine; or, if its civil

[154] *Remarks on Dr. Wiseman's sermon on the Gorham case,* London, 1850.

[155] *Church Matters in 1850: A Call to Speak Out,* p. 8.

[156] *Loc. cit.,* p. 31.

and social position equitably interfere with its freedom in this respect, to be allowed at least a choice which of the two it will forego?' 'The imposition of any doctrine by such an evidently human institution as that (the Crown),' wrote Mr. W. J. E. Bennett to Lord John Russell,[157] 'would be the very severest of tyranny.' 'Men have not yet learned,' the same clergyman complained again,[158] 'to separate the spiritual power of the Church from the temporal . . . the royal supremacy in civil matters, as well as in ecclesiastical matters, as long as they are merely ecclesiastical and not spiritual; also in all temporal matters, causes and trials, arising out of them we cheerfully acknowledge: but the royal supremacy in the doctrines of our Blessed Lord, in the discipline of the Church within, in the regulation of her pastors, in the enunciation of her doctrines, we utterly and explicitly deny.' 'If the decision of the Judicial Committee be the voice of the English Church,' protested Mr. J. M. Neale,[159] 'she is actively committed to heresy.'

Of the meaning of such an attitude there can be no question; it is simply the assertion of the sovereignty of the Church over its own concerns. Naturally, this is even more vehemently asserted by those whom the decision drove into the Roman

[157] *A letter to the Rt. Hon. Lord J. Russell on the Present Persecution of a certain portion of the English Church,* London, 1850, p. 11.

[158] *Op. cit.,* p. 49.

[159] *A Few Words of Hope on the present Crisis in the English Church,* London, 1850, p. 5.

Catholic Church. 'He found,' wrote Mr. Allies,[160] 'that supremacy of the civil power to consist in a supreme jurisdiction over the Establishment in matters both of faith and of discipline, and in the derivation of Episcopal mission and jurisdiction—not as to their origin indeed, but as to their exercise—from the Crown or the nation. The writer at once felt that he must repudiate either that supremacy, or every claim of the Church, that is the one divinely-constituted society to which the possession of the truth is guaranteed, . . . the royal supremacy and the Church of God are two ideas absolutely incompatible and contradictory.' For assuredly a Church that claims to derive its character from divine institution can not admit of human interference. What she is, she is by virtue of her origin, nor does she need the aid of the State to complete her social powers. This was very distinctly proclaimed by Manning. 'The Church of England,' he said,[161] 'then being thus an integral whole, possesses within itself the fountain of doctrine and discipline, and has no need to go beyond itself for succession, orders, mission, jurisdiction and the office to declare to its own members in matters of faith, the intention of the Catholic Church.' He emphasised the fact that the royal supremacy was in no sense 'spiritual or ecclesiastical—understanding the word ecclesiastical

160 *The See of St. Peter,* London, 1850, p. 8.

161 *A letter to the Rt. Rev. Ashurst Turner, Lord Bishop of Chichester,* London, 1850, p. 5.

to mean anything beyond a civil power accidentally applied to ecclesiastical persons or causes. To make this as clear as I can, I would further add that I know of no supremacy in ecclesiastical matters inherent in the civil power or prince but either (1) such power as all princes, Christian or heathen, alike possess; or, (2) such as has been received by delegation from the Church itself."[162] The claim to complete independence could hardly be more incisively stated. Nor would he have any compromises. 'It seems to me,' he wrote of Mr. Gladstone's proposal,[163] 'a plan to amuse and lull real intentions.' He felt himself compelled to admit that laws he held divine had been violated. 'My contest now,' he told his sister,[164] 'is with the State and the world, with secular churchmen, and those who of a divine would make it a human society, or at the best a Protestant Communion.' 'A body,' he said again,[165] 'which teaches under the authority of human interpretation descends to the level of a human society,' and he felt keenly that the whole ἦθος of the Church would disappear were the bishops to betray their trust and admit the judgment. He felt that 'all Divine authority in England is at stake,' and urged to Robert Wilberforce the necessity of bearing witness 'against the whole Reformation schism, which is

[162] *Op. cit.*, p. 6.
[163] *Life*, I, 539.
[164] *Life*, I, 547.
[165] *Letter to Rev. Ashurst Turner*, p. 15.

a national and corporate private judgment."[166] Obviously his mind turned more and more against the Erastian nature of the sixteenth century settlement. 'Surely,' he wrote a little later,[167] 'the Reformation was a Tudor statute carried by violence and upheld by political power; and now that the State is divorcing the Anglican Church, it is dissolving.' The Reformation had shut out 'the authority of the living and universal church' for three hundred years until it was no longer a Church of Christ.[168] And it was essentially the implicit Erastianism of the Gorham judgment which for him was decisive. 'The violation of the doctrine of baptism,' he wrote in his diary nearly forty years later,[169] 'was of less gravity to me than the violation of the divine office of the Church by the supremacy of the Crown in Council.'

This same feeling clearly underlay the conversion of Dodsworth.[170] The attitude of the Establishment he held to be 'simply one of non-resistance, of acquiescence in what the State pleases to dictate to it,"[171] and therefore was no part of the Church at all. It is plain, he argued,[172] 'that the whole spiritual supremacy over the Church, en-

166 *Life,* I, 555.

167 *Loc. cit.,* I, 556.

168 *Loc. cit.,* I, 565.

169 *Loc. cit.,* I, 558, n. 1.

170 For Manning's opinion of him see Purcell's *Life,* I, 547. For Pusey's relations with him see Liddon's *Life of Pusey,* III, 263 ff.

171 See his *Anglicanism Considered in its Results,* p. 5, London, 1851. It was written after he became a Roman Catholic.

172 *Ibid.,* p. 56.

joyed by the Pope before the Reformation . . . has been transferred to the Crown and is now exercised by it, or rather by the State of which the Crown is the executive.' It does not matter that this power is exercised constitutionally since 'this would not relieve men's consciences, which are compelled to reclaim against the spiritual jurisdiction of the Crown, or of the State, in whatever way exercised.'"[173] It is to enter the one society which can claim the possession of Catholic principles that he is compelled to leave the Church of England. The Church has lost its ἦθος as it has lost its constitution and its freedom.[174]

III

The Oxford Movement, so far as the working out of the principles of 1833 are concerned, ended with the defection of Manning. Yet because the principles for which it stood lie buried as deeply as the origins of the Church itself they are no less living to-day. If the State has ceased to invade the functions of the Church with the ruthless determination of the last century, Erastianism is far from dead, and so long as it remains Tractarianism can not die. For, in its essence, Tractarianism is essentially the plea of the corporate body which is distinct from the State to a separate and free existence. It is a denial that

[173] *Ibid.*, p. 61.
[174] *Ibid.*, p. 65 ff.

the members of the Church are as its members no more than individuals, living under the all-inclusive sovereignty of the Crown. Certain churchmen have striven increasingly to stress its corporateness, its sense of a real life to which it is of right entitled. The Church has striven to free itself from Newman's reproach that it is 'nothing more nor less than an establishment, a department of government, or a function or operation of the State—without a substance, a mere collection of officials, depending on and living on the supreme civil power. Its unity and personality are gone . . .'[175] Where the hand of the State has seemed to imperil the right of the Church to its own life, distinguished churchmen, willing to repudiate the State-connexion have not been wanting. 'Once free from State-control,' wrote Father MacKonochie,[176] 'we shall begin, I trust, to feel as a body and not merely as individuals, that we belong to a 'kingdom which is not of this world.' Our bishops will know that their power is that of servants of Christ, not Lords of Parliament. We of the clergy shall be free from the temptations to worldly gain and ambition with which an Establishment surrounds men; and our people will receive or reject us for Christ's sake, not as ministers appointed by the State.'

175 Ward, *Life of Newman,* Vol. I, p. 234. The quotation is from the Lectures on the Difficulties of Anglicans.

176 See a letter in the London *Times,* January 11, 1869.

A similar spirit is to be observed among those who have been responsible for the growth of ritualism in the English Church. It was Dean Church who condemned what he called the 'short and easy' method of dealing with the ritualists on the ground that 'English clergymen are ministers of an Established Church, and are therefore as much bound to submit to all that Parliament orders as any other public functionary.' 'If the Church be supposed to have an existence and powers of its own,' he said,[177] 'besides what the State gives it, and, however closely joined with the State, to be something which the State, though it may claim to regulate, may neither create nor destroy—then the debate is open whether the conditions of union and co-operation have been observed on either side.' The Royal Commission on Ecclesiastical Discipline of 1906 contains a series of comments on the Erastianism of the Supremacy of the Crown which might well date back to 1833. Clergyman after clergyman unhesitatingly rejected the right of the Judicial Committee to deal with matters of ritual. 'I deny,' is the usual formula,[178] 'the competence of that tribunal as a court of final appeal in matters relating to the doctrine, discipline, and ceremonial of the Church.' Lord Hugh Cecil, in his very remarkable evidence, insisted on the distinction between Church and State. 'It is untruthful

[177] *Life and Letters of R. W. Church,* p. 284.

[178] *Report,* Vol. I, *e.g.,* pp. 15, 18, 27, 44, 48, 53, etc.

and pernicious,' he said,[179] 'to go on making believe that the Church and the State are one set of people considered in different aspects. They must be now thought of as distinct bodies.' From that unhesitating rejection of Arnoldism, he drew the obvious conclusion. 'I could not, so far as I am concerned, approve of any settlement which still left it possible for any one except the bishops to define the doctrine of the Church in the course of an ecclesiastical judgment and to make that definition binding upon the whole body of the Church.'[180] 'For my action as a priest of the Church,' one witness informed the Commission,[181] 'I am responsible to the bishop alone, to whom I am ready at all times to give account, not to the Privy Council.' Mr. G. J. Talbot, one of the most distinguished of ecclesiastical lawyers, urged that the Judicial Committee as an ecclesiastical tribunal was theoretically indefensible and practically a failure.[182] The Bishop of Exeter drew an interesting distinction between the legal and moral sovereignty of Parliament. 'While according to our constitution,' he said,[183] 'Parliament has unlimited power, the effect of its legislation must depend on the moral power behind it, and churchmen generally will distinguish between legislation invited by the Church, and legislation merely forced upon

179 *Report,* Vol. II, p. 216, Q. 10510.
180 *Report,* Vol. II, p. 221, Q. 10587.
181 *Report,* Vol. I, p. 36, Letter of Rev. G. Tremenheere.
182 *Report,* Vol. II, p. 447, Q. 14120.
183 *Report,* Vol. II, p. 484, Q. 14706.

the Church from without.' The Bishop of Birmingham repudiated the sovereignty of the State outside the temporal sphere in no less uncompromising fashion. 'The Church,' he said,[184] '. . . has become only one of many religious bodies in the State . . . and in consequence the legislative and judicial authorities of the State have ceased to be in any real sense . . . capable of claiming the allegiance of churchmen in spiritual matters.' The attitude was that of Bishop Blomfield in 1850. 'I rest my case,' he said,[185] 'on the inherent and indefeasible right of the Church to teach and maintain the truth by means of her spiritual pastors and rulers, a right inherent in her original constitution.' We are clearly dealing again with the notion of a *perfecta societas* set over against the State. There is no room in such conception for that stern Erastianism of Sir William Harcourt when he urged, with reference to this controversy,[186] 'if there is to be such a (national) church, it must be based upon national authority, and the only national authority which we recognise is that of the Crown and of Parliament.' The very strength of such contrast is a measure of the Tractarian achievement.

It is not a little curious that more attention should not have been paid to the remarkable analogy between the Oxford Movement and the

184 Vol. II. Cf. *Report*, p. 499, Q. 14953.

185 See Lord H. Cecil's evidence.

186 *Lawlessness and the National Church*, 1899, p. 13.

Disruption of 1843 in the Established Church of Scotland.[187] Each was essentially an anti-Erastian movement. It was against an all-absorptive State that each group of men was contending. There is a striking temporal parallel between the two movements. That of Oxford, in the narrower sense, begins in 1833 and ends with the conversion of Newman in 1845; that of which Chalmers was the distinguished leader begins in 1834 with the abolition by the General Assembly of lay patronage, and ends in 1843 with the secession of those who refuse to accept what they term an invasion of their peculiar province by the State. In each case, as was well enough admitted by contemporaries, the attempt was made—and in the case, particularly of Presbyterianism, this lay at the very root of its theory—to work out a doctrine of the Church which, neglecting the State, gave the Church the general organisation of a perfect society. In each case, that attempt was resisted by Parliament on the one hand, and by the Courts on the other. The State claimed a sovereignty against which, as it deemed, no part of itself might contend. But to this it was in each case retorted that Church and State were in essence distinct from one another, that each was a self-sufficing society, into the province of which the other might not wander. Both to Chalmers and Newman it seemed very clear that to admit a right of control on the part of the State was to deny that divine consti-

[187] See the *Political Theory of the Disruption, supra.*

tution to which their churches laid claim. They would have urged, with Warburton, that the two societies are 'sovereign and independent of each other;' but they would have denied his conclusion that 'their joint forces must co-operate thus to apply and enforce the influence of religion"[188] if in that union the sovereignty of the Church was impaired. If, as seems probable, the effort of Chalmers was more logical and more consistent than the somewhat chaotic antagonism of the Tractarians, that was rather because he had inherited a definite theory of Church and State, which Newman and his followers had to hammer out for themselves. Both Chalmers and Newman believed in a purified Establishment;[189] but each also asserted roundly that the benefit was derived by the State rather than the Church. It was when it was conceived that the fact of a statutory alliance involved also the idea of a statutory control, that they found themselves compelled to abandon the Church of their origin.[190]

It was a definition of the Church that the Tractarians attempted, and they found almost immediately that to define its identity was to assert

188 See his *Alliance of Church and State,* p. 86.

189 Chalmers himself actually lectured on their benefits in London in 1838.

190 Though of course Newman claimed that in 1845 he was joining the true Catholic Church, just as Chalmers looked upon the Free Church as the true Presbyterian Church. The other had abandoned the Headship of Christ in his view and had therefore lost its identity with the Church of Knox and Melville which he still represented.

its exclusiveness. If it was created by God it could not be controlled by man; if it was created by God, it was not subject to the ordinances of a man-created institution like the State. They would never have accepted the federalism of Nicholas of Cusa, with its implied admission that the State might reform the Church;[191] between *jus publicum* and *jus sacrum* they drew a firm distinction. In reality, their position is singularly medieval: it is almost an adequate description of their attitude to the State to say that it is a Guelfic attitude. It was against the pretensions put forward in the name of the Prince by men like John of Paris[192] that they were contending, of Wyclif,[193] of Hus,[194] and of Gregory of Heimberg.[195] For, in all these cases, the position of the controversy between Pope and Emperor had led the imperialists to assume the superiority of kingly power, and, as a consequence, the right of the Crown to deal as it would with the Church; just as Lord John Russell in 1833 implicitly assumed the right of the State to deal with the Irish Church. Marsilio of Padua's claim that the Church is no more than an institution within the State,[196] was exactly the expression of the Whig government's attitude. With him it

[191] *Works, De Concordantia Catholica,* 11. c. 40.

[192] See his *Tractatus de potestate regia et papali* in Goldast, II, p. 108 ff., esp. c. 21.

[193] Cf. De Officio Regis, esp. pp. 34-36, 137, 138.

[194] Goldast, I, 232-242.

[195] Goldast, I, 559-560.

[196] Cf. Defensor Pacis, cc. 5-6.

would have said that the ecclesiastical sovereign was the body of the faithful, just as he would, with their approval, identify the faithful with the nation as a whole. The whole foundation of Tractarianism lies in the fact that this had ceased to be the case. They argued, therefore, that the change meant logically the impossibility of confiding the government of the Church to those without its fold. This sense they felt so passionately is already fully developed in Thomas Aquinas,[197] and in him, as in them, this led to the common notion of the Church itself as a State;[198] and in the Middle Ages not even the stoutest imperialist denied the truth of this, even when he repudiated its connexion with worldly concerns.[199] So that it is not difficult to understand the medievalism of the Oxford Movement. It is therein but seeking its natural affiliations. If it goes back for its atmosphere to those beginnings of the controversy it so strikingly illustrates, that is because it is itself the continuator of that controversy. The Reformation had decided the battle in favour of the State, but it had secured rather independence than sovereignty for the State and sovereignty the Church could still, and does still, challenge. If it seems, as with the Tractarians, to have put aside the dreams of men like Gregory

[197] *E.g.,* Summa Cont. Gent., IV, 76.

[198] *E.g.,* the Gloss on C. 3. X. I, 41. and Hostiensis. Summa, I, 1, nr. 4.

[199] The Somnium Vidarii, I, c. 1-16. Ockham. Dialog., I, 6, c. III. John of Paris, Tract, Introd. and c. 13-14. The references can be multiplied almost indefinitely.

VII with his absorption of Church in State,[200] that is, as the work of W. G. Ward makes very clear, rather from necessity than from desire. They realised that the time for a world-church had passed away. It seemed then natural to demand that what remained of her mighty dominion she should have the right to cultivate undisturbed.[201]

It is in one significant sense alone that they have advanced beyond the prevalent conceptions of medieval thought. Where, to men like Baldus and Innocent IV, the Corporation of the State—whether that State be lay or ecclesiastical—is essentially a fictitious thing, the Tractarians had transcended the limited conception of personality as associated only with the individual life. One who reads the sermons of Newman, above all that most eloquent and most tragic of farewells before his Hegira to Littlemore, will not doubt that to him than the Church there is no life more real or more splendid. She is his mother; it is for her infinite woes that above all he has concern. In her is all the richness of his life, and her injury brings to him what is worse than desolation. Nor is that sense less keenly felt, even if it finds a less eloquent expression, in Pusey and Keble. To all of

200 Cf. the striking phrases in the *Registrum,* Bk. IV, ep. II (1076), pp. 242-243.

201 The introductory lecture of Dr. Figgis, *From Gerson to Grotius* works out this conception most admirably. I should say that the substantial difference lies in the fact that the Church has become separate from the State to the Tractarians whereas to the medieval publicist the State was, in Dr. Figgis' phrase, the 'police-department of the Church.'

them to be members of a Church was to be of a fellowship the more precious because in its life they found the mysterious oneness of a vivid personality.[202]

IV

It is becoming more and more clear that the future trend of political theory is away from that attitude which bids us read all things in their relation to the State. Certain things that body will not undertake because it is not competent to undertake them. It will cease to attempt the control of religious doctrine. The tribunals of the State no less than its legislature only interfere with the most precious part of corporate freedom when, though an alien organisation, they attempt a perilous invasion. The Church has its history, its laws, its doctrines; the State can not, from a stunted theory of its sovereign power, attempt the fusion of her customs with its own.[203] It will rather leave her free to work out, as she best may, the grave and complex problems that confront her. From her own sense of righteousness it will welcome the good. From her own right to freedom it will cherish the beneficent product. From a new

202 Dr. Figgis, in the brilliant little essay on Newman which he has printed as an appendix to his *Fellowship of the Mystery* has made this very clear. It is of course merely one result of that realism which Gierke and Maitland have taught us to understand.

203 As in Rev. v. Dibden [1910], P. Q. 57; Thompson v. Dibden [1912], A. C. 533. The whole mass of ritual cases is of course another aspect of the same problem.

world, moreover, that has been perhaps untrammelled by the struggles of the old, it will learn certain great and significant lessons. Where civil right is not directly concerned, it will, as in America,[204] maintain that it has no jurisdiction. It will say that Church membership is a Church right not a civil right,[205] Church discipline a matter for the ecclesiastical tribunal. It will realise that, should the Church use her powers ill, she and she only, will suffer. She will forfeit her privileges not because they are conditional, and therefore subject to revocation,[206] but because where men are wronged they will renounce their membership of the State, be its nature lay or clerical. And the State will understand that the degree of her freedom will be the measure of her progress. In that event the tragedies of Oxford will not have been vain.

[204] Fitzgerald v. Robinson, 112 Mass. 371. Shannon v. Frost, 3 B. Mon. (Ky.), 253, 258. Dees v. Moss Point Baptist Church, 17, So. 1 (Miss.). Waller v. Howell, 20 Misc., 236, 45 N. Y. Supp., 790.

[205] Grosvenor v. United Society of Believers, 118 Mass., 78; and even more striking, Fitzgerald v. Robinson, 112 Mass. 371. Farnsworth v. Storrs, 5 Cush. (Mass.), 412, 416.

[206] It is, I think, the natural deduction from Jarves and Hatheway, 3 Johns. (N. Y.), 180; cf. Konkle v. Haven, 140 Mich. 472, 478.

CHAPTER IV

THE POLITICAL THEORY OF THE CATHOLIC REVIVAL[1]

I

WITH the passage of the Roman Catholic Relief Act of 1829, a body of men who had been for too long excluded from political privilege became once more citizens of the State.[2] The grounds for their exclusion had been, for the most part, based upon a single fact. 'The modern theory,' writes Lord Acton,[3] 'which has swept away every authority except that of the State, and has made the sovereign power irresistible by multiplying those who shared it, is the enemy of that common freedom in which religious freedom is included. It condemns, as a State within the State, every inner group and community, class or corporation, administering its own affairs; and, by proclaiming the abolition of privileges, it

[1] The best general work on the Catholic Revival in England is that of M. Thureau-Dangin: 'La Renaissance Catholique en Angleterre au XIXme siècle.' This has been translated. To M. Thureau-Dangin, however, the movement is entirely non-political.

[2] The story of the emancipation may now be consulted in Monsignor Bernard Ward's *Eve of Catholic Emancipation*. It is, however, weak on the non-religious side.

[3] *History of Freedom*, p. 151.

emancipates the subjects of every such authority, in order to transfer them exclusively to its own.' The divine right of kings, was, in fact, replaced by a right divine inherent in the State; and it was argued that men owed to it an allegiance that should be undivided. But the Pope was a temporal sovereign, and to him, as the head of their Church, the Catholics owed a full allegiance. They were a close and united body, the typical *imperium in imperio* of which Lord Acton wrote; and it was perhaps logical, even if it was ungenerous, that men should deem it impossible for such allegiance to be compatible with loyalty to the British Crown.[4] That argument had, during the previous half-century, prevailed no less against the calm and splendid philosophy of Burke, than against the annual eloquence of Grattan.[5] Sir H. Parnell had summed up their unanswerable case in a single sentence, when he asked if Catholic emancipation could have other than beneficent effect. 'What,' he demanded,[6] 'can be its certain and practical effect on the Catholic body at large but universal content and unqualified gratitude to the legislature that granted it?' Yet the musty prejudices of two centuries, and the unthinking obstinacy of George III proved too strong for the principles of political

4 See, for example, Lord Redesdale in Hansard, New Series, Vol. XXXIV, p. 1251.

5 See Charles Butler's tribute to him in *Historical Memoirs,* Vol. IV, p. 392.

6 Hansard, 2d Series, Vol. XXXI, p. 477.

reason, until the genius of Daniel O'Connell perceived the value of militant agitation.[7]

It was, prejudice apart, emphatically a question of unity of allegiance which had lain at the root of the Catholic difficulty. To the majority of statesmen and ecclesiastics—there are certain noble exceptions—Great Britain was still the country of 1688,[8] essentially a Protestant country of which the identity would be destroyed by the admission of Catholics to political power. The practical unanimity of the bishops on this question is little less than amazing. They seemed united in what Andrew Marvell—confronted by a not dissimilar problem—gaily called 'pushpin theology'—the theory that 'there can not be a pin pulled out of the Church, but the State immediately totters.'[9] 'The reason for adhering to this principle in this country,' the Bishop of Worcester told the House of Lords,[10] 'was particularly forcible, as the Protestant religion was so intimately woven with the whole system of the Constitution.' 'Be allegiance what it will,' said the Bishop of Norwich,[11] 'if that allegiance is divided between the king of the country and the foreigner, the king of the country has not the

7 Monsignor Ward, *op. cit.*, Vol. III, Chapters 40, 43, 46, adds much to our knowledge of this part of the history.

8 Cf. Mr. Russell Smith's valuable little work, *Religious Liberty under Charles II and James II*, especially Chapter 2.

9 *Rehearsal Transposed*, p. 132.

10 Hansard, 2d Series, Vol. XL, p. 390, May 17, 1819.

11 *Op. cit.*, p. 395.

share he ought to have and which in this country he really has from members of the Established Church.' 'Such exclusion,' urged the Bishop of Llandaff,[12] 'may be justified on grounds of civil delinquency . . . the allegiance of the churchman is entire—he acknowledges the king as supreme in matters ecclesiastical as well as civil . . . but if a Church is governed by a foreigner who has neither dependence on, nor a common interest with, the king of the country, the civil allegiance of those who belong to that Church can not fail to be weakened by their ecclesiastical allegiance. . . . They are not so good and so useful members of the State as members of the Establishment.' It was in a similar vein that the Bishop of Ossory argued that by their principles the Catholics must attempt the destruction of the Established Church, which would place the State in grave danger. 'Pushpin theology' may be; but it was keenly felt. 'They were,' he said,[13] 'so intimately connected that whatever tended to injure the one must infallibly injure the other.' The principle of Lord Liverpool's uncompromising antagonism was in no wise distinct from this episcopal opposition. The State had need of the Church, and the Revolution of 1688 had 'settled that the principle of our government in all its parts was Protestant . . . the moment you throw open your door to equal and general concession . . .

12 Hansard, 2d Series, Vol. XXXVI, p. 616, May 16, 1817.
13 Hansard, *loc. cit.*, p. 642.

Parliament will cease immediately to be a Protestant Parliament."[14] Nor did the pamphleteers feel otherwise. The government, 'Julius' told the people of England,[15] 'is not only essentially, but vitally Protestant. And it is thus that the admission of persons professing Catholic tenets to political power, either now or at any time hereafter becomes a thing literally impossible.'

The supporters of the Catholics realised quite clearly that the fundamental question was that of the nature of the State. Plunkett urged that their exclusion on religious grounds 'was calculated to impress an opinion that religion was only an instrument for State purposes."[16] The constitution was to him essentially secular in its nature. His attitude was very like that of Penn and the Tolerationists of the seventeenth century. As to the latter it seemed evident that 'religion is no part of the old English government,"[17] so to Plunkett the law enjoined certain duties, and whoever performed those duties was entitled to the privileges of citizenship.[18] Canning admitted that there had been a time when Catholic and Protestant had struggled 'to see which should wed the State and make her exclusively its own. But the time of combat had passed—the Catholics tendered a

[14] Hansard, *loc. cit.*, p. 647.

[15] See his able little pamphlet, *First Letter to the People of England on the Catholic Question*, London, 1829.

[16] Hansard, 2d Series, Vol. V, p. 965, February 28, 1821.

[17] Penn, *England's Present Interest Discovered*, p. 32 (1675).

[17] Hansard, New Series, Vol. V, p. 969, February 28, 1821.

willing submission . . . the Protestant religion and the Constitution were inseparably united' so that no danger need be apprehended from Catholic antagonism to the Church of England."[19] And Sidney Smith, who perhaps more than any other writer made plain to humble men the Catholic argument,[20] went directly to the charge of divided allegiance as the root of the matter. The Catholics were charged with owing allegiance to one who might dethrone kings, and were themselves bound to destroy heretics. 'To all of which,' wrote Smith,[21] 'may be returned this one conclusive answer that the Catholics are ready to deny these doctrines upon oath. And as the whole controversy is whether the Catholics shall by means of oaths be excluded from certain offices in the State, those who contend that the continuation of these excluding oaths is essential to the public safety, must admit that oaths are binding upon Catholics, and a security to the State that what they say is true.' Nor did he fear the fact that the Catholics owed an allegiance no less to the Pope than to the British Crown. The one was spiritual, and not even distantly connected with the second, which was concerned with civil policy. 'What is meant by allegiance to the crown,' he said,[22] 'is, I presume obedience to Acts of Parliament and a

[19] Hansard, New Series, Vol. VII, p. 517, May 10, 1822.

[20] It is a pity that Monsignor Ward in his three volumes should not have paid Sidney Smith the tribute his *Letters of Peter Plymley* merit.

[21] *Collected Works,* p. 250.

[22] *Collected Works,* p. 684.

resistance to those who are constitutionally proclaimed to be the enemies of the country. I have seen and heard of no instance for this century and a half past, where the spiritual sovereign has presumed to meddle with the affairs of the temporal sovereign. The Catholics deny him such power by the most solemn oaths which the wit of man can devise. In every war the army and navy are full of Catholic soldiers and sailors; and if their allegiance in temporal matters is unimpeachable and unimpeached, what matter to whom they choose to pay spiritual obedience, and to adopt as their guide in genuflexion and psalmody? Suppose these same Catholics are foolish enough to be governed by a set of Chinese moralists in their diet, this would be a third allegiance; and if they were regulated by Brahmins in their dress, this would be a fourth allegiance; and if they received the directions of the Patriarchs of the Greek Church in educating their children, here is another allegiance; and as long as they fought and paid taxes, and kept clear of the Quarter-Sessions and Assizes, what matter how many fanciful supremacies and frivolous allegiances they choose to manufacture or accumulate for themselves?' Here, at any rate, Sidney Smith was as irresistible in his logic as in his humour.

The attitude of the Catholic authorities was in no wise different from that of their Protestant supporters. From the early days of the struggle, they tried to make it plain that, whatever their connexion with the Church of Rome, the loyalty they owed the British Crown in civil affairs was unexcepted and entire. 'We acknowledge,' wrote the Vicars Apostolic of England in 1813,[23] 'that we owe to the State a proof of our civil allegiance and security against all treasonable designs. You (the Catholic laity) in common with us . . . have given to our country the strongest proofs of civil allegiance, and an abhorrence of all treasonable designs by the profession of your religious principles, by the solemn oaths you have taken with unquestionable sincerity, and by the known loyalty of your conduct. . . . We are all British-born subjects, and as such we feel an interest and a glory in the security and prosperity of our country. We can no more betray our country than our religion.' This is a sufficiently clear pronouncement. Yet two years later O'Connell made an even more striking repudiation of any claim of the Pope to temporal allegiance. 'I deny,' he said,[24] 'the doctrine that the Pope has any temporal authority, directly or indirectly, in Ireland, we have all denied that doctrine on oath, and we would die to resist it.' 'I know of no foreign prince,' he went on to assert,[25] 'whom, in temporal matters the Catholics of Ireland would more decidedly resist than the Pope.' Nor did Charles Butler—whose great legal powers give to

23 Ward, *op. cit.*, Vol. II, p. 65.
24 Ward, II, 143.
25 *Op. cit.*, II, p. 148.

his declaration a peculiar value—speak otherwise. 'If the Pope,' said the pamphlet reprinted by him,[26] 'should pretend to dissolve or dispense with his Majesty's subjects from their allegiance, on account of heresy or schism, such dispensation would be vain and null; and all Catholic subjects notwithstanding such dispensation or absolution, would still be bound in conscience to defend their king and country at the hazard of their lives and fortunes (as far as Protestants would be bound) even against the Pope himself, in case he should invade the nation.' To the same effect was the petition of the Catholic Board to the king. 'To your Majesty,' it says,[27] 'they swear full and undivided allegiance; in your Majesty alone they recognize the power of the civil sword within this realm of England. They acknowledge in no prince, prelate, State, or potentate, any power or authority to use the same within the said realm, in any matter or cause whatever, whether civil, spiritual or ecclesiastical.' Dr. O'Hanlon of Maynooth told Lord Harrowby's commission that the college virtually taught Gallicanism. 'We teach in Maynooth,' he said,[28] 'that the Pope has no temporal power whatever, direct or indirect. We have affirmed that doctrine upon our solemn oaths, and we firmly maintain it. . . . We hold the same

[26] *Op. cit.*, II, 302. The author of the pamphlet is unknown, but it was reprinted by Butler with emphatic approval, as an appendix to his *Historical Memorials* in the later editions.

[27] Ward, *op. cit.*, II, 302.

[28] *Quarterly Review*, 1875, p. 494.

doctrine in regard to the Church.' In 1826, all the Catholic bishops united in a declaration that in civil matters 'they hold themselves bound in conscience to obey the civil government of this realm . . . notwithstanding any dispensation or order to the contrary to be had from the Pope or any authority of the Church of Rome.'[29] And Dr. Doyle, the most influential, if the youngest,[30] of the Irish Catholic bishops, assured Lord Liverpool that 'Papal influence will never induce the Catholics of this country either to continue tranquil or to be disturbed, either to aid, or to oppose the Government; and that your lordship can contribute much more than the Pope to secure their allegiance or to render them disaffected.'[31]

It is obviously a political question as to the nature of sovereignty that is at the bottom of this discussion; and the attitude of Parliament, on the one hand, and of the Catholics on the other, to the problem of security against Roman aggression throws this aspect of emancipation into very striking relief. The fear clearly is that the nature of their religious allegiance will compel Catholics to endanger the Protestant nature of the State. Means must therefore be had to make the government sufficiently in control of Catholic loyalty as to guard against that risk. In Grattan's Bill of 1813 a long oath of loyalty was inserted by Can-

29 *Declaration of the Catholic Bishops,* etc., London, 1826, p. 14.

30 See the amusing opinion expressed of him by the voluble and excitable Milner. Ward, *op. cit.,* III, 153.

31 *Letter to Lord Liverpool on the Roman Catholic Claims,* p. 115.

ning intended to secure Great Britain against Roman interference. A Board of Commission, selected from distinguished Catholics, was to be chosen and was to accept all appointees to vacant bishoprics in the Roman Church, and to examine all documents from Rome before admitting them into the country.[32] But this measure raised in its turn a curious problem. While it did not hurt the implicit Gallicanism of men like Butler, it was unalterably opposed by the redoubtable Milner and by the Irish bishops. It was, said the latter,[33] 'utterly incompatible with the discipline of the Roman Catholic Church and with the free exercise of our religion,' since it involved the admission that the State had the right to interfere with the internal affairs of the Church. The bill, said Milner,[34] 'was contrived with a heart and malice which none but the spirits of wickedness in high places . . . could have suggested to undermine and wither the fair trees of the English and Irish Catholic Churches.' Nor would he admit the rescript of Monsignor Quaranotti, the sub-prefect of Propaganda, who, in the enforced absence of the Pope as Napoleon's prisoner, approved the proposal.[35] O'Connell even went so far as to assert that not even the Pope himself would make

[32] The text of these amendments is given in *Parliamentary Debates*, Vol. XXVI, pp. 88 *seq.*

[33] Ward, II, 37.

[34] Ward, II, 41. The 'heart and malice' is that of Charles Butler to whose Gallicanism Milner was unalterably opposed. See Ward, *passim.*

[35] Ward, II, pp. 71 *seq.*

him admit such an invasion of Catholic integrity.[36] 'The Catholics of Ireland,' said the *Dublin Daily Chronicle,*[37] 'will not recognise any of its acts as binding and obligatory . . . they have distinctly and on their solemn oaths protested against the recognition of any foreign temporal authority.' By 1817, it was clear that Catholic opinion would tolerate neither the royal approval of bishops, nor the regulation of ecclesiastical intercourse with Rome.[38]

The reason is sufficiently plain. The Roman Catholic Church has always claimed that the Church is itself a perfect society, and as such it could hardly acknowledge the supremacy of the State. Milner, indeed, from this standpoint insisted, and logically, that no Catholic could swear undivided allegiance to the temporal sovereign 'as there might always be occasions when the authority of the State might be at variance with that of the Church';[39] and he seems to have objected to the limited sense in which the Catholics interpreted allegiance. Securities of any kind seemed to him 'Bills of Pains and Penalties' which struck at the root of Catholic independence, and he actually organised a petition against a Relief Bill of Plunkett's on this ground.[40] His

36 *Life and Speeches,* Vol. II, 178. Ward, II, 143.

37 Ward, II, 150.

38 See the abortive resolutions proposed by Bishop Poynter. Ward, II, 242.

39 Ward, III, 58.

40 Ward, III, 63.

position seems to have won the support of the Roman authorities, who expressed surprise and sorrow that the laity of the Church should have presented a petition to the king 'in which they have protested that they acknowledge in no one but himself any power or authority, either civil, spiritual or ecclesiastical' and emphasised their opinion that such an attitude would be 'unlawful and schismatical.'[41] The reason of this attitude becomes clear from a note of Bishop Milner's on what he understood allegiance to mean under the laws of England. It is not to allegiance itself 'which means nothing more than the duty which a subject owes to the Prince or State under which he lives' that he objected, but, 'as it is gathered from the laws of the country which invested the king with the power of excommunication, or cutting off from the body of Christ, and of reforming all heresies, and, therefore, of judging of them.'[42] It was thus against the theoretical limitations upon all bodies not the State which is implied in the doctrine of parliamentary sovereignty that he made his protest. He could owe allegiance to the State only so far as it did not conflict with the loyalty his Church had the right to demand.

A twofold tendency within the Catholic fold was clear thus early. Men like Butler were Gallican in their attitude,[43] willing to combine with the

[41] Ward, III, 77.

[42] Ward, III, 158.

[43] Manning's attacks on the Gallicanism of the old Catholics are well known. See Purcell, II, pp. 217, 308.

Unitarians to secure emancipation on the broad basis of a general religious toleration;[44] while others, like Milner, were profoundly Ultramontane in temper. It was with the first body of thought that general English sentiment allied itself. 'You will consider,' said the Speech from the throne announcing the Relief Bill,[45] 'whether the removal of these disabilities can be effected consistently with the full and permanent security of our establishments in Church and State.' It was the knowledge at Rome that this feeling must be respected which had prevented the recognition of the Jesuits in England;[46] and when, in 1815, Cardinal Gonsalvi had visited England he had, in deference to public sentiment, not only put aside the ordinary robes of his office, but had been most careful to avoid all questions of precedence.[47] For the old prejudices were far from dead. As late as 1827, Arthur Hallam told Mr. Gladstone how the gibes in 'King John' against the Pope had met with eager applause; and the Oxford bedmakers thought separation might be preferable to emancipating the Catholics.[48] When the Bill actually came, the concession to this sentiment was apparent. The oath was of the most drastic nature, and prevented any Catholic from attempting to secure a change in the character of the

44 Ward, III, 168.
45 Ward, III, 247.
46 Ward, III, 21.
47 Nielson's *History of the Papacy*, I, 350.
48 Morley, I, 40.

State.[49] The Catholics were forbidden to take the names of Protestant sees for their bishoprics—a clause which, ignored in Ireland, was in England to lead to serious trouble.[50] Catholics were forbidden from religious celebration outside a church or private house, and from wearing the habits of their orders.[51] The Jesuits were prohibited from entrance into England.[52] On the more negative side, Catholics were not to hold certain offices, nor were they to have direct concern with religious appointments.[53] Gifts to religious orders were made void,[54] and the rule against tracts for superstitious purposes was sufficient to invalidate such bequests as one for masses or prayer for the repose of souls.[55] It is perhaps worth noting that in the year before the passage of the Relief Act, a bequest for inculcating the doctrine of the Pope's supremacy was declared illegal;[56] and it was not until 1836 that a Roman Catholic marriage became valid in the eyes of the law.[57]

The Relief Act clearly bears upon its face the marks of the difficult circumstances under which

49 Ward, III, 362, and see his comment at pp. 254-255.

50 Ward, III, 257, and see below.

51 This has practically been inoperative.

52 This again has been inoperative.

53 10. G. IV.

54 SS. 12, 17, 18; and in connexion with his ownership of an advowson, see 3 Jac. I, c. 5. s. 13. and I, W. & M. C. 26. s. 2.

55 This is of old standing, see *e.g.*, Adams v. Lambert (1602), 4 Co. Rep. 104. West v. Shuttleworth, (1835), 2 My. & K., 684. Heath v. Chapman (1854), 2 Drew, 417, 425.

56 De Themmines v. De Bonneval (1828), 5 Russ. 288.

57 Dicey, *Law and Public Opinion* (Second ed.), p. 345.

it was passed. It is evident that most Englishmen suspected the Catholic religion of sapping the foundations of civic loyalty; and the Act rather lulled than removed that suspicion. The securities were plainly enough the mark of a fear that the sovereignty of the Crown might suffer impairment; for if, as Plunket had stated fifteen years before, the 'true principles of the Constitution' were 'the safety of the Established Church and of the Protestant throne,'[58] and if no concession not consistent with these could be yielded, it was clear not only that religious proselytisation must be circumscribed but also that enthusiasts would hesitate to suffer such a limitation of religious freedom as was here implied. Certainly Bishop Doyle's way out of the impasse was more casuistically ingenious than politically logical.[59]

The fact of the matter is that, as is usually the case, English practice was better than English theory. The Irish difficulty apart[60]—and only complete emancipation could be its solution—to the attitude of men like Charles Butler it was scarcely possible even for the most bigoted of Protestants to take political exception. He admitted the authority of common law and statute law, both of which he had himself illuminated by his profound learning. He did not hesitate to accept the claims of constituted jurisdiction in all

58 See his collected speeches, ed. Hoey (1855), p. 117.

59 *Life,* Vol. II, p. 126.

60 Plunket has stated its nature very eloquently and unanswerably. *Collected Speeches,* pp. 111-135.

civil and religious matters that did not touch his conscience. He repudiated the temporal supremacy of the Pope. To have excluded him from the exercise of political power when, without its possession, he had been for so long loyal to the British Crown, would have been to create an allegiance which no thinking man could accept. The Catholic had been 'a marked man and a plotting sectary'[61] in the eyes of the populace for more than two hundred years, yet he had not attempted the destruction of an oppressive State. Emancipation came as the half-unwilling and half-accomplished recognition of the error inherent in a theory of sovereignty which, because it makes political outcasts of those whose intimate beliefs it fails to control, is at war with all the deeper realities of human life.

II

If the Papacy, as Thomas Hobbes so scornfully remarked, be no more than the 'ghost of the Holy Roman Empire sitting crowned upon the ruins thereof,' it has not seldom possessed sufficient substantiality to cause Englishmen some vigorous tremors. Whatever its defects, Ultramontanism has, at any rate in its broader form, the merit of a respectable pedigree. Nor has the attitude of England to its demands changed very greatly in the centuries since the Reformation Parliament

[61] The phrase is Plunket's. *Collected Speeches*, p. 217.

bestowed on the omnivorous Henry the attributes of papal sovereignty.[62] But an Anglican usurpation was not likely to decrease the pretensions of that organism of which changelessness was the proud boast. The claims of Gregory VII and Boniface VIII may have slumbered; but dead they were not. Certainly to the divines of the seventeenth century it was the supreme merit of the Reformation that it prevented an allegiance to the sovereign which had been heretofore precarious because divided.[63] But the condition of its removal was a narrow and uncritical antagonism to whatever savoured of Roman practice. The penalisation of the Catholic religion turned it once more into a secret society—mistakenly since the Armada had sufficiently proved the implicit Gallicanism of the English Catholics. Nevertheless it was true that they owed allegiance to an ecclesiastical monarch who claimed the deposing power. Men never forgot the Bull of Pius V, and they were determined not to endure a repetition of his offence. So that when an enlightened opinion at length admitted of a fair measure of toleration, it was upon conditions that the boon was extended. The fear of Rome was far from dead; it was rather the suspicion of the English Catholics that had been removed and the latter were to find how

62 For some striking remarks on the Byzantinism of Henry VIII see Maitland's *English Law and the Renaissance*, especially pp. 14 ff.

63 This is the essential argument of such works as Leslie's *A Battle Royal*, Barrow on the Pope's Supremacy, Jackson on Christian Obedience, and the like.

easily the lightest indiscretion might fan those suspicions once more into flame.

The twenty years succeeding emancipation were used by the Catholics in reaping the harvest that had been so long and so painfully sowing.[64] They were not unfortunate in their position. Englishmen discovered that the Catholic gentry had virtues very similar to their own. The reputation of statesmen like Montalembert, the history of thinkers like Schlegel, and, from 1846, the suspected liberalism of Pius IX, but, above all, the influence of the Oxford Movement and the skilful social ability of Cardinal Wiseman, were all bound to add greatly to the prestige of their situation. People began with interested amazement to hear O'Connell declare that the Catholic Church had ever been on the side of democracy,[65] and the corrosive sublimate of which Hurrell Froude's mind was mainly composed assisted in the dissolution of Newman's evangelical suspicions.[66] The Napoleonic adventure, moreover, had done much to check men's fears of a Catholic revival. The political edifice of the temporal power seemed less secure than at any former time in modern history. The things of which De Maistre did not lightly

[64] In his two recent volumes, *The Sequel to Catholic Emancipation,* Monsignor Bernard Ward has related the internal history of the Catholic Body in England to the re-establishment of the hierarchy. See also Mr. Wilfrid Ward's able *Life of Cardinal Wiseman.*

[65] Cf. Acton, *History of Freedom,* p. 190.

[66] See Newman, *Difficulties of Anglicans* (ed. of 1908), Vol. I, pp. 37 ff.

dream, the *Symbolik* of Möhler, the grave charm of the Münich reaction—all these might logically lead to a reformulation of the Catholic political system, but it was a reformation of which men had ceased to be afraid.[67] Newman, Manning, Gladstone—all of them visited Rome in the full vigour of early manhood; but if they were historically impressed, they were in nowise religiously convinced.[68] And even the rosy optimism of Pius IX was quite early to expect the fall of the temporal power.[69]

Then, suddenly, there came a change. From an attitude of watchful waiting, Wiseman, who in 1847 had become pro-Vicar Apostolic of the London district, assumed a critical offensive. In the *Dublin Review* he had an admirable means of propaganda—and that the more important since it was an age when men still read theology with interested acumen. A skilful controversialist, he followed the fortunes of the Oxford Movement with unfailing eagerness; nor had he failed to contribute his observations. An article on the Donatist schism in 1839 had perhaps done more than any other single event to convince Newman that the 'via media' was untenable.[70] He perhaps

67 Indeed, as Acton pointed out in 1858, it was doubtful if there was a Catholic political system at all. See his essay, 'Political Thoughts on the Church' in the *History of Freedom.*

68 Cf. Newman's *Apologia* (ed. Ward), p. 133, and Morley's *Gladstone,* (Pop. ed.), I, 65.

69 See the preface to Dollinger's *Kirche und Kirchen,* where he gives an account of this prophecy made to the Archbishop of Rheims.

70 Ward, *Life of Wiseman,* I, 321.

did more, as Mr. Ward reminds us, to reawaken Englishmen to the historic significance of his Church than any other Catholic of the age.[71] It was the beginning of the Romeward movement. The folly of Oxford completed in W. G. Ward a process that logic had already begun. Dalgairns, St. John and Richard Stanton followed, while Newman, as Dean Stanley caustically put it, 'had recourse to whispering, like the slave of Midas, his secret to the reeds.'[72] Then he, too, went and with his conversion a flood-gate of proselytisation seemed open. The secession, says Mr. Lecky,[73] 'was quite unparalleled in magnitude since that which had taken place under the Stuarts.' It was no wonder that Wiseman rejoiced. The accession of so strong a body of intelligence seemed to synchronise naturally with his plans for broadening the basis of English Catholic culture.[74] Then in 1846 came the election of the new pope and the dawn, as men thought, of a new liberal Catholicism. It seemed clear to Wiseman and his colleagues that this was a time for action. On a visit to Rome in 1847,[75] he first broached his plans for the restoration of the Catholic hierarchy in England. There were good reasons for his plan; though at the time the antagonism of Cardinal Acton and the excitement of the crisis at Rome was sufficient to delay

[71] *Op. cit.*, I, 330.
[72] *Op. cit.*, I, 425.
[73] *History of Rationalism*, I, 159.
[74] *Life*, I, 440.
[75] *Ibid.*, I, 474 ff.

any action, Wiseman himself was able to secure the exercise of Lord Palmerston's influence against Austria and the despatch of an unofficial but important envoy—Lord Minto—to the papal Curia.[76] Though the negotiations for the hierarchy were in abeyance, they were by no means forgotten. By 1848 the Papacy was convinced; and Lord John Russell, on behalf of the English government, had made public announcement that though he would not assist, at any rate he would not interfere.[77] In 1850 the expected event took place. Wiseman was created Cardinal-Archbishop of Westminster and the Pope's brief of September 29 re-established the hierarchy.[78] In his famous Pastoral of October 7, 'from out of the Flaminian Gate' Wiseman, dramatically perhaps, but with an intelligible pride, announced the event to the Catholics of England.

He had anticipated no storm. It had seemed to him that the matter was one of no more than Catholic concern, the announcement of a metropolitan that the method of internal ecclesiastical administration had been changed. Yet he had, perhaps, been supremely unfortunate in the method of reporting he chose to adopt. Himself a man of exuberant temperament, it was with some genial bombast that the good news was told. 'So that at present' ran the Pastoral,[79] 'and till such time

[76] *Ibid.*, I, 480 ff.

[77] *Ibid.*, I, 492-494.

[78] *Ibid.*, I, 529.

[79] *Ibid.*, I, 543.

as the Holy See shall think fit otherwise to provide, we govern, and shall continue to govern, the counties of Middlesex, Hertford and Essex as Ordinary thereof, and those of Surrey, Sussex, Kent, Berkshire and Hampshire, with the islands annexed, as Administrator with Ordinary jurisdiction.' He was, of course, doing no more than marking the confines of his ecclesiastical jurisdiction. But it was not thus that his action was interpreted. The claim of government was at once taken in its fullest and most literal sense. The Pope was claiming to supersede Queen Victoria; nothing less than her supersession was intended. He was the new Hildebrand aiming at a new Canossa. 'We can only receive it,' said the *Times*,[80] 'as an audacious and conspicuous display of pretensions to resume the absolute spiritual dominion of this island, which Rome has never abandoned.' Nor did the *Times* alone fan the flame of popular resentment. In an extraordinary letter to the Bishop of Durham, Lord John Russell gave full rein to his feelings. 'There is an assumption of power in all the documents which have come from Rome,' he wrote,[81] 'a pretension to supremacy over the realm of England, and a claim to sole and undivided sway which is inconsistent with the Queen's supremacy, with the rights of our bishops and clergy, and with the spiritual independence of the nation as asserted even in Roman Catholic

[80] October 19, 1850.
[81] *Life of Wiseman*, I, 548.

times.' But the pretensions would be resisted. 'No foreign prince or potentate will be permitted to fasten his fetters upon a nation which has so long and so nobly vindicated its right to freedom of opinion.' The legal position of Dr. Wiseman would be considered and due steps taken to enforce the law.

For four months England luxuriated in a recrudescence of all its ancient prejudices. The Lord Chancellor quoted *King John* at the Guildhall. Bishops vied with one another in the choice of extravagant epithets and addressed a petition of loyalty and remonstrance to the Queen. In reply the sovereign was made to assure them of her 'determination to uphold alike the rights of my crown and the independence of my people against all aggressions and encroachments of any foreign power.'[82] Meetings of protest were held all over the country; everywhere, too, since Russell's letter happily coincided with Guy Fawkes' Day, Pope and Cardinal were committed in effigy to the flames. Crowds broke the windows of Roman Catholic churches. So serious did the feeling become that the Catholic authorities were doubtful if it was wise for Wiseman to return.[83]

But the Cardinal was equal to the occasion. He hurried back to England and immediately issued an able 'Appeal to the English Nation' which not only did much to quieten public sentiment but even

[82] *Ibid.*, I, 551.
[83] *Ibid.*, I, 553.

was successful in procuring a reluctant retractation from the *Times*.[84] In a skilful letter Disraeli sneered gracefully at the whole affair, while Mr. Roebuck publicly rebuked Russell as the successor of Lord George Gordon.[85] Wiseman himself, in certain lectures at St. George's Cathedral, explained the decree in detail and in circumstance. What, perhaps, did most to assuage popular indignation was the passage of the Ecclesiastical Titles Bill which received the Royal Assent in August, 1851. The declaration that Roman Catholics should not assume titles of bishoprics under penalty of fine nor publish papal bulls seemed to act like a soothing charm.[86] By the end of 1851 the excitement had entirely disappeared.

The episode is perhaps more theoretically than practically important. It is clear that to the majority of Englishmen the effect of the new Ultramontanism was to invade the integrity of English sovereignty. 'The day is coming,' said the *Edinburgh Review*,[87] 'when either the Ultramontane theory, as developed by such writers as De Maistre, will be universal and paramount, or the theory of the infallibility and supremacy of the Church of Rome will crumble to atoms. The theory of a divided allegiance the nations will at length find untenable.' Lord Shaftesbury seems particularly to have feared the introduction of the

84 *Ibid.*, II, 3.

85 *Ibid.*, II, 6-9.

86 The text of the Act is given in the *Life of Wiseman*, Vol. II, p. 585.

87 April, 1851, p. 574.

Roman Canon law. 'Do you know what the Canon law is?' he asked a great meeting.[88] 'It is a law incompatible with the civil law of this realm; it is subversive of all religious liberty; it permits—nay, enjoins—persecution of heresy, it elevates the Pope as God, and asserts that he is superior to all human and national laws. We deny synodal action to our own Church—shall we allow it to a rival and hostile body?' A section of Catholic opinion seems to have concurred in these views. 'The late bold and clearly expressed edict of the Court of Rome,' wrote Lord Beaumont,[89] 'can not be received or accepted by English Roman Catholics without a violation of their duties as citizens.' 'I should think,' said the Duke of Norfolk,[90] 'that many must feel, as we do, that Ultramontane opinions are totally incompatible with allegiance to our Sovereign and with our Constitution.' Though Macaulay himself had no fear of the Bull, some of his friends were 'angry and alarmed' and he did not regret their fright 'for such fright is an additional security for us against that execrable superstition.'[91] Mr. Gladstone seems to have disapproved with vehemence of the papal action but desired to draw a distinction between the action of Rome and the attitude of the English Catholics.[92]

88 Hodder, *Life of Shaftesbury,* Vol. II, p. 332.
89 *Life of Wiseman,* II, 15.
90 *Ibid.*
91 Trevelyan's *Life* (Nelson's ed.), Vol. II, p. 275.
92 Morley, *Life,* I, 304 ff.

It is clearly the old argument against Catholic emancipation clothed in a newer garb. The demand from Catholics is for an undiluted loyalty, and it is believed that such loyalty is incompatible with their spiritual allegiance. The answer made by the Catholics is masterly alike in form and substance. It is admitted by Wiseman that for the Pope to appoint Catholic bishops in England is a virtual denial of the royal supremacy in ecclesiastical affairs. But he correctly pointed out that this denial was not confined to members of the Catholic faith. 'The royal supremacy,' he wrote,[93] 'is no more admitted by the Scotch Kirk, by Baptists, Methodists, Quakers, Independents, Presbyterians, Unitarians and other Dissenters than by the Catholics.' He quoted Lord Lyndhurst to the effect that so long as no mischievous temporal consequences ensue from Catholic recognition of the papal supremacy, it was lawful for them to hold that belief. 'If the law,' said Lord Lyndhurst,[94] 'allowed the doctrines and discipline of the Roman Catholic Church, it should be allowed to be carried on perfectly and properly.' Not to do so was a practical refusal of religious toleration. 'To have told Catholics,' Lord Lyndhurst added,[95] ' "you have perfect religious liberty, but you shall not teach that the Church can not err; or, you have complete toleration but you must not presume to

93 *Life of Wiseman*, I, 560.

94 Hansard, 2d Series, Vol. LXXXVIII, p. 1261, Speech of April 20, 1846.

95 *Ibid.*

believe holy orders to be a sacrament" would have been nugatory and tyrannical.' Wiseman was able to show that Lord John Russell himself had admitted that the introduction of papal bulls was essential to Church discipline. 'There are certain Bulls of the Pope,' Russell had told the House of Commons,[96] 'which are absolutely necessary for the appointment of Bishops and pastors belonging to the Roman Catholic Church. It would be quite impossible to prevent the introduction of such Bulls.' But this was all that Wiseman had brought. And his case was strengthened by the fact that in Canada the local governments admitted the titular creations of the colonial hierarchy and had incorporated them by name in acts of Parliament.[97] He very pertinently enquired what distinction existed between the papal act of 1850 and the creation by Act of Parliament of the Anglo-Prussian bishopric of Jerusalem. 'Suppose,' asked Wiseman,[98] 'his Majesty of Abyssinia or the Emir Beshir had pronounced this to be an intrusion "inconsistent with the rights of bishops and clergy and with the spiritual independence of the nation" how much would this country have cared?' The ground he took in the St. George's Cathedral lectures was exactly similar. People complained that 'it was the State in every department which was invaded . . . the Crown was wounded in its

[96] Hansard, 2d Series, Vol. LXXXVIII, p. 362.
[97] *Life of Wiseman,* II, 566.
[98] *Appeal,* etc., p. 23.

prerogative, its supremacy, its right to allegiance, its very sovereignty . . . suppose that any one had told you six months ago that the Bishop of Rome had it in his power to throw this vast empire into convulsions; to upheave by the breath of his nostrils the granite foundations of the noble British constitution; to shake to its basis the throne of our gracious Queen . . . you would have laughed to scorn the man who would have presumed to tell you that he had such tremendous power. And if, by way of jest, or through curiosity, you had asked the fanatic who told you so by what wonderful machinery, by what magical agency he could do all this; and he had answered you "by a scrap of paper, wherein he should desire the Catholic districts of England to be henceforth called dioceses, and the Bishop of Trachis to be called Bishop of Beverley and the Bishop of Tloa to be called Bishop of Liverpool," you would, I am sure, have considered the man little better than an idiot who asserted or believed in such effects from such a cause."[99] Nor was he alone in his contempt for this agitation. Roebuck pointed out to Lord John Russell that if Catholic allegiance was divided as he asserted, the issue of a papal bull dividing England into dioceses would in nowise alter their situation. 'Let us, if we will,' he wrote,[100] 'fulminate an Act of Parliament against the Catholics; does any one suppose that

[99] *Life of Wiseman,* II, 17 ff.
[100] *Ibid.,* II, 3.

their faith will be in the slightest affected thereby? We can not make people loyal by Act of Parliament; we can not by excluding certain names, keep out the doctrines of the Catholic religion.' This practical limitation on a theoretical power was ably insisted upon by the *Westminster Review*. It pointed out that the claim of the Catholic Church to be a heaven-appointed body made it theoretically impossible for a human organisation to live upon amicable terms with it. 'Those who wield the sceptre of the Most High,' it urged,[101] 'will pay small heed to the bâton of the constable. Where the Almighty reigns what room will there be for the police magistrate? and where Omniscience directs, for debates in Parliament? What natural function can fail to undergo eclipse where the mystic shadow of the supernatural traverses the air?' But the wide claims of the imagination suffer diminution amid the stress of everyday life. '*De jure*,' as it wisely suggested,[102] 'the divine commission extends to everything and might absorb this planet into the Papal State; *de facto* it includes what it can, and stops where it must.' And amid its gibes and protests the *Edinburgh* was constrained to admit[103] that 'we do not for a moment question either the loyalty or the patriotism of the mass of our Roman Catholic fellow-subjects. We believe that, whether consistently or

101 *Westminster Review*, 1851, Vol. LIV, p. 450.

102 *Ibid.*, p. 454.

103 *Edinburgh Review*, April, 1851, p. 538.

not, they would be as ready as were their Roman Catholic ancestors, or as are their Protestant contemporaries, to resist any aggression on the civil or political supremacy of England.' But, as Professor Dicey has admitted,[104] no absolute theory of sovereignty can ever be consistent since it is always subject to the opinions of those it commands. And it is immensely difficult to understand why the Catholics should have been subject to a political logic which never has and never will be put into operation.

The argument for the Roman Catholic upon the basis of toleration seems well-nigh unanswerable. 'It is a mockery of toleration,' said the *Westminster Review,*[105] 'to permit people to believe in a divine corporation, and then to refuse them their corporate offices.' Sir George Bowyer, in an exceedingly able pamphlet, pointed out that 'the Pope has only created certain offices in a Church which is, in the eye of the law a dissenting body, and as much a voluntary society as any other incorporated body enjoying no legal privileges or franchises. And the theological claims of our Church do not alter the case. They belong to religion, and are within the inviolable rights of liberty of conscience over which no human power can exercise jurisdiction.'[106] They were doing no more than attend to the internal organisation of

104 See his *Law of the Constitution* (7th ed.), pp. 74-82.

105 *Westminster Review,* 1851, Vol. LIV, p. 458.

106 *The Cardinal Archbishop of Westminster and the New Hierarchy,* London, 1851, p. 20.

the Church. They submitted to the law 'as good Englishmen and loyal subjects . . . but we claim full liberty so long as we do not infringe the law and the rights of our fellow-countrymen.'[107] It was ridiculous to talk of toleration if this was not the case. 'If we are not allowed by law to hold a doctrine,' he said,[108] 'without which we should cease to be Roman Catholics, it obviously and inevitably follows that the law does not permit us to be Roman Catholics at all, which is absurd. Persecute us, drive us out of the realm altogether and into perpetual banishment, but do not hold out to us the delusive phantom of an apparent toleration, and then deny us the liberty to hold that doctrine on which the very existence of our Church, as the Catholic Church . . . most undeniably depends.' And Roebuck pointed out that dangerous consequences would ensue from this lack of toleration. 'Will not Catholics in Ireland,' he asked,[109] 'assert their own pre-eminence in that country and insist upon equality at least in the baneful right of persecution?' Mr. Bright had no doubts about the policy of Russell's government. Lord John's speech, he said, would have been 'very good if delivered some three hundred years ago,' and he denounced the measure as 'nothing better than a sham.'[110] But he opposed it on higher and

[107] *Ibid.*, p. 36.
[108] *Ibid.*, p. 18.
[109] *Life of Wiseman*, Vol. II, p. 9.
[110] Trevelyan, *Life of Bright*, 193.

more splendid grounds. 'The course on which the noble Lord has been so recklessly dragging us,' he told the House of Commons,[111] 'is fruitful in discord, hatred, religious animosities—it has separated Ireland from this country, has withdrawn her national sympathies from us, and has done an amount of mischief which the legislation of the next ten years can not entirely, if at all, abate. The noble Lord has drawn up an indictment against eight millions of his countrymen; he has increased the power of the Pope over the Roman Catholics, for he has drawn closer the bonds between them and their Church, and the head of their Church. The noble Lord has quoted Queen Elizabeth and the great men of the Commonwealth, as though it were necessary now to adopt the principles which prevailed almost universally two hundred years ago. Does the noble Lord forget that we are the true ancients, that we stand on the shoulders of our forefathers and can see further?' It was, however, reserved for Mr. Gladstone in a speech which Lord Morley has placed among his 'three or four most conspicuous masterpieces' to make plain the essential wrongness of the government measure. 'Recollect,' he reminded the House,[112] 'that Europe and the whole of the civilised world look to England at this moment not less, no, but even more than ever they looked to her before, as the mistress and guide of nations

[111] *Ibid.*, 194, Speech of May 12, 1851.
[112] Morley, I, 306.

in regard to the great work of civil legislation. . . . Show, I beseech you—have the courage to show the pope of Rome, and his cardinals, and his Church, that England, too, as well as Rome has her *semper eadem,* and that when she had once adopted some great principle of legislation, which is destined to influence the national character, to draw the dividing lines of her policy for ages to come and to affect the whole nature of her influence and her standing among the nations of the world—show that when she has done this slowly and done it deliberately, she has done it once for all; and that she will no more retrace her steps than the river which bathes this giant city can flow back upon its source. The character of England is in our hands. Let us feel the responsibility that belongs to us, and let us rely on it; if to-day we make this step backwards it is one which hereafter we shall have to retrace with pain. We can not change the profound and resistless tendencies of the age towards religious liberty. It is our business to guide and control their application; do this you may, but to endeavour to turn them backwards is the sport of children, done by the hands of men, and every effort you may make in that direction will recoil upon you in disaster and disgrace.' Rarely have the principles of religious toleration been more splendidly vindicated with a more profound sense of the issues at stake. 'O'u se réfugiera la liberté religieuse,' wrote de

Tocqueville to Senior,[113] 'si on la chasse de l'Angleterre?' It was fortunate for the good sense of Englishmen that their practice was an advance upon their precept. The act was never put into operation. 'The weapon that had been forged in this blazing furnace by these clumsy armourers proved blunt and useless; the law was from the first a dead letter, and it was struck out of the statute book in 1871 in Mr. Gladstone's own administration.'[114]

It is of interest to go back to the summer of 1850, when the first of English theologians was explaining to the Church he had deserted the principles of that which had gained his powerful allegiance. The essential point of his effort was the demonstration that Church and State ought to be separate organisations, that the one can not rightly invade the province of the other. 'The life of a plant,' he wrote,[115] 'is not the same as the life of an animated being, and the life of the body is not the same as the life of the intellect; nor is the life of the intellect the same as the life of grace; nor is the life of the Church the same as the life of the State.' It was this distinction the movement of 1833 had endeavoured to emphasise; but, as he conceived it was foreign to the spirit of the National Church. For that organisation is not its

[113] De Tocqueville, 'Correspondence,' III, 274, quoted in Morley's *Life*.

[114] Morley, I, 308.

[115] *Difficulties of Anglicans* (ed. of 1908), I, 44.

own mistress, it is nothing but the creature of the State. It is not, like the Catholic Church, a perfect society living a life of its own. When the test of separateness is applied, it is seen at once to fail. What is the test? 'We know,' he argued,[116] 'that it is the property of life to be impatient of any foreign substance in the body to which it belongs. It will be sovereign in its own domain, and it conflicts with what it can not assimilate into itself, and is irritated and disordered until it has expelled it.' The Church of Rome fulfils this test of separate identity, for over itself it is essentially sovereign. It has, as Möhler argued, its own special character and genius, stamped infallibly in its every act.[117] With the heresy of Erastus which, politically, is the Royal Supremacy, it can make no alliance of any kind. 'Erastianism, then,' he said,[118] 'was the one heresy which practically cut at the root of all revealed truth. . . . dogma would be sacrificed to expedience, sacraments would be rationalised, perfection would be ridiculed, if she was made the slave of the State.' It was here that Anglicanism essentially was distinguished from the ideals of Rome as the Oxford Movement gave expression to them. For while the Establishment desired nothing more than to be 'the creature of Statesmen,' the ambition of the Tractarians was to force it to self-action. It was not 'contented

[116] *Ibid.*, I, 52.

[117] The reference is to the *Symbolik* (Robertson's translation), II, 36-39.

[118] *Difficulties of the Anglicans,* I, 102.

to be the mere creation of the State, as schoolmasters and teachers may be, as soldiers or magistrates, or other public officers.'[119] The Roman Church could not but regard the question of ecclesiastical liberty as the fundamental question. Her independence was no theological question to be proved by theological argument. 'If the Church is independent of the State in things spiritual,' he scornfully said,[120] 'it is not simply because Bishop Pearson has extolled her powers in his exposition of the Creed, though divines are brought forward as authorities too; but by reason of "the force of that article of our belief, the one Catholic and Apostolic Church."' The source of her power is a divine mystery which, because reason may not penetrate it, that reason may never resolve. She has her unvarying principles and dogmas which do not change with the shifting sands of time. Nor is the Catholic Church a national church since that must, man's nature being what it is, be necessarily Erastian. For if the Church be Erastian it can not be independent; yet her independence is the very root of her nature. 'You hold and rightly hold,' he told his audience,[121] 'that the Church is a sovereign and self-sustaining power in the same sense in which any temporal State is such. She is sufficient for herself; she is absolutely independent in her own sphere; she has

[119] *Ibid.*, I, 107.
[120] *Ibid.*, I, 131.
[121] *Ibid.*, I, 173.

irresponsible control over her subjects in religious matters; she makes laws for them of her own authority, and enforces obedience on them as the tenure of their membership with her.' He admits that membership of the Church will coincide, in many cases, with membership of the State; but the distinction is nevertheless clear. 'There is no necessary coincidence in their particular application and resulting details, in the one and the other polity, just as the good of the soul is not always the good of the body; and much more so is this the case, considering there is no divine direction promised to the State, to preserve it from human passion and human weakness."[122]

Difficulties, of course, abound; and Newman does not fail to recognise their existence. 'It is not enough,' he says,[123] 'for the State that things should be done, unless it has the doing of them itself; it abhors a double jurisdiction, and what it calls a divided allegiance; *aut Caesar aut nullus* is its motto, nor does it willingly accept of any compromise. All power is founded, as it is often said, on public opinion; for the State to allow the existence of a collateral and rival authority is to weaken its own.' Clearly, if the State desires to be an Austinian sovereign, collision is inevitable, and Newman admits that the State is physically the superior power. The problem then becomes the search for means whereby the Church 'may be

122 *Ibid.*
123 *Ibid.*, I, 175.

able to do her divinely appointed work without let or hindrance' from an organisation that has been 'ever jealous of her, and has persecuted her from without and bribed her from within.' One way, he decides can alone be found. 'If the State would but keep within its own province, it would find the Church its truest ally and best benefactor.' Her principles are the principles of the State. 'She upholds obedience to the magistrate; she recognises his office as from God; she is the preacher of peace, the sanction of law, the first element of order, and the safeguard of morality, and that without possible vacillation or failure; she may be fully trusted; she is a sure friend, for she is defectible and undying.'[124] He urges this the more strongly since the Church is anxious to avoid collision. The quarrel of Becket and Henry, with its appeals and counter appeals, its legatine commission, its papal rebukes of the Saint, seems to him the proof of its forbearance.[125] He contrasts that humility and patience with what seems to him the proud Gallicanism of Louis XIV and the insolent Byzantinism of Joseph II.[126] They recognised the value of controlled religion to the State. 'The State wishes to make its subjects peaceful and obedient; and there is nothing more fitted to effect this object than religion.'[127] For the Church that aims at universality this is, of course, an

124 *Ibid.*, I, 175.
125 *Ibid.*, I, 181 f.
126 *Ibid.*, I, 185.
127 *Ibid.*, I, 187.

impossible attitude. However disguised, it is still Erastianism; and it is the nature of the Catholic Church to be proof against that heresy.[128] He reinforces that conclusion by urging that the Church has a mission fundamentally distinct from that of any other society. It is on the ground of 'tangible benefits' that the State claims the loyalty of its subjects;[129] but the Church is the sole guardian of a truth which none but her children may understand. 'She is the organ and oracle, and nothing else, of a supernatural doctrine, which is independent of individuals, given to her once and for all, . . . and which is simply necessary to the salvation of every one of us . . . hence, requiring, from the nature of the case, organs special to itself, made for the purpose, whether for entering into its fulness, or carrying it out in deed."[130]

Here, surely, is the basis upon which the Hierarchy of 1851 was re-established. The bare statement does less than the merest justice to the splendid eloquence with which it was adumbrated. The theory is not original with Newman; its origins are to be found in the fifth century of the Christian era. Confronted by difficulties which were not in essence distinct from those which had called forth the Durham letter from Russell, Gelasius I had constructed a theory of Church and

[128] *Ibid.*, I, 196.
[129] *Ibid.*, I, 213.
[130] *Ibid.*, I, 218

State of which the main characteristic is the dualism for which Newman had argued. Felix II had already urged the Emperor Zeno to leave ecclesiastical affairs to the ecclesiastical authorities;[131] and Gelasius added, as Newman would have added, that while the imperial authority was divine, it does not extend to control of the Church.[132] Gelasius points out that there was a time—witness Melchisedech and the Pontifex Maximus—when Church and State were capable of identification; but with the coming of Christ, the two were separated and to each distinct functions were assigned.[133] Within its sphere each power is supreme, nor should it suffer interference with its independence. The theory exercised a profound influence upon medieval thought. In the ninth century it was the basis of the episcopal definition sent to Lewis the Pius;[134] it was accepted by Hincmar of Rheims.[135] But already the incidence of the theory had changed. Where Gelasius found the two societies in the world, the bishops saw but one Church,[136] and the obvious inference, when there came the struggle between Papacy and

131 Ep. Felix II, Ep. VIII, 5. in Thiel. *Epistolae Romanorum Pontificum.*

132 Gelasius, I, Ep. X, 9. and I, 10. in Thiel., *op. cit.*

133 *Tractatus,* IV, 11.

134 *Monument,* Germ. Hist., Sec. 11, Vol. II, No. 196.

135 Ad. Episcop. De Inst. Carol, cap. 1 in Migne, *Patrolog,* Vol. CXXV.

136 Cf. the emphatic words in the document referred to above, 'Quod eiusdem æclessiae corpus in duabus principaliter dividatur eximiis personis,' etc.

empire, was to argue the inferiority of the secular branch. This is, of course, but fitfully apparent in the ninth century, when papal pretensions are almost at their minimum;[137] but when it is apparent in the letters of court favourites like Alcuin,[138] its reality is hardly to be doubted. And in the claim that the priest is responsible to God for the acts of kings there is room for illimitable expansion.[139] And when the problem of delimitation becomes difficult it was inevitable that use should be made of the implicit elasticity of the Gelasian theory. Mr. Carlyle has pointed out the irony with which Stephen of Tournai repeats the tradition he had inherited.[140] We can not here narrate the transformation which the views of Gelasius were to undergo in the hands of men like Hildebrand and Boniface VIII. Certainly the attempt at dualism was given up. The Church wins its victory only to promote a return, fostered by the revival of the study of Roman law in the eleventh century,[141] and the birth of nationalism in the fifteenth, to the older and better conception.[142] Newman's attitude, as it

137 As evidence, for example, in the purgation of Leo III; the clause about his freewill is clearly the merest sop to his dignity.

138 Cf. for instance Mon. Germ. Hist. Ep., IV. Alcuin, Ep. XVIII, 108.

139 Carlyle, *Med. Pol. Theory,* I, 281. Mr. Carlyle quotes from Jonas of Orleans with whose work, however, I am not acquainted.

140 Carlyle, II, 199.

141 Cf. the important remarks of Mr. Sidney-Woolf in his brilliant essay on Bartolus, pp. 101-107.

142 As pointed out by Mr. Figgis in the essay, 'Respublica Christiana,' which he has reprinted as an appendix to his *Churches in the Modern State.*

was evinced in his *Difficulties of Anglicans* seems to represent the end of the reaction against Hildebrandinism—the end, because, with the revival of the Jesuit power, the official theory of the papal Curia becomes once more monistic in character.[143]

A rigid adherence to Newman's attitude was compatible enough with the utmost loyalty the English crown could have desired. If it is true, as a Catholic historian a little maliciously reports,[144] that when Queen Victoria read Cardinal Wiseman's Pastoral she remarked, 'Am I Queen of England or am I not?', she showed a lamentable misunderstanding of the nature of sovereignty. Hume had long ago emphasised the dependence even of the most despotic power on public opinion; and the wise remark of the *Westminster* reviewer that the divine commission 'includes what it can and stops where it must'[145] might have suggested the obvious limits to Wiseman's claims. As a fact, it is clear enough that the Cardinal did not himself intend—whatever he may ultimately or secretly have desired—any more than the fullest spiritual jurisdiction permitted by the peculiar organisation of the papal Curia. The English challenge to that claim was, in effect, a denial of the right of private judgment in religious matters. It was an old

143 I assume that nobody now doubts that the Jesuits were responsible for the Syllabus of 1864 and the Decree of 1870. Cf. Acton, *History of Freedom,* p. 498 ff., and Janus' *The Pope and the Council, passim.*

144 *Sequel to Catholic Emancipation,* II, 287.

145 See above, note 102.

objection. Underlying it was the ancient desire for unity, perhaps, also, for uniformity, of which Dante's *De Monarchiâ* is so supreme an expression. To the Protestant statesman of the mid-Victorian age, the single society which Hildebrand envisaged had become the English State. The ecclesiastical ideal Cavour had embraced seemed to him open to the most grave theoretical advantages even while he practically admitted its completest consequences. But a genius for political abstractions is perhaps no part of the English heritage.

III

The establishment of the Hierarchy in England coincided with perhaps the greatest change in the character of the Papacy since the Council of Trent.[146] The failure of Rosmini's mission and the murder of Rossi[147] seem to have convinced the Pope that the Jesuits might, after all, be right, and henceforward there were but fitful gleams of his ancient liberalism. The assassination of the minister was followed by the flight to Gaëta and the attainment of Antonelli to supreme power.

[146] The best general work on the Papacy during the nineteenth century is that of Bishop Nielsen. Friedrich's *Life of Dollinger* contains a mass of information upon what is perhaps its most important episode. The historical perspective will always be set by Janus' *The Pope and the Council.*

[147] Rosmini's *Della Missione a Roma* is our best authority on this critical episode. For his interpretation of Rossi's appointment, see *op. cit.*, p. 53.

The use of the latter synchronised with the condemnation of Rosmini which Antonelli seems to have thought essential to his security.[148] Pius' interest in reform seemed almost immediately to vanish. It was said openly by the Pontiff and his minister that there was no compatibility possible between the spiritual supremacy of Rome and the gift of a free constitution to the Papal States.[149] As the Romans mockingly but truly said, it was a *Pio nono secondo* who returned to Rome.[150] Simultaneously the General of the Jesuit Order, Father Roothaan, came back from a voluntary exile, and the publication of the notorious *Civiltà Cattolica* was begun.[151] Within six months, the restoration of the English hierarchy followed. The imprisonment of Franceso Madiai and the prohibition of a new edition of Muratori showed clearly how thoroughgoing was the reaction.[152] Two years later Pius, already more bold than his reactionary predecessor, promulgated the dogma of the Immaculate Conception,[153] which Schräder was later to interpret as the inferential claim of papal

148 Nielsen, II, 173.

149 See the very interesting note of Antonelli in Bianchi's *Storia documentata della diplomozia Europea in Italia,* Vol. VI, p. 238, *seq.*

150 Nielsen, II, 181.

151 Nielsen, II, 182. For Dollinger's opinion of the change, cf. his *Kleinere Schriften,* p. 582 ff.

152 Nielsen, II, 184. Lord Palmerston obtained his release in characteristic fashion by threatening to send some English warships to the Mediterranean.

153 Nielsen, II, 191 f. For the attitude of Gregory XVI, see *op. cit.,* II, 76 f.

infallibility.[154] Pius had already embarked on the path which led directly to the catastrophe of 1870.

It was inevitable that English Catholicism should respond to the eddies of this reaction. Nor was the ground unprepared. W. G. Ward's genial remark that he would 'like a new Papal Bull every morning with my *Times* at breakfast'[155] was in fact symptomatic of a whole philosophy. It is possible to trace two, and perhaps three, definite schools of thought among English Catholics of the time. Ward himself, and Manning also when he came to a position of influence in the Church of his adoption, was thoroughly in sympathy with the reactionary ideas of continental Ultramontanism.[156] It seemed to him that between thoroughgoing skepticism on the one hand, and an equally uncompromising conservatism on the other there could be no alternative. His political philosophy was that of De Maistre, and he would have asserted with the latter that it was Rome which gave its stability to the Christian world.[157] De Maistre identified sovereignty with infallibility,[158] and Ward would have followed him blindly in that striking claim. He himself, in the *Dublin Review* of which in 1859 he became editor,[159] devoted his

154 Schräder, *Pius IX als Papst und als König*, 12.

155 Wilfrid Ward, W. G. Ward, and the *Catholic Revival*, p. 14. I owe much to this able and fascinating book.

156 Cf. W. Ward, *op. cit.*, Chapter V, for a general discussion of his father's position.

157 Cf. Du Pape (ed. of 1837), Vol. I, p. 345.

158 *Ibid.*, I, 23.

159 Wilfrid Ward, *op. cit.*, p. 141.

energies to combating religious liberalism in every shape and form. He believed whole-heartedly 'in shutting the intellect within the sacred influences which the Church supplies, in order to preserve it from error. The freedom which leads to anarchy is the danger; the surrender to restraint and authority is the safeguard."[160] It is obvious that such an attitude must have led very easily and naturally to Ultramontanism. It was the more inevitable where the thinker was, once his premises had been reached, so rigorous a logician as Ward. Nor did he confine his doctrine to religion alone. He could not separate out the realms of thought. The world had to be drummed into subjection and the universal supremacy of the Pope was the weapon with which the change was to be effected. Few men have had so genuine and whole-hearted a belief in the medieval theocracy as Mr. Ward. A friend called him a 'theo-politician' and the epithet was literally true.[161] The Holy Roman Empire most nearly achieved his ideal. He admired the 'civil intolerance of heresy.' In that time 'it was the civil ruler's highest function to co-operate with the Church in preserving unshaken the firm conviction of Catholic truth, and in preserving unsullied the purity and unearthliness of Catholic sentiment.' But that day has passed and the Church has lost its hold on the minds and hearts of men. 'They give

160 *Op. cit.*, p. 133.
161 *Op. cit.*, p. 134.

far more of their obedience to the Church than of their loyalty and affection; they give to her, and to God whose representative she is, but a divided allegiance.'[162] So the unity of the Church's sovereignty is broken with the onset of liberalism. An aggressive campaign was essential if the enemy was to be defeated.[163] In the true ethics of Catholicism it could bear no part.

The school of ecclesiastical thought most antagonistic to Ward was nobly represented by Lord Acton. To the study of a man who so strenuously devoted a whole life to the understanding of liberty it is difficult to approach without emotion. Acton's life was spent in repelling at once the claims either of Church or State to a unique sovereignty over the minds of men. He saw that a State which attempts the control of ecclesiastical authority is virtually denying the right of religious freedom.[164] He no less equally and thoroughly condemned the whole effort of the Catholic Church after religious uniformity.[165] He saw the inevitability of a certain convergence between Church and State. 'She can not,' he wrote of the Church,[166] 'permanently ignore the acts and character of the State or escape its notice. While she preaches submission to authorities ordained by God, her

162 *Op. cit.*, 176.

163 *Op. cit.*, p. 186.

164 *History of Freedom*, p. 151.

165 This is apparent in the famous essay on the massacre of Saint Bartholomew.

166 *History of Freedom*, p. 246.

nature, not her interest, compels her to exert an involuntary influence upon them. The jealousy so often exhibited by government is not without reason, for the free action of the Church is the test of the free constitution of the State, and without that free constitution there must necessarily be either persecution or revolution. Between the settled organisation of Catholicism and every form of arbitrary power there is an incompatibility which must terminate in conflict. In a State which possesses no security for authority or freedom, the Church must either fight or succumb.' The Catholic Church was thus a weapon in the search for liberty. Toleration was an essential part of its method. 'Persecution is the vice of particular religions,' he argued;[167] 'and the misfortune of particular stages of political society. It is the resource by which States that would be subverted by religious liberty escape the more dangerous alternative of imposing religious disabilities. The exclusion of a part of the community by reason of its faith from the full benefit of the law is a danger and disadvantage to every State, however highly organised its constitution may otherwise be. But the actual existence of a religious party differing in faith from the majority is dangerous only to a State very imperfectly organised. Disabilities are always a danger. Multiplicity of religions is only dangerous to States of an inferior type.' Ultimately and funda-

167 *Ibid.*, p. 250.

mentally the object of the Church and the State was not dissimilar. It was this essentially which prohibited the possibility of intolerance. Nor should the Church attempt to enslave the secular organ. 'The direct subservience of the State to religious ends,' he said,[168] 'would imply despotism and persecution just as much as the pagan supremacy of civil over religious authority.'

These, it is clear, are the watchwords of liberalism. Nor did he hesitate to draw from them certain obvious conclusions. The Papacy must suit its activities to the needs of the age. The *plenitudo potestatis* of Boniface VIII was no universal right which defied the problem of time. 'The political power of the Holy See,' he wrote,[169] 'was never a universal right of jurisdiction over States, but a special and positive right, which it is as absurd to censure as to fear or to regret at the present time. Directly, it extended only over territories which were held by feudal tenure of the Pope, like the Sicilian monarchy. Elsewhere the authority was indirect, not political but religious, and its political consequences were due to the laws of the land.' He points out that the Pope can not interfere between the Crown and its subjects. 'The idea of the Pope stepping between a State and the allegiance of its subjects is a mere misapprehension. The instrument of his authority is the law, and the law resides in the State.' The

168 *Ibid.*, p. 251.
169 *Ibid.*, p. 256.

old notion of a right to depose was fundamentally at variance with the nature of ecclesiastical authority. 'A moral, and, *à fortiori,* a spiritual authority moves and lives only in an atmosphere of freedom.'[170] A control over every sphere of life it was not possible for the Church to claim. The spiritual world was hers; 'but the ethical and intellectual offices of the Church, as distinct from her spiritual office, are not hers exclusively or peculiarly.'[171] The worlds of politics and intelligence move on lines parallel to that of the spirit. The latter dare not challenge their right. 'A political law or a scientific truth may be perilous to the morals or the faith of individuals, but it can not on this ground be resisted by the Church. . . . A discovery may be made in science which will shake the faith of thousands, yet religion can not refute it or object to it.' 'Within their respective spheres,' he said again,[172] 'politics can determine what rights are just, science what truths are certain . . . they have become, not tools to be used by religion for her own interests, but conditions which she must observe in her actions and arguments.' The attempt to put truth into blinkers which W. G. Ward so vehemently condoned seemed to him a profound mistake. It was making principles of no more than temporary value. Nor, in the end, was anything gained.

[170] *Ibid.*, p. 257.
[171] *Ibid.*, p. 448.
[172] *Ibid.*, p. 453.

'They have betrayed duties more sacred than the privileges for which they fought,' he said in eloquent condemnation of the Ultramontane School,[173] 'they have lied before God and man; they have been divided into factions by the supposed interests of the Church, when they ought to have been united by her principles and her doctrines; and against themselves they have justified those grave accusations of falsehood, insincerity, indifference to civil rights, and contempt for civil authorities which are uttered with such profound injustice against the Church.' 'Modern Society,' he urged,[174] 'has developed no security for freedom, no instrument of progress, no means of arriving at truth, which we look upon with indifference or suspicion.'

It is clearly a concordat with modern society that he is proposing, and perhaps no finer defence of religious liberty has ever been penned.[175] No less is it obvious that the proposal was utterly out of harmony with the dominant Catholicism of the time. Acton's own journalistic experiences were sufficient proof of the antithesis.[176] The very article in which his most eloquent defence of liberalism appeared was itself an announcement

173 *Ibid.*, p. 455.

174 *Ibid.*, p. 457.

175 What freedom meant to Acton the reader can gather—his own writings apart—from the famous passage in Lord Bryce's *Contemporary Biography.* Cf. also Figgis, *Churches in the Modern State,* pp. 253-265.

176 Cf. the introduction to Gasquet's *Lord Acton and His Circle.*

that those enterprises were concluded.[177] For the alliance between scholarship and Catholic theology for which his whole life was so moving a plea was exactly the antithesis of that which the ecclesiastical authorities were willing to admit. His liberalism dethroned the Church from its position of universal sovereignty. It asked that control be surrendered over all save the sphere of the spirit. But this was to make an end of the 'intellectual captivity' which Ward and Manning deemed so essential. It was to expose the Catholic to disturbing influences he was perhaps unfitted to encounter. It gave a loophole to that 'thätige skepsis' of which the consequences could be seen in men like Darwin and Huxley. But its intellectual dangers apart, it contained implications which could never be admitted. The papal dominions apart, it entirely nullified the dream of a territorial sovereignty for Rome. It suggested that there was a system of rights in which heretics might be entitled to share. It drew a distinction between religious and political salvation. It implied the existence of a moral code to which the Roman Church, as any ordinary, and human, institution was subject. It gave to the laws of men a validity in their own sphere no less absolute than that which the Church had urged its own dogmas could alone enjoy. It was, in fact, the negation of every dogma of the Ultramontane belief. Nor did Acton take pains to conceal his antagonism.

177 'Conflicts with Rome,' *Home and Foreign Review*, April, 1864.

Ultramontanism seemed to him politically dangerous and—he would perhaps have identified the two—morally corrupt. 'A speculative Ultramontanism,' he wrote many years later,[178] 'separate from theories of tyranny, mendacity, and murder, keeping honestly clear of the Jesuit with his lies, of the Dominican with his fagots, of the Popes with their massacres, has not yet been brought to light.' It was obviously no more than a moral influence in the sphere of politics that Acton desired for his religion. He seems to have regarded it, in England at least, as a voluntary and dissenting sect, which, if in his eyes it enshrined the truth, might yet be held by others untrue, and could not force itself upon an unwilling people.[179] But so to believe in the age of Pius IX was to invite the onset of ecclesiastical tragedy.

The position of Newman is most difficult, at any rate before 1870, to understand.[180] The implicit liberalism of his *Difficulties of Anglicans* has already been noted. He was sympathetic towards Acton in his journalistic difficulties. His struggle for a freer Catholic education suggests an acceptance of some of the most fundamental of liberal ideas.[181] His antagonism to Manning is one of the

[178] *Letters of Lord Acton to Mary Gladstone* (2d ed.), p. 104.

[179] This, I take it, is the basic thought of the 'Political Thoughts on the Church,' *History of Freedom,* p. 188, *seq.*

[180] Cf. the comments of Lord Acton in *Letters to Mary Gladstone,* pp. 35 and 107, especially p. 35.

[181] Cf. Wilfrid Ward, *Life of Newman,* Chapters XXI and XXIV.

most famous episodes in his career. Yet his liberalism is always wavering and hesitant, hedged about by subtle reservations and implied doubts so that it is dangerous to affix to him the label of any party. The attitude of W. G. Ward he stigmatised as 'preposterous,'[182] yet he did not hesitate to accept the *Encyclical* of 1864. He believed in papal infallibility because, seemingly, he did not deem it could be dangerous; 'I am confident,' he told Pusey,[183] 'that it must be so limited practically that it will leave things as they are.' To the latter he defended the Jesuits—the main weapon in the service of reaction.[184] He had written a famous article in the *Rambler* on the place of the laity in the Catholic Church which struck a serious blow at the notion of despotic ecclesiasticism.[185] He hated passionately the extreme Ultramontane views of Ward and Louis Veuillot,[186] which seemed to him to commit Catholic theology to a view entirely out of accord with historic tradition. Yet he insisted always on the necessity of implicit loyalty to the Pope. 'As a matter of Principle,' he wrote to Pusey,[187] 'the Pope must have universal jurisdiction' because otherwise there would be no bond of unity in the

182 Wilfrid Ward, *Life of Newman,* II, 101.
183 *Ibid.,* II, 101.
184 *Ibid.,* II, 114.
185 Cf. *Life,* Vol. II, Chapter XXV, for an account of the Curia's attitude to it.
186 Cf. the impressive comment of Mr. Wilfrid Ward, *Life,* II, 213.
187 *Life,* II, 223.

Church. 'An honorary head,' he said,[188] 'call him primate, or premier duke, does not affect the real force, or enter into the essence of a political body and is not worth contending about.' Yet at the same time that he endorsed this virtual Austinianism he noted the limitations in practice. 'His abstract power is not a practical fact. . . . I observe it is not so much even an abstract doctrine as it is a principle; by which I mean something far more subtle and intimately connected with our system itself than a doctrine, so as not to be contained in the written law, but to be, like the common law of the land, or rather the principles of the Constitution, contained in the very idea of our being what we are."[189] It is perhaps not difficult to understand why the abstractly logical mind of Ward should have been puzzled by the tortuous subtleties of Newman's attitude. He does, in fact, seem, on occasion, to have been rather the master, than the servant of truth.

IV

At Rome there were few hesitations. The dogmatisation of the Immaculate Conception was essentially a Jesuit victory,[190] and it was the Jesuits who were the main upholders of papal infalli-

[188] *Ibid.* and cf. his emphatic protest against the idea that he was a minimiser, *Life,* II, 218.

[189] *Life,* II, 218.

[190] Nielsen, II, 195.

bility.[191] Ten years after its promulgation, on the eighth of December, 1864, came the Encyclical *Quanta Cura,* and its accompanying Syllabus of errors.[192] In these Pius virtually declared war on modern society. The encyclical condemned the application of naturalism to civil society, liberty of conscience, the right of public worship, the freedom of the press. Communism was condemned as a 'destructive error'; excommunication was launched against those who should attack either the rights or the property of the Church.[193] But striking as was the papal brief, it was almost weak by the side of the formidable Syllabus. Theological questions apart, the denunciations wandered boldly into the civil sphere. It was no longer permissible to argue that either popes or councils had exceeded their power;[194] that the Church could not avail herself of force or of direct or indirect temporal power;[195] that National Churches could be established;[196] that the civil law ought to prevail in a contest between Church and State;[197] that Church and State should be separated;[198] that the civil authority may pronounce marriages dis-

191 Acton, *History of Freedom,* p. 496.

192 The authoritative exposition on the papal side is Schräder, *Die Encyclika* (1865).

193 Cf. Nielsen's comment, *op. cit.,* II, 259.

194 Syllabus section 23.

195 Section, 24.

196 Section, 37.

197 Section 42.

198 Section 55.

solved;[199] that a civil contract can constitute a true marriage;[200] that the Catholic religion need no longer be the only religion of the State;[201] and, finally, there came the last and most tremendous of anathemas against the thought that the Roman Pontiff could or should reconcile himself with progress, liberalism and modern civilisation.[202]

The promulgation of this tremendous indictment had not been made without opposition or careful thought. The task had occupied four able theologians of the Curia almost ten years.[203] Dupanloup had urged Antonelli to withhold it on the ground that trouble would be bound to follow its publication; and the Archbishop of Tours had given similar advice.[204] It was probably the growth of liberal Catholicism in France and Belgium which finally provoked its promulgation. In the Congress of Malines in 1863, Montalembert had read a brilliant essay on a 'Free Church in a Free State' and had been immediately delated to Rome.[205] The publication of most of the Syllabus in France was actually prohibited by the French government.[206] In England, Newman insisted that

199 Section 67.

200 Section 73.

201 Section 79.

202 Section 80.

203 Nielsen, II, 262.

204 Dupanloup's protest is very striking. See the life by Lagrange, II, 279.

205 The essay was published in 1865. For the charge of heresy, see Oliphant, *Memoir of Montalembert,* II, 268.

206 Nielsen, II, 265.

the document did not come from the Pope;[207] but W. G. Ward immediately accepted it as infallible, and seems to have rejoiced in the variety of subjects with which it dealt.[208] It seems probable that Newman's view was the more correct; for Lord Acton has pointed out that the officials of the Curia emphasised the informality of the Syllabus and that Pius himself did not dare to repudiate the minimising interpretations.[209] But when all the explanations had been made, the document still remained as a forcible and thoroughgoing challenge.

A yet more striking determination was to come. Even before the issue of the Syllabus, his decision to effect the restoration of the papal power had made Pius convinced of the necessity of a General Council.[210] The need of the Church, doctrinally, politically, intellectually, was immense, and the decision was in a high degree intelligible. Nor was care lacking to obtain a general consensus of ecclesiastical opinion before any decisive step was taken.[211] By 1867, Pius had finally made up his mind; and some of the bishops who were at Rome for the celebration of the eighteenth celebration of St. Peter urged the need for a definition of papal

207 *Life*, II, 101.

208 *W. G. Ward and the Catholic Revival*, p. 248.

209 *History of Freedom*, p. 496. Lord Acton's testimony is the more important since he probably had access to what he called the 'esoteric' sources.

210 *History of Freedom*, p. 492.

211 Nielsen, II, 291.

infallibility. 'To proclaim the Pope infallible,' says Lord Acton,[212] 'was their compendious security against hostile States and Churches, against human liberty and authority, against disintegrating tolerance, and rationalising science, against error and sin.' Even at the time when the dogma of the Immaculate Conception had been promulgated, the idea of infallibility had been in Pius' mind.[213] Manning, then in Rome, had taken a vow to devote his utmost efforts to secure the publication of the new dogma; and on his return to England he began to move Catholic opinion in that direction.[214] The Jesuits, of course, were wholeheartedly enthusiastic; and the presence of three of their leading members upon the dogmatic commission seemed to point to the direction in which affairs would trend.[215]

The determination was not made known without grave misgivings on the part of those outside the Ultramontane party. Manning tells us that Baron Hübner, then Austrian ambassador at Rome, felt it would injure the Church;[216] even the ecclesiastically minded Ollivier feared that the omission of an invitation to the sovereigns of Europe was tantamount to the separation of

212 *History of Freedom,* p. 495. Cf. Manning, *True Story of the Vatican Council,* p. 53.

213 Friedrich, *Tagebuch,* p. 294.

214 Purcell, *Life of Manning,* II, 420.

215 *History of Freedom,* p. 500.

216 Purcell, II, 457.

Church and State.[217] Prince Hohenlohe, then foreign minister of Bavaria, urged the governments of Europe to intervene;[218] and the publication of Janus' *Pope and the Council* gave the liberal Catholics possession of an overwhelming historical indictment against the projected definition which neither the action of the Index nor the reply of Hergenröther could adequately efface. Hefele, greater as a historian than as a bishop, condemned infallibility in a stinging phrase.[219] In England, Newman did not conceal his fears. He stimulated Father Ryder to write a trenchant attack on Ward's extremism, and personally identified his views with those of the pamphlet.[220] He urged a friend to discuss the condemnation of Pope Honorius, one of the crucial cases in the argument against infallibility.[221] The dogma itself he regarded not as certain but as probable and 'anyhow it . . . must be fenced round and limited by conditions.'[222] While he did not doubt that what the General Council pronounced would be the word of God, 'still we may,' he wrote to Canon Walker,[223] 'well feel indignant at the intrigue, trickery and imperiousness which is the human side of its history—and it seems a dereliction of

217 Nielsen, II, 296.
218 *Ibid.*, II, 301.
219 *Ibid.*, II, 310.
220 *Life*, II, 224.
221 *Ibid.*, II, 235.
222 *Ibid.*, II, 236.
223 *Ibid.*, II, 240.

duty not to do one's part to meet them.' He criticised with scornful indignation the '*ὕβρις ὀρ θίων κνωδάλων*, the arrogant *ipse dixit* of various persons who would crush every opinion in theology which is not theirs,'[224] and elsewhere he stigmatised the extreme Ultramontanes as an 'insolent and aggressive faction.'[225] He prayed 'those great early Doctors of the Church . . . to avert so great a calamity. If it is God's will that the Pope's infallibility should be defined, then it is his blessed will to throw back the times and moments of that triumph He has destined for His Kingdom.'[226] What is done, he told Ambrose de Lisle,[227] 'I will accept as His act; but until then, I will believe it impossible.' Nor did he like the atmosphere in which the proposed definition was enshrouded. 'To outsiders like me,' he told Father Whitty,[228] 'it would seem as if a grave dogmatic question was being treated merely as a move in ecclesiastical politics,' and he pointed out its effect in causing a recrudescence of anti-Catholic sentiment in England. It is clear that Newman was absolutely convinced of the impolicy of the Jesuits' decision even while he was prepared loyally to abide by its consequences.

Protests of all kinds, were, however, unavailing; and after some stormy scenes the Council passed

224 *Ibid.*, II, 241.

225 For the curious history of this epithet see the *Life*, II, 289-290.

226 *Life*, II, 288.

227 *Ibid.*, II, 293.

228 *Ibid.*, II, 298.

the dogma on the eighteenth of July, 1870.[229] Amid the horrors of the Franco-German War and the almost immediate fall of Rome men perhaps hardly realised that the event had come to pass. It had, of course, its tremendous consequences. The excommunication of Dollinger deprived the Church of its greatest living historian;[230] and if Hefele submitted it was permissible to doubt whether he believed.[231] Infallibility did not prevent the confiscation of Church property in Italy,[232] and in Germany it gave birth to the famous Falck Laws. Bavaria did not permit the publication of the Bull which announced the definition on the ground that priests could no longer be loyal subjects of the Crown.[233] France was too occupied with its internal reconstruction to pay much attention to the change; and, in any case, nationalistic sentiment would probably have been sufficient to prevent any action similar to that of Germany. It was on political and diplomatic grounds that the publication of Veuillot's paper, *L'Univers,* was forbidden.[234]

In England, for the moment, the definition made little stir. Statesmen were more interested in the Franco-German War, and its possible relation to

[229] Nielsen, II, 371 f. *History of Freedom,* p. 549.

[230] A very beautiful little volume translated in England as *Letters and Declarations on the Vatican Decrees* gives the history of Dollinger's relation to the Church after the definition.

[231] Cf. Schulte, *Die Altakatholicismus,* pp. 222, 223-228.

[232] Nielsen, II, 431.

[233] Nielsen, II, 431.

[234] Nielsen, II, 449.

Belgium to give heed to the politics of ecclesiasticism. Measures like the Education and Land Bills were more than sufficient to absorb their attention. But in 1873, Mr. Gladstone's Irish University Bill failed and the Irish Catholic bishops were mainly responsible for its failure.[235] In the next year Mr. Gladstone retired from the leadership of the Liberal party, and, in his leisure, had the opportunity to renew his acquaintance with Dr. Dollinger. Not unnaturally he studied anew the problem of infallibility and he could not help being moved to indignation at the sufferings of a man whose only faults were his scholarship and his honesty. With Mr. Gladstone, thought was commensurate with action. On his return to England he launched a bitter attack on the Ritualist movement in the Anglican Church. He traced its existence to the new and vaunting pretensions of the Roman Curia. It has, he wrote,[236] 'substituted for the proud boast of *semper eadem* a policy of violence and change of faith . . . when no one can become her convert without renouncing his moral and mental freedom, and placing his civil loyalty and duty at the mercy of another.'

These were hard words, and it was perhaps not unnatural that they should have aroused keen resentment.[237] But it was not Mr. Gladstone's

235 So Ward in the *Life of Newman,* II, 401, and Gladstone, *Vaticanism,* p. 41.

236 *Contemporary Review,* 1874, p. 671.

237 *Vatican Decrees,* p. 7. I use an edition of 1874 published in New York by Appletons.

habit to shrink from justifying his conclusions. In his *Vatican Decrees in their bearing on Civil Allegiance* he explained at length the causes which had led to his angry outburst. The Church of Rome, he argued, occupied a position essentially different from all other churches. While they loyally accepted the sovereignty of the State in return for their religious freedom, the Church of Rome, like the medieval Church, desired to lord it over the world.[238] That desire might be resisted as of old were not Rome now fighting with new weapons; for she had made a claim to the acceptance of her demands incompatible either with civil right or the duty of obedience.[239] He urges that in the Syllabus of 1864, 'Rome has refurbished and paraded anew every rusty tool she was fondly thought to have disused.'[240] The effect of this novelty is to bring once more into the field of discussion certain civil questions which must be answered differently from the reply given at the time of Catholic emancipation. He points out that the strength of antagonism to Catholic liberties 'had lain in the allegation that it was not possible for the consistent Roman Catholic to pay to the Crown of this country an entire allegiance, and that the admission of persons, thus self-disabled, to Parliament, was inconsistent with the safety of State and nation.'[241] But satisfactory assurances

[238] *Ibid.*, p. 11.
[239] *Ibid.*, p. 12.
[240] *Ibid.*, p. 16.
[241] *Ibid.*, p. 25.

were given, and the emphatic denial of civil responsibility to the Pope made by men like Bishop Doyle, the declaration of the Vicars Apostolic, and the Hierarchy, was sufficient to make men accept as a limitation in theory what was inevitably necessary as a limitation in practice.[242] But the situation, in Mr. Gladstone's view, had now changed. 'Since that time,' he wrote,[243] 'all these propositions have been reversed. The Pope's infallibility, when he speaks *ex cathedra* on faith and morals, has been declared, with the assent of the Bishops of the Roman Church, to be an article of faith, binding on the conscience of every Christian; his claim to the obedience of his spiritual subjects has been declared in like manner without any practical limit or reserve; and his supremacy, without any reserve of civil rights, has been similarly affirmed to include everything which relates to the discipline and government of the Church throughout the world. And these doctrines, we now know on the highest authority, it is of necessity for salvation to believe.'

This seemed to him a claim to universal sovereignty. It would of necessity involve the State no less than the individual. The medieval history of the Papacy showed how easily the gap between individual and corporate difficulty might be bridged. There were cases of national protest and

[242] *Ibid.*, p. 31-33.
[243] *Ibid.*, p. 33.

the Papacy did not always emerge successful from the conflict. Yet, on the whole, a theory of separate spheres, such as was the basis of the Roman Catholic Relief Act, was worked out—a theory for which it seems that Mr. Gladstone did not hesitate to claim divine sanction.[244] But of this an end had been made. The stern demand for absolute obedience 'swept into the papal net whole multitudes of facts, whole systems of government, prevailing, though in different degrees, in every country in the world.'[245] It denied the severance of Church and State even while it asserted the superiority of the former organisation. It drew within the ecclesiastical domain much of what had formerly been deemed matter for the State's decision. The result was that 'this new version of the principles of the papal Church inexorably binds its members to the admission of these exorbitant claims, without any refuge or reservation on behalf of their duty to the Crown.'[246] The civil loyalty of Catholics was thus made impossible since their ecclesiastical sovereign had claimed the rights of their temporal sovereign also.

If this was a logical deduction from the Decree of 1870 two conclusions seemed to Mr. Gladstone to follow. Either the Catholics must reject the possible civic interpretation of the new dogma, or the assurances of the twenties must be repeated.

244 *Ibid.*, p. 41.
245 *Ibid.*, p. 43.
246 *Ibid.*, p. 45.

For the claims had substance behind them. It was true that the Court of Rome could neither secure an invasion of England, or fulfil the visions of Gregory VII.[247] But a contest with civic authority Rome was determined to have, and the result of the Falck Laws seemed to him to demonstrate that she was merely fighting her enemies one by one.[248] The events in Germany and the intransigeant policy of Rome in Italy seemed to him to portend danger of no mean kind. It was a serious incentive to European wars because the possible disaffection of Roman Catholic subjects might hinder the action of the State.[249] He seems to suggest that the type of influence which the Dogma of Infallibility of 1870 is bound to extend was shown in the influence of the Irish prelates over the Nationalist members in 1873.[250] The attitude of converts to Rome seems to him fraught with danger. The phrase 'a Catholic first, an Englishman afterward' seems to him now to mean 'that the "convert" intends, in case of conflict between the Queen and the Pope, to follow the Pope, and let the Queen shift for herself; which happily, she well can do.'[251] Before 1870 Mr. Gladstone felt that he could ask for religious liberty 'for whatsoever be the follies of ecclesiastical power in his Church, the Church

[247] *Ibid.*, p. 47.

[248] *Ibid.*, p. 50.

[249] *Ibid.*, p. 52. It is curious to speculate how differently Mr. Gladstone would have written in 1916.

[250] *Ibid.*, p. 62.

[251] *Ibid.*, p. 64.

itself, has not required of him, with binding authority, to assent to any principles inconsistent with his civil duty.'[252] But of that consolation he has been deprived even though he will continue to urge the necessity of toleration. For, at bottom, he believes in the loyalty of English Catholics. What they did in the sixteenth century they will, he hopes, do in the nineteenth. He hopes it, and expects that it will be so. And into the hateful path of religious persecution England will not be drawn by the 'myrmidons of the Apostolic Chamber.'[253]

If it is in no sense an original thesis, it is, at all events, an ably argued one, and it derived a peculiar significance when maintained by the most important of English statesmen. The whole point of Mr. Gladstone's thesis was in his emphasis on the novelty of the position in which English Catholics had been placed: they had before been able truthfully to make declaration of their loyalty; now they were compelled to make choice between Queen and Pope. But, as a fact, Mr. Gladstone's argument was vitiated by exactly the same fallacies as those which, half a century before, had been used to defeat Catholic emancipation. He depicted Vaticanism as an attack on the sovereignty of the State. The sphere of the latter body was invaded if the implications of papal infallibility were fulfilled. But that was in its turn to imply that

252 *Ibid.*, p. 65.
253 *Ibid.*, p. 67.

the claims were possible of fulfilment, and of this Mr. Gladstone himself made emphatic denial. It was exactly that old problem of a unified allegiance which, as Sydney Smith had so whimsically shown, no man can have if his interests are of a varied character.[254] It was not very serious that Pius IX should make claim to the lordship of the world if he could not make good his pretensions. If Catholics did not obey the Papacy in the sixteenth or in the seventeenth century, when the reality of its power was a far more powerful tradition with men, it was hardly likely that they would bow to it in the nineteenth, when its temporal possessions were gone and it stood as a forlorn ghost of a glory which now adorned a novel and secular power. To a claim of spiritual supremacy Mr. Gladstone could raise no objection; he had himself often enough lamented the Erastianism of the English State.[255] If, as it seemed, the spiritual demand was justified, and the temporal was unimportant, Mr. Gladstone was fighting a shadow. The sovereignty he feared had no more than a historic interest. It depended, as he must have realised, on the consent of men; and there was no evidence that that consent could in any dangerous degree be obtained.

The answers to Mr. Gladstone's pamphlets were varying in nature, and perhaps of a greater interest than his own attack. Manning at once declared

[254] *Supra,* n. 22.

[255] Morley, *Life,* I, 282.

that the decrees 'have in no jot or tittle changed either the obligations or the conditions of civil allegiance' of Catholics whose 'civil allegiance is as undivided as that of all Christians, and of all men who recognise a divine or moral natural law'; but he was careful to emphasise that 'the civil allegiance of no man is unlimited, and therefore the civil allegiance of all men who believe in God, and are governed by conscience, is in that sense divided.'[256] Lord Acton pointed out that the claims of the Ultramontane school had a far longer history than Mr. Gladstone cared to admit, and he wisely, if a little sardonically, suggested that to repel the demand of the Pope needed a little more than 'a written demonstration.'[257] 'The fact is,' said Lord Emly, one of the most distinguished of Catholic laymen,[258] 'we should deal with a Pope's orders to be disloyal as Stephen Langton and the Barons of Runnymede dealt with a similar order.' Lord Camoys and Mr. Henry Petre spoke in similar fashion.[259] Nor were Protestants wanting to repudiate Mr. Gladstone's contentions. His assumptions appeared to the *Edinburgh Review* entirely erroneous. 'English Roman Catholics,' it wrote,[260] 'are quite as loyal now as they were in the days of Lord Howard of Effingham and the Spanish Armada . . . all men in some degree hold

256 *Times* of November 9, 1874.
257 *Times,* same date as the letter of Manning.
258 *Life of A. P. de Lisle,* Vol. II, p. 56.
259 *Annual Register* for 1874, p. 105.
260 *Edinburgh Review,* July, 1875, p. 557.

a divided allegiance to conscience and the law. A Quaker who refuses to take an oath . . . A Nonconformist who refuses to pay a Church rate, . . . the High Church party in England, are continually setting the law at defiance. We think these conscientious people are mistaken, but we do not accuse them of throwing off their allegiance,' and, in an admirable sentence it pointed out that 'Catholics do and can give their consciences the benefit of the great "nevertheless."'[261] The *Times,* while pointing out that certain claims of Dr. Manning would 'possess the power of determining for Queen Victoria and her subjects the bounds of their mutual obligations,' did not fear the claims. 'The guns may look very formidable,' it argued,[262] 'but they require men to fire them; and if the word of command should ever be given, the obedience rendered to it will be too irregular to produce any dangerous result.' Father Reilly protested that a truly divine religion could not possibly make its members disloyal subjects of society.[263] Clearly, here, the notion of an absolute sovereignty is disregarded altogether. Your sovereign obtains what obedience he can, and it seems to be admitted that the judgment, or the conscience, of men, is in truth the actual arbiter of events.

Yet different interpretations were not wanting.

[261] *Ibid.,* p. 559.

[262] *Times* of November 14, 1874.

[263] See the quotation from his pamphlet in the *Dublin Review* for 1876, p. 83.

W. G. Ward boldly stated that the Bull *Unam Sanctam* was his ideal and that he had 'no other wish than that its doctrines may find acceptance in Europe.'[264] The ground of his attitude is quite evident. A Catholic theocracy on earth was his ideal and without the absolute supremacy of the Pope it seemed to him that anarchy would follow.[265] Ambrose de Lisle, on the other hand, thought 'it dangerous and untrue' thus to assert the superiority of the ecclesiastical to the civil power, or to suggest that the former defined the limits of the latter.[266] The distinguished historian Thirlwall echoed with grave concern Mr. Gladstone's theories. 'It has now become impossible,' he said,[267] 'for a Roman Catholic, consistently with the first principles of his religion, to be a loyal subject of any government which is not itself subject to the Pope.' Canon Oakeley, one of the most distinguished of the Newmanite converts, argued that the Syllabus and its consequences embodied no more than the natural consequences of the Oxford Movement. 'There is not,' he told Mr. Gladstone,[268] 'one of the popular maxims condemned in the Syllabus which such men as Mr. Keble and Mr. Hurrell Froude would not have held in utter detestation,' and he argued for the dutiful reception of the Vatican decrees. But the two fullest

[264] *Dublin Review,* 1875, p. 179.
[265] *Ibid.,* p. 197.
[266] *Times* of November 23, 1874.
[267] *Charges,* Vol. II, p. 302.
[268] *Annual Register* for 1874, p. 107.

answers, on the Ultramontane side, to Mr. Gladstone, came from Manning, and his subordinate, Monsignor Capel. Cardinal Manning, in his brief note to the *Times,* had already explained that the civil allegiance of Catholics was unimpaired by the promulgation of the dogma. He now explained the grounds upon which his assertion was based. He pointed out again that no allegiance is undivided. 'Every moral being,' he wrote,[269] 'is under two authorities, human and divine. The child is under the authority of parents, and the authority of God; the subject is under the authority of the Civil State and the divine authority of natural or revealed religion. Unless we claim infallibility for the State, its acts must be liable to revision and resistance by natural conscience. An unlimited obedience to parents or to States would generate a race of unlimited monsters.' So far he had done no more than to give an admirable criticism of Austinianism. But he proceeded to questions of a different kind. He urged that to allow complete liberty of conscience was virtually to allow anarchy and against this the Church must provide corporate protection. The sixty-third proposition of the Syllabus adjudged anathema against him who rebelled against legitimate princes. 'The political conscience of Catholics,' he said,[270] 'is not left to the individual judgment alone. It is guided by the whole Christian morality, by the greatest system

269 *The Vatican Decrees,* London, 1875, p. 37.
270 *Ibid.,* p. 38.

of ethical legislation the world has ever seen, the Canon Law and the Moral Theology of the Catholic Church.' But this was virtually to admit that the Church controlled the Catholic as a citizen, which was exactly the position against which Mr. Gladstone had made his protest. Nor did Manning stop here. While he admitted that, within his own sphere, the State was a perfect and supreme society, he denied that it was the highest society on earth;[271] the Church was higher than the State because it had a higher aim and was therefore supreme above the State. What did that supremacy imply? One thing only to his mind: that the Church only can fix the limits of its own jurisdiction;[272] and he admitted that if it can fix the limits of its own jurisdiction, it can fix the limits of all other jurisdictions. From this, as he conceived, two consequences followed: the Church did not concern itself with temporal matters, and in all things which hinder or promote the eternal happiness of men, the Church has a power to judge and enforce.'[273]

It will perhaps be admitted that the argument is more controversially interesting than historically accurate. Its truth can only be maintained by giving to the word 'eternal' a connotation which includes all temporal things. But temporal things had been adjudged the province of the State, and

[271] *Ibid.*, p. 46.
[272] *Ibid.*, p. 54.
[273] *Ibid.*, p. 55.

on that basis Manning had suggested that if each organisation kept to its rightful sphere, collision was impossible. He did not doubt which was the offender. 'Modern Liberalism,' he wrote in 1877,[274] 'is the Caesarism of the State. Liberalism seems to believe that "all power in heaven and on earth" was given to it—that the State has power to define the limits of its own jurisdiction and also those of the Church. All sin and blasphemy against God is forgiven to men. There is only one unpardonable sin. Any one who speaks a word against the omnipotence of the State is disloyal, and shall never be forgiven.' So thoroughgoing a criticism leaves no doubt as to the direction in which Manning's sympathies lay. Theoretically, it seems clear that his attitude lays itself open to the objections urged by Mr. Gladstone. If only the Church could define the limits of her jurisdiction, and if she chose, as under Gregory VII and Innocent III, the medieval Church seems to have chosen, to interfere with every possible domain of civilised life, then collision between Church and State was not merely possible but inevitable. That, in fact, was the central problem of Ultramontanism. It postulated a theocracy of which the Pope was the Austinian sovereign. It could hardly then be surprised if those out of sympathy with Catholic ideals showed themselves unwilling to admit such unlimited power. Cardinal Manning, indeed, when confronted with the facts, seems to have

274 *Nineteenth Century,* 1877, Vol. I, p. 804.

been driven to that conclusion. 'The first principles of morals,' he wrote in a very striking paragraph,[275] 'forbid the extension of the supreme judicial power of the Church on such a civil order as that of England. When it was *de facto* subject to the Church, England had, by its own free will, accepted the laws of the Church. It can never again be subject to such laws except on the same condition—namely, by its own free will. Till then the highest laws of morality render the exercise of such Pontifical acts in England impossible.' It is difficult to see exactly why this should be the case unless the Austinianism for which Manning had previously contended becomes impossible. For whereas he had argued for a papal sovereignty based upon Divine Right, now he does not ask for its exercise except upon the basis of human consent to its activities. In such a connotation the Austinian spectre is more formidable in appearance than in reality.

Monsignor Capel went even further in the direction of an extreme interpretation than Manning. His historical disquisition it is probably unnecessary at this date to treat with any seriousness; it is in his political theses that the interest of his pamphlet lies.[276] He explains that God has established on earth three powers, paternal, civil and spiritual. 'Each of these powers is supreme and independent in its own province; has full and

[275] *Vaticanism*, p. 79.

[276] *A Reply to Mr. Gladstone's Political Expostulation*, London, 1875.

free activity in its own order; preserves its own autonomy; and ought never to be absorbed by either of the other powers.'[277] We have, in fact, a kind of Presbyterian doctrine of three kingdoms instead of two, and since allegiance to each is absolute, the theory is really, on the surface at least, a theory of toleration and liberty. But then Monsignor Capel begins to introduce curious limitations. He explains that the Spiritual Power is pre-eminent over the other two not only because of 'its nobler end and greater empire, but also in its very nature'; for that reason 'it is manifest that this power is not exercised directly in its own sphere, but likewise indirectly over the actions of the other two powers. In this sense, it is supreme, and the other powers are subordinate to it.'[278] So that the freedom and independence of which he had previously spoken are not really existent. He explains the cause of this seeming contradiction. 'The Church has held,' he writes,[279] 'that politics, or the science which treats of the State, must necessarily, from its ethical character, present many points of contact with revealed truth. The principles on which it is based flow from the natural law. They can never, therefore, be in real contradiction with the precepts of the divine and positive law. Hence the State, if it only remain true to its fundamental principles, must ever be in the completest harmony

[277] *Ibid.*, p. 53.
[278] *Ibid.*, p. 54.
[279] *Ibid.*, p. 55.

with the Church and Revelation. Now so long as this harmony continues, the Church has neither call nor right to interfere with politics, for earthly politics do not fall within her jurisdiction. The moment, however, the State becomes unfaithful to its principles, and contravenes the divine and positive law, that moment it is the Church's right and duty, as the guardian of revealed truth, to interfere, and to proclaim to the State the truths which it has ignored, and to condemn the erroneous maxims which it has adopted.' So that, in the last analysis, the Ultramontanism of which Capel was representative is only willing to allow the State its freedom so long as its actions meet with the approval of the Church. It goes back to medieval ideas, and reduces politics to a branch of theological study of the truth of which it is necessarily and obviously the sole arbiter.[280] So that we ultimately have a State that finds the expression of its freedom in compliance with the wishes of the Church; and the Church, we are told, has judged of the conduct of States as a consequence of the universal desire of nations.[281] It is perfectly clear, therefore, that Monsignor Capel's theories of the Church make it logically impossible to hold the idea of separate supremacies which he had previously put forward; for a supremacy that is not supreme seems rather to

280 Cf. the very valuable remarks of Dr. Figgis on this nation in the introductory lecture to his *Gerson to Grotius.*

281 *A Reply to Mr. Gladstone's Political Expostulation,* p. 61.

belong to a Looking-Glass world than to a well-reasoned political treatise. It was essentially to bring out the implications of this Ultramontanism, historically and politically, that Dollinger had written his *Pope and the Council* and Mr. Gladstone his pamphlet. Logically, Monsignor Capel, like Manning, virtually admits the main conclusions at which Mr. Gladstone arrived, and in theory their conclusions led exactly to that questionable loyalty of which he spoke as established by the new dogma. Where both he and they were in error was in their regarding an Austinian sovereignty as a working hypothesis. Theoretically admirable, in practice it would not work. Mr. Frederic Harrison made this abundantly clear in an admirable letter. 'Exeter Hall denounced the opium war,' he wrote,[282] 'some of our civil and military officers are under the inspiration of Exeter Hall; therefore we may expect them to desert to the enemy in a possible war with China. These exercises of irritating logic are as easy as they are puerile. If every opinion a man may hold is to be followed out to what we think its logical result, and every man is to be supposed in any dilemma which our ingenuity can frame, every man is a rebel.' The pity was that the advocates of Ultramontanism did not see the application of these remarks no less to their own demands upon

282 In a letter to the New York *Herald* quoted in Monsignor Capel's pamphlet, p. 67. The whole letter is an admirable exposition of the real meaning of sovereignty.

the minimisers of their own faith, than to the criticism passed upon them by Mr. Gladstone.

For the fact is, that in any contest between life and logic, it is not logic that is successful. It required a man whose philosophic outlook was essentially based upon this realisation to understand the actual nature of the debate. Newman's *Grammar of Assent,* then but four years old, was above all things a study of the psychology of mental processes, and a demonstration that certain dormant conceptions, when once aroused, would justify convictions for which no logic could adequately account.[283] But the line between belief and action was not very wide and it required but a step to transfer the ideas of the philosophical volume to the political arena. Quite early in the controversy with Mr. Gladstone he determined to speak out his mind, and though his 'old fingers'—he was then seventy-three—'did not move quick,' he seems to have worked with astonishing rapidity.[284] The *Letter to the Duke of Norfolk,*[285] the *Apologia* apart, was Newman's masterpiece. Its profound psychology, its subtlety, its humour, its loyalty to his friends, its whimsical castigation of his enemies, place it in

283 It would be interesting to trace the relation of this attitude to the current psychology of the unconscious. It is of course the argument of James in the famous lecture on Bergson in his *Pluralistic Universe.*

284 The *Letter to the Duke of Norfolk* was begun in October, 1874, and published in January, 1875. Ward, *Life of Newman,* II, 402-403.

285 I use an edition published by the Catholic Truth Society of New York in 1875 and all references are to that edition.

a class by itself of the controversy of which it formed a part. But it is more than a piece of ephemeral argument. It remains with some remarks of Sir Henry Maine and a few brilliant dicta of F. W. Maitland as perhaps the profoundest discussion of the nature of obedience and of sovereignty to be found in the English language. In the reply to his critics which Mr. Gladstone published it is clear that of this argument alone did he take serious account.[286] For Newman, even apart from his theology, was an able political thinker who had devoted the twelve years of his connexion with the Oxford Movement to the study of the problem of sovereignty in its acutest phase—that of Church and State. The pamphlet, in a sense, was the summation of his life's work. He seems to have felt that the clouds which had gathered about so much of his early life were now dispersing and that he might hope, if not for justification, at any rate for peace.[287] And it is difficult not to feel that the service he rendered to his Church upon this occasion was closely connected with the bestowal of that honour which was his official vindication. But in the hearts of Englishmen it was a vindication he did not need.

Newman was quick to see that the central problem was the relations of sovereignty to alle-

[286] Cf. his phrase p. 11, 'Dr. Newman is like the sun in the intellectual hemisphere of Anglo-Romanism' and note the different way in which throughout he deals with the criticism of Newman compared with other replies.

[287] Cf. the beautiful letter to Blachford. *Life,* II, 408.

giance on the one hand, and to conscience on the other. The Pope was sovereign and infallible, said Mr. Gladstone; therefore no British subject can be at once loyal to the Crown and a Catholic. But Newman at once points out that there are degrees of obedience and that they determine the nature of sovereignty. Mr. Gladstone, as he said, objected to the 'supreme direction' exercised by the Pope over Catholics.[288] But Newman urges that the State, through the law, makes a precisely similar claim. 'The State,' he said,[289] 'as well as the Church, has the power at its will of imposing laws upon us, laws bearing on our moral duties, our daily conduct, affecting our actions in various ways, and circumscribing our liberties; yet no one would say that the Law, after all, with all its power in the abstract, and its executive vigour in fact, interferes either with our comfort or our conscience.' But the papal activity is less than this. 'At first sight,' Newman says,[290] 'I have not known where to look for instances of his actual interposition in our private affairs.' The fact is that, of necessity, whatever be the claims of the Papacy, it can in practice do no more than lay down perfectly general laws and trust to the good sense of Catholics for their wise application to the facts of any particular case.[291] And he goes on to show how Catholic loyalty to the Pope must receive

288 *Letter to Duke of Norfolk,* p. 52.
289 *Ibid.,* p. 53.
290 *Ibid.,* p. 54.
291 *Ibid.,* p. 57.

limitation in the event. 'Suppose England,' he wrote,[292] 'were to send her ironclads to support Italy against the Pope and his allies, English Catholics would be very indignant, they would take part with the Pope before the war began, they would use all constitutional means to hinder it; but who believes that when they were once in the war, their action would be anything else than prayers and exertions for a termination?' In so difficult a case, in fact, Catholics would do no more than play the perfectly constitutional part of an opposition in Parliament, as did John Bright during the Crimean war. But what, Newman asks, would Catholics do if a direct command from the Pope came actively to oppose their country? If, for example, Parliament forced Catholics to attend Protestant service weekly, and the Pope told Catholics to disobey the law, he would obey the Pope. To Mr. Gladstone's argument that such a case is impossible he replies by admitting it, and, almost in Mr. Harrison's words he points out the obvious circumscription to which an absolute obedience is subject.[293] He would not obey the Pope if, as a Privy Councillor, he was ordered to give acknowledgement to a Prince of Wales who became a Roman Catholic. He would not obey the Pope if, when a soldier or sailor, the Pope ordered all Catholics to retire from the services. In extreme cases, in brief, that is 'when his conscience

292 *Ibid.*, p. 64.
293 *Ibid.*, p. 66.

could not be reconciled to any of the courses of action proposed to him by others,' he will follow the dictates of his conscience as men like Turrecremata and Bellarmine have alike argued he must do.[294] For such a demand of absolute obedience 'would be transgressing the laws of human nature and human society' since 'there is no rule in this world without exceptions.'[295] He is careful to point out that this is not the doctrine of private judgment as held by Protestants; for while with the latter private judgment is the arbiter of common events, with him it is decisive only 'in very extraordinary and rare, nay, impossible cases.' The term 'conscience' must not be misunderstood. 'Conscience is not a longsighted selfishness, nor a desire to be consistent with oneself, but it is a messenger from Him who, in nature and in grace, speaks to us behind a veil and teaches and rules us by his representatives.'[296] Such a freedom of conscience no Pope dare deny; did he do so 'it would be a suicidal act. He would be cutting the ground from under his feet . . . on the law of conscience and its sacredness are founded both his authority in theory and power in fact.'[297] If he trampled on the consciences of men thus conceived he would meet his due reward. And conscience thus conceived is the real abiter of conduct. Nor can it collide with infallibility. For the one, he

[294] *Ibid.*, p. 68.
[295] *Ibid.*, p. 69.
[296] *Ibid.*, p. 73.
[297] *Ibid.*, p. 77.

says, quoting St. Thomas, is engaged only with immediate things while infallibility deals with general propositions.[298] And he is careful to point out that the Pope 'is not infallible in his laws, nor in his commands, nor in his acts of state, nor in his administration, nor in his public policy.'[299] He is infallible only when he speaks ex cathedra in the name of the Church; and it is a difficult theological problem to decide when he does so speak. Newman feels certain that the essence of Catholic doctrine is the duty of obeying conscience 'at all hazards.'[300] 'If I am obliged,' runs his striking conclusion,[301] 'to bring religion into after-dinner toasts (which indeed does not seem quite the thing), I shall drink—to the Pope if you please—still to Conscience first, and to the Pope afterwards.'

The argument seems complete. Man should do that which he deems morally right, and the only obedience he can render is the obedience consonant with his ethical standards. Clearly in such a view the sovereign of Austin, the superior who always receives submission to his views, is an unthinkable thing. He is unthinkable because so long as men live they will vary in opinion on fundamental questions, and varying will follow their individual bent. Whether so minimising an interpretation represents with any accuracy the policy of Rome

298 *Ibid.*, p. 80.
299 *Ibid.*, p. 81.
300 *Ibid.*, p. 83, and see the interesting citations he gives on this point.
301 *Ibid.*, p. 86.

is another and very different question.[302] Certainly one may doubt whether it would have met with the approval of *il diavolo del' Concilio,* Manning. For it deprives the Pope of his sovereignty at exactly the point where it is most needed—the crucial instance where it might be put to the test of the event. It is a theory of liberty since it bases power and obedience on the consent of men. In such a view, for instance, Newman has not the right to doubt the morality of Dollinger's secession; for the highest motives—as was universally admitted—actuated the great historian in the course he took. Certain words of Mr. Gladstone, when he closed this momentous debate, contain a truth of profound importance. 'It may be true,' he said,[303] 'that the men of good systems are worse than their principles, and the men of bad systems better than their principles.' Theories which depend for their translation into terms of the event upon an irrevocable certainty in human nature are psychologically fallacious. Men, for the most part, have an unknown factor in their every political equation. Dogma may dream that it has extinguished right at law, and it yet will be found to suffer defeat. Divine right does not prevent the execution of kings. So long as our theories have to validate themselves in practice we may perhaps fear little the remorselessness of their logic. For human nature has evolved its separate guarantees.

302 Newman claimed for it the sanction of Bishop Fessler—the Secretary-General of the Council. *Ibid.,* p. 105.

303 *Vaticanism* (New York, Harpers, 1875), p. 85.

V

The problem of Church and State is in reality, as Mr. Figgis has so ably argued,[304] but part of the larger problem of the nature of civil society. To distrust the old theory of sovereignty is to strive towards a greater freedom. We have been perhaps too frankly worshippers of the State. Before it we have prostrated ourselves in speechless admiration, deeming its nature matter, for the most part, beyond our concern. The result has been the implicit acceptance of a certain grim Hegelianism which has swept us unprotestingly on into the vortex of a great All which is more than ourselves. Its goodness we might not deny. We live, so we are told, but for its sake and in its life and are otherwise non-existent. So the State has become a kind of modern Baal to which the citizen must bow a heedless knee. It has not been seen, or perhaps has been too truly seen, that the death of argument lies in genuflexion.[305]

It is an inadequate attitude thus to perpetrate a meaningless uniformity of outlook. Societies are persons as men are persons. They have—the word matters but little—their ethos, character, nature, identity. They are born to live within the pale of human fellowship. They may be wrong, as men

304 In his *Churches in the Modern State.*

305 I should like to refer to Mr. Barker's brilliant paper on the 'Discredited State' in the *Political Quarterly* for May, 1915, for a very full expression of this attitude. I think, however, that he unduly narrows the meaning of personality.

and women are wrong, and the rules of human conduct which the processes of evolution have developed for the individual must be applied to them also. It is no answer to assert the theoretical infallibility of the State to us who possess the record of history. To acquiesce in its sin, to judge of it by criteria other than those of individual action, is to place authority before truth. The sovereignty of the State will pass, as the divine right of kings has had its day. It has been no more than a sword forged in one of the mightiest of political conflicts. It has been a victorious sword but it must be replaced by newer weapons. No dogma can hope for immortality since we live in an age of readjustment and of reconstruction.

There is an etching of Brangwyn's in which the artist has depicted the break-up of a discarded vessel. It lies on its side, dominating the picture. It overawes by its impressiveness, by its suggestion of a mighty past. One sees it as a stage in the evolution of sea-craft, a vessel which, in its day, was a very giant of human invention. Then it enabled those who piloted it through unknown and uncharted seas to do voyage of service and discovery. But it is at length cast aside. Vessels built on principles more consonant with modern knowledge take its place. So, with its past splendour borne clearly in mind, it is held to have served its purpose. What it has been, what it has accomplished, is remembered by those who plan the evolution of that science of which it is part;

whatever there is in it of good, goes to the making of its successor. So should it be with the dogmas of political thought. At a time when the organisation of the State was the essential need, the dogma of its moral sovereignty was of the highest value. But newer knowledge has come, and with it the need of change. And it is sheer tragedy that men should be unwilling to realise that the majesty of the State is in nowise diminished by a frank recognition of its imperfections. The State, like man, ceases to be human when it is exalted into Godhead. We dare not so exalt it lest we be imprisoned by the errors of the past. For it is ours to hand down undimmed the torch of conscious life.

CHAPTER V

DE MAISTRE AND BISMARCK[1]

I

THE Catholic Revival and the growth of nationalism are perhaps the two most fundamental facts in the history of the nineteenth century. Round them may very largely be grouped the ideals from which its ultimate canon may be evolved. They are largely antithetic movements; for the series of facts which each sought to control were for the most part identical. It is thus perhaps superficially difficult to discover grounds of intimate resemblance between the greatest of those who gave to the Roman Catholic system the chief rationale of its renascence, and the supreme master of nationalist statesmanship. The nineteenth century, after all, is essentially an anti-theological age. It is the age which contributed most to the dissolution of ecclesiastic structure, the age in which Cavour destroyed the political foundations of the Church, in which Darwin cast

[1] It is perhaps unnecessary to express the obligation this paper owes to the essay by Lord Morley in the first volume of his *Miscellanies*, to that of Sainte-Beuve in his *Portraits littéraires*, Vol. II, and above all to the masterly analysis of Faguet in his *Politiques et Moralistes.* See also the brilliant little study by M. Georges Cogordan.

the corrosive sublimate of demonstrated evolution upon the basis of dogmas which had boasted of their eternal nature. De Maistre, it is clear enough, stands for that old medieval theocracy which the Revolution had made finally impossible. The frank opponent of Bacon, the contemptuous critic of Locke, the unmitigated hater of Voltaire, he seems essentially unaffiliated to the modern world. He is like one of those curious instances of atavism for which the science of heredity is so signally unable to account. It seems at first sight illogical to connect his thought with that of Bismarck who, in creating the German empire, was perhaps instrumental more than any other statesman of his time in rendering impossible the fulfilment of the dream of which De Maistre was the chief exponent. Bismarck was, with Cavour, the most national of nineteenth century statesmen, and it was of nationalism that the Ultramontane theory has been the uncompromising antagonist. He was the foe of the Roman Church. For more than a decade he pursued it with a hostility that was at once bitter and unrelenting. His outlook seems antithetic to that of De Maistre. Yet the differences are more apparent than real; and examination suggests that in the search for an adequate perspective they are unimportant. Each aimed, fundamentally, at the same goal; and it was only the formal structure in which their ideas found realisation that marks a distinction in the basis of their thought.

II

There is no problem as to the origin of De Maistre's fundamental ideas. He was born to hate the Revolution and in his examination of its character he found no signs of good. Every institution he cherished it had overthrown. Every dogma he accepted it had cast away. It had tyrannised over the Church, it had mocked religion, it had executed the king. 'France was dishonoured by more than a hundred thousand murders and the soil of that noble kingdom was strewn with scaffolds.'[2] The foundations of political authority were overthrown and with them the structure of ecclesiasticism seemed to perish. It was De Maistre's task to suggest the basis of their reconstruction.

The character of his response was in a large degree determined by his early life. The member of a distinguished family, he was, as M. Faguet has well pointed out,[3] essentially a patrician by nature. His early career had fastened on him the disposition of the bureaucrat who loves order and to whom chaos is the first of sins. He had, even from childhood, a high regard for authority; and even when at the University, he read no book without the permission of his father. Nor can the fact that the Jesuits of Chambéry played their

[2] *Considérations sur la France,* p. 13. I use an edition published in 1910 by Roger and Chernoviz of Paris.

[3] *Politiques et Moralistes,* p. 5.

part in the determination of his career have been without its influence; and we know that to his mother the suppression of that order in France was a serious blow to religion.[4] To an intelligence so trained a shock more deep than that which the ideas of the Revolution must have suggested it is impossible to imagine. The blow came, moreover, when he was nearly forty years of age,[5] at a time when the main lines of intellectual development have been finally determined.

He desired a reconstruction of society and it was such a method as his education had familiarised him with that he applied to his work. In no sense of the word a psychologist, it was a logical analysis of the problem that he made. He found a new dogma—the sovereignty of the people—popularised by the Revolution. No item in the term was defined, no implications had been studied. The magic of a phrase had enthralled the intelligence of men. There was easy talk of the rights of men, and, once more, no shadow of precision in the talk.[6] Society, he pointed out, was not born, as Rousseau devoutly urged, from deliberation; for that term itself implies the organisation which is society. Nor can we predicate a society before we have a sovereign, in order that we may refer authority to a popular origin. The very idea of human intercourse implies, to his mind, the idea

[4] Sainte-Beuve, *Portraits littéraires,* Vol. II (ed. of 1862), p. 389.
[5] He was born in 1753.
[6] See the biting attack on Rousseau in the *Mélanges,* pp. 188-192.

of sovereignty; 'for the term "people" suggests an organisation built round a common centre, and without sovereignty there can be neither union nor political unity."[7] He is equally opposed to the suggestion that man is in any sense an independent being. He admits that the thought is an easy one, but it is founded upon a mistaken interpretation of freedom.[8] We have to accustom ourselves to grasp firmly the idea of a divine will as the foundation of human society, and only in so far as man acts in harmony with that will is he capable of constructive achievement.[9]

It is easy to see the direction in which his thought is moving. To conceive of man as an isolation is to build a State upon the basis of his separatism.[10] But that is to neglect the fact that the State is essentially an unity, over and above its constituent parts. The attempt to base it upon separatism results in an undue stress of the individual on the one hand, and of reason on the other. Reason is useless in the preservation of a political society,[11] and the essence of patriotism is that abnegation of the individual which a separatist theory denies.[12] That corporate soul which is the centre of national power can never be constructed from thought. 'If every man thinks out for

7 *Mélanges,* p. 192.

8 *Principe Générateur,* No. X. Cf. No. XLV.

9 *Mélanges,* p. 192.

10 Cf. the valuable remarks of M. Faguet, *op. cit.,* p. 10.

11 *Mélanges,* p. 247.

12 *Ibid.,* p. 249.

himself the principles of government,' he says, 'civil anarchy and the destruction of political sovereignty must quickly follow.' So that the consequence is clear. If reason is insufficient, we must have faith; if argument is inadequate we must have authority. And since what man alone achieves is not destined to endure, he has need of the work of God. As in the Hebraic and Mohammedan systems, the wise legislator will make his political theory a religion also; so will the fidelity of his citizens become a faith and their obedience be exalted into a fanatic enthusiasm.[13] Religion to him is the keystone of the arch of social structure, and the deeper the study of history the more certain becomes the realisation of how indispensable is its alliance.[14] That was, as Cicero realised,[15] the secret of Roman success. The statesman dare not neglect it since, crime apart, the best means are the most successful.[16]

We have abandoned reason and the individual and their main weapon must follow. If it is necessary to introduce a certain mysticism into the texture of the State, it must be preserved in all its dignity. So he urges that a written constitution is an error. The danger of its accessibility apart, it contains the stupid error of supposing that the makers of laws are men, that laws are documents, that a nation can be constituted with a pen and

[13] *Ibid.*, p. 230.

[14] *Ibid.*, p. 236.

[15] *De naturâ deorum*, II, 4.

[16] *Lettres sur l'Inquisition*, I.

paper. History gives evidence to the contrary. The more feeble the institution the more does it tend to take a written form.[17] Men do not respect that which they see created. A real constitution man can not create; for his function in nature is only to transform. 'Man,' he urges,[18] 'can not give laws to himself. He can do no more than defend what is dispensed to him by a higher power. These rights are beneficent customs which are beneficent because they are unwritten and because we know neither their beginning nor their author.' And the declaration of custom should be avoided since not only is it either the effect or the cause of great evil, but it also is invariably more costly than it is worth.[19]

So that it is to authority we are driven back and of its worth he has no doubt. He has emphasised the value of patriotism of which the essence is an undeliberating and heedless devotion, a sacrifice of oneself to the corporate good. Under what form of State may it be best attained? Of democracy he takes but little account; it is to be defined as an association of men without sovereignty, that is to say, without control over themselves.[20] It lacks the essential conditions of stability and of justice. It gives too great a handle to selfishness, it has not the distinction of ranks which is the foundation of

17 *Principe Générateur,* Nos. 19, 20, 21.

18 *Mélanges,* p. 244.

19 *Principe Générateur,* No. 28.

20 *Mélanges,* pp. 246, 347.

power.[21] Aristocracy he conceives to have more merit though he allows it vigour only in proportion as it approximates in character to a monarchy.[22] For it is in monarchy that he places all his confidence. It is the natural form of government. It permits that concentration of sovereignty which allows the manifestation of its real virtues. Even if it has its dangers, nevertheless history gives to it a splendid justification and history is experimental politics.[23] It is in a monarchy that the vices of sovereignty are least apparent.[24] It permits, above all, of unity—an inestimable virtue in his eyes; since in the rule of many the subjects of the crown delight in its dissection and thus deprive it of its majesty.[25] But kingship gives to sovereignty a character of intensity which increases its value. 'The name of king,' he writes,[26] 'is a talisman, a magic power, which gives to every force and intent a central direction.' It is the personalisation of that authority which is the pivot of De Maistre's political system.

No one can doubt the reasons for his attitude. 'Ainsi donc, Madame,' he wrote to a Russian lady,[27] 'plus de pape, plus de souveraineté; plus de souveraineté, plus de unité; plus d'unité, plus

21 *Ibid.*, p. 359.
22 *Ibid.*, pp. 332 *seq.*
23 *Ibid.*, pp. 201 *seq.*
24 *Ibid.*, p. 309.
25 *Ibid.*, p. 313.
26 *Ibid.*, p. 323.
27 *Oeuvres Choisies de Joseph de Maistre,* Vol. IV, p. 179.

d'authorité; plus d'authorité, plus de foi.' It is the bitter protest of the medievalist against the Revolution. Doubt is sin, and to prevent its birth we must form a political system in which it shall have no place. The antithesis of doubt is faith and faith must be imposed. It must come from without, and authority is therefore its inevitable accompaniment while sovereignty is no more than its full expression in political terms. It is, too, clear why he desired unity so deeply. Where men begin to differ change must result; and change is the child of that discussion which can be born only of scepticism. We recognise the medievalism of an attitude which is clearly identifying heresy with rebellion and finding therein political reason for its suppression. So long as there is unity there is peace which is the sole guarantee of survival. De Maistre can not doubt that the guarantee of a continuance of political life is the erection of a system impermeable to the currents of change. Man's truest ideas are the primeval feelings of his heart, and he could see no adequate ground for their discussion. Herein is the result of his experiences of the eighteenth century; for to deny the value of reason and of argument is to deny the fundamental purpose for which it conceived itself to exist.[28] He opposes the splendour of a stable civilisation to the bewildering variety for which the age in which he lived stood sponsor. For in that variety is involved a denial of the sovereignty of

[28] Cf. Faguet, *op. cit.*, p. 15.

the State, the division of its powers, the erection of antithetic systems of rights; and from them is born revolution.[29] If you suggest that from revolution good may accrue, he will point out that between the conduct of France and the qualities of which virtue is composed there is a direct antithesis. 'Cette plaie,' he wrote angrily,[30] 'est du vol . . . cette habitude du vol, cette scandale donné et reçu mutuellement tous les jours, et tout le jour sur toute la surface de la France, ont produit à la fin un état de chose dont on ne se forme ancune idée juste si on ne l' a vu de près . . . Il y a une antipathie naturalle et invincible entre la République Française et toutes les vertus.'

We need, then, a formula against revolution and it is in the sovereignty of authority that we find it. One tremendous consequence must result immediately from such a conclusion: our theologico-political system can not be Protestant in character. De Maistre was too bold a thinker not to admit the logical deduction from his premises and he was unsparing in his criticisms of Protestantism. It is a word that must be effaced from the language of Europe if religion is to be re-established and the foundations of political authority strengthened.[31] In its various forms, as Calvinism, more insidiously as Jansenism,[32] it has declared war on

29 *Fragments*, p. 34.

30 *Ibid.*, p. 57.

31 *Du Pape, Conclusion* (ed. of 1910), p. 354.

32 The reader will wish to consult Sainte-Beuve's reply to De Maistre's attack, *Porte-Royal,* Vol. III (ed. of 1888), p. 233 *seq.*

every sort of authority. It is protestant against sovereignty for its only dogma is to have no dogmas.[33] The French Revolution is the inevitable and disastrous consequence of its principles; it has almost annihilated Christianity in Europe.[34] For it is a philosophy of scepticism. 'C'est l' insurrection de la raison individuelle,' he wrote,[35] 'contre la raison générale, et par conséquent c'est tout ce qu'on peut imaginer de plus mauvais. C'est l'ennemi essentiel de tout croyance commune à plusieurs hommes: ce que constitue ennemi du genre humain.' By nature it is rebellious, for doubt is its foundation and doubt is the mother of rebellion. History gives proof of this statement. With the Reformation came the religious division of Christianity and the political division of Europe.[36] Its force even then was not expended. To test the doctrines of Luther it cast Germany into the horrors of the Thirty Years' War. The execution of Charles I is traceable directly to its influence. If it urges the inhumanity of Saint Bartholomew the necessity of that massacre is the proof of its inherent danger.[37] It is in fact anti-sovereign, and therefore anti-authoritarian by nature. It is the very mainspring of inquietude. For sovereignty in its essence is indivisible, and Protestantism makes of each man his own sover-

33 IVme lettre *sur l'education publique en Russie.*

34 Vide his *Sur l'État du Christianisme en Europe.*

35 *Mélanges,* p. 510.

36 *Ibid.,* p. 513.

37 *Ibid.,* p. 516.

eign.[38] It places faith in the category of sin, and examines dogma only to reject it. For in that desire for investigation lies the yearning for novelty, and the distrust of existing things, as is instanced in the manner in which one whom De Maistre signalises as perhaps the most odious of the Revolutionists, Condorcet, was the eager friend of reform.[39] It is the sans-culottisme of religion. It is inferior as a political system even to paganism or to the theories of Mahomet which realised the necessity of dogma and faith.[40] It has taken the security of the State to cast it heedlessly among the multitude.

The criticism has at any rate the merit of certitude and it is also the logical result of his beliefs. For when he had based his monarchy on miracle, De Maistre had in fact placed it beyond the reach of argument, and his salvation must find itself in a political theory in which reason was but a secondary consideration. The necessities of his outlook are clear. He has his organic state, of which the nature and origins are alike enwrapped in mystery. He has asserted the need of corporate government which can not, in its turn, exist without sovereignty. For there is no adequate rule that is not absolute. If it is said that absolutism is bound to issue in injustice, he will retort that injustice is at the basis of life. It is upon sacrifice

[38] *Ibid.*, p. 227.
[39] *Ibid.*, p. 542.
[40] *Ibid.*, p. 547.

that existence is founded, and if the innocent die they will at any rate have the satisfaction of remembering that the executioner is the corner-stone of society. If it be retorted that this is irrational, he will then answer that he is thereby the more certain of its truth. So to him even Christ can be no more than 'une victime sanglante,' and M. Faguet has acutely suggested that his Christianity was basically pagan; for it lacks the very idea of love of which the Gospel is the written expression.[41] This, clearly, is the cause of his profound hatred of the Greek spirit. For he found there the same lack of vigour, of hardness of certitude, the same anxiety to examine and to doubt, which is the root of the egoism of the Protestant.[42] Nothing is more characteristic of his temper than the singular but striking judgment of Plato that as a Greek he is wearying to a degree; 'il n' est grand, sublime, pénétrant que lorsqu' il est théologien; c'est à dire lorsqu' il énonce des dogmes positifs et éternels séparés de toute chicane.'[43] The Greek mind was for him too pliable, too yielding, too curious to command either his affection or his admiration. What he sought for were the premises of life, and, once given, as he could not doubt they were given to the world in the Christian philosophy, the sole problem was to give them an unchangeable political expression.

[41] Faguet, *op. cit.*, p. 59.
[42] *Du Pape*, Bk. IV, Caps. VII-XI.
[43] *Du Pape* (ed. of 1910), p. 331.

The discussion of Christianity itself became thus unimportant. For, once given, it was outside the realm of argument. It was in this way that De Maistre became above all a political theorist. He could subordinate philosophy and theology to his theory of the State simply because they required no more than the statement to merit acceptance. That is why, as M. Faguet has pointed out, his earliest work is a political treatise; for at the very outset of his career his other views were indelibly fixed, were, indeed, the foundation of his political thought.[44]

III

With the rejection of Protestantism he is thrown back on the Catholic theory, and to this he gave an uncompromising and unquestioning acceptance. The book was in the nature of a personal apologia; for in the stress of the Napoleonic conflict he had spoken disrespectfully of the Holy Father, and *Du Pape* was written as a method of reparation.[45] Certainly the Papacy has good reason to give thanks to the ability of its enthusiastic champion; for with the possible exception of Augustinus Triumphus no one has given such entire allegiance to the gravest extremism of Hildebrand and of Innocent III., and De Maistre is superior to his

[44] Faguet, *op. cit.*, p. 5.

[45] Brandes, *Main Currents of XIXth Century Literature*, Vol. III, p. 105.

predecessor in that he has the important merit of being readable.

It is not difficult to understand the cause of De Maistre's papalism. *Semper eadem* might have been the motto of his thought, as it was the Catholic challenge to a revolutionary age. The Papacy had endured unchanged for eighteen hundred years. It was almost the parent of dogma. Its very life depended on the imposition of its authority. It was the guardian of a mystery into which faith alone could penetrate. Its sanction was divine; it spurned the power of human thought; it was the proud claimant of infallibility. What institution could be more fitted to rule the world?

It claimed infallibility. That was to mark it as a sovereign power, since infallibility is only the spiritual synonym of sovereignty.[46] That it should claim infallibility did not mean that it asked the possession of any special privilege, but only that the Church was a monarchy and demanded the natural attributes of its character.[47] It meant that error could not be charged against it, that its decisions must be accepted without question. If it be suggested that its infallibility is impossible, since Popes have erred, the reply is simply that infallible it must be since without it unity becomes impossible.[48] Nor is it worth while to raise the

46 *Du Pape,* Bk. I, Chap. I (ed. of 1910), p. 44.
47 *Ibid.,* p. 45.
48 *Ibid.,* p. 47.

objection, since the Catholic Church does not enter into argument. 'Elle croit,' he says almost with affection,[49] 'elle croit sans disputer; car la foi est une croyance par amour, et l'amour n' argumente point.' It has the even greater merit of finding at once its visible unity in the Pope. De Maistre makes short work of conciliar claims. Their infrequency, the manner in which they have themselves acclaimed the papal supremacy, the analogy with the relation of States-General to King, the witness of Gallican Church and Jansenist schismatics, of Protestant theologians like Calvin and heretic jurists like Pufendorf, are all dragged, some little matters of history notwithstanding, into the service of this supremacy.[50] Rome, he says with Calvin, is the centre of the world, *umbilicus terrae*.[51]

He is not afraid of despotism; for the Pope will be governed by the laws of his being, which are divine in character. And in any case he alone is the judge of those laws and must be obeyed without conditions unless anarchy is to result. The descent from absolute sovereignty to utter confusion is single and precipitous. Infallibility has been established in order that it may be avoided.[52] If it be said that Popes have meddled too intimately with the lives of men, he will reply that it has never

[49] *Ibid.*, p. 49.
[50] *Ibid.*, Bk. I, Chaps. II-IX.
[51] *Ibid.*, p. 79.
[52] *Ibid.*, p. 123 (Bk. I, Chap. XVI).

been without justification, and to Catholics who cherish such a thought he gives the warning that it implies a human judgment upon a divine institution.[53] Everything, in short, that can be known of the papal structure justifies the conclusion that it fulfils all the necessary conditions of social permanence. 'Il ne peut avoir de société humaine sans gouvernement,' he said in tremendous words,[54] 'ni de gouvernement sans souveraineté, ni de souveraineté sans infaillibilité, et ce dernier privilège est si absolument necessaire, qu' on est forcé de supposer l'infaillibilité, mêmes dans les souverainetés temporelles (où elle n'est pas) sans peine de voir l'association se dissoudre.' Law, then, is simple enough. It is what the sovereign commands, and that sovereign must be unique that he may escape destruction.

There is a tinge of fatalism in so terrible a logic, but De Maistre is ready with explanations of its necessity. Man, he holds, is a curious mingling of good and evil, and has need of government that he may be social. The law courts—we must remember that De Maistre was for long a judge—make us understand why that government must be absolute. Where there is no sentence given dispute immediately arises; and sovereignty arising to prevent the disaster which would result therefrom. Man desires to be just, and sovereignty provides the

[53] *Ibid.*, p. 129 (Bk. I, Chap. XVIII).
[54] *Ibid.*, p. 132 (Bk. I, Chap. XIX).

means for the attainment of that end.[55] It is true, of course, that dangers can result from its exercise; but they are less than the dangers which would result from its absence. And those who urge that the difficulty may be avoided by the erection of constitutions and of fundamental laws forget that the individual or the institution which carries them into effect will be in fact sovereign; so that in our effort to avoid it we attain it.[56] It is useless to object, for instance, that the difficulty has been evaded in the limited monarchy of England; for, as he urges, what has been limited in England is royalty while the king in Parliament still remains supreme.[57] It can do all it desires, and there is no legal limitation upon its will. He does not deny that kings may act wrongly; but in that event they will be subject to the indirect power of the Pope, who, as the direct representative of God, can release their subjects from their oath of fidelity. It is in this case only that there exists a right of resistance in the subject. Or, rather, it is not a right of resistance so much as a duty, since it is a command laid upon them by the most supreme of powers.[58] Nor have the Popes ever misused their power. If they have fought with sovereigns, with abstract sovereignty itself they have never con-

[55] *Ibid.*, p. 138-139 (Bk. II, Chap. I).
[56] *Ibid.*, p. 140 (Bk. II, Chap. II).
[57] *Ibid.*, p. 145 (Bk. II, Chap. III).
[58] *Ibid.*, p. 148 (Bk. II, Chap. IV).

tended. They have enforced the divine law of which they are the chosen delegates, and its very exercise has exalted the peoples of the earth.[59] They have defended the sanctity of marriage;[60] they have maintained the laws of the Church and the customs of the priestly caste;[61] they have upheld—De Maistre speaks in all seriousness—the liberty of Italy;[62] it is an enviable record.

The power thus theoretically conceived is justified in its practical results. It is untrue to urge, as is customary with the opponents of the Papacy, that it has plunged Europe into strife and fanaticism. The Popes are charged with the execution of a supreme power—that of excommunication—and they have used that power for public welfare. Where its use has resulted in tumult, it is due to the resistance they have encountered.[63] The medieval exercise of their right saved Europe from the catastrophes of barbarism. They can do so again, after the latest of barbarian irruptions, if men would but realise their power instead of remaining blinded by appearances. The good the Popes have conferred upon men is manifest in work such as missionary enterprise which is the harbinger of civilisation.[64] It is seen in their

59 *Ibid.*, p. 149 (Bk. II, Chap. V).
60 *Ibid.*, p. 166 (Bk. II, Chap. VII).
61 *Ibid.*, p. 173.
62 *Ibid.*, p. 180.
63 *Ibid.*, Bk. II, Chap. IX.
64 *Ibid.*, Bk. III, Chap. I.

struggle for civil liberty,[65] in the admirable results that have followed on the institution of clerical celibacy[66]—a good which Protestantism has sought to destroy—in their almost miraculous preservation of monarchy at a time when the decay of the Roman empire, and the barbarian invasions from the North seemed destined to achieve its destruction.[67] In its new infancy it was cherished and strengthened by the papal arm.[68] Where kings have been obedient to the Pope their reigns have been long and prosperous—clearly a sign of virtue.[69] Without the Pope, in short, a true Christianity would have been impossible. 'Des Papes,' he writes,[70] 'furent les instituteurs, les sauveteurs, et les veritables génies constituantes de l'Europe.' It thus becomes impossible to judge of kings save in their papal context, and its achievements are the solid demonstration that the papal monarchy is the best because the most permanent and the most natural.

To such a view his theory of schism is the logical conclusion. A schismatic church is a Protestant Church, for it is destroying the essential unity of civilisation.[71] The heretic churches are so many

65 *Ibid.*, Bk. III, Chap. II.
66 *Ibid.*, Bk. III, Chap. III.
67 *Ibid.*, Bk. III, Chap. IV.
68 *Ibid.*, p. 287.
69 *Ibid.*, Bk. III, Chap. V.
70 *Ibid.*, p. 303.
71 *Ibid.*, Bk. IV, Chap. I.

evidences of division and thus so many proofs of danger. They have no common name, their character is mutually alien, they attack each others' dogma, they have no means of final decision between their errors.[72] To sympathise with their variety is to invite the onset of a cataclysm.

What, then, is the conclusion to which his speculations lead? The faulty systems of the eighteenth century must be cast aside; they have deprived the half of Europe of its Christianity.[73] The institution which alone has lasted for eighteen centuries can serve as the natural centre of a new political system which will be the old. It is necessary for the preservation of Christianity that Rome should undertake that leadership. She only has the power and the majesty. She only emerges unharmed from the ruthless attacks to which she is subjected. She only can guarantee unity and faith. Divine in her origin, she has been splendid in her past and is destined to a more glorious future. God has watched over her with a special love, and thus fitted her to be the protector of nations. She holds in her hands the future happiness of men. If she has to face doubt and vice and rebellion, yet is she destined to triumph. 'Hydra-headed error will be vanquished before indivisible Truth: God will reign in the Temple as He reigns in heaven, in the blessed communion of his Saints.'[74]

[72] *Ibid.*, p. 321 ff.
[73] *Ibid.*, p. 347.
[74] *Ibid.*, p. 365.

IV

Lamartine has somewhere remarked that De Maistre's political thought is at the service of his religious instincts and this must be the main and abiding impression of any one who analyses his work. His was that fanatic devotion to a cause which examines all dogmas save his own. His own faith he did not examine, for he had placed it outside the realm of discussion; and to have admitted that it was capable of analysis would have been for him the admission that it might be annihilated. It is an admirable position; and it would demand the highest reverence did it possess the single merit of truth. For it was here that the immense fallacy lay in De Maistre's argument. He had already determined his conclusions before he began his enquiry. In the result, he became not the judge but the advocate who uses history as the great storehouse of political examples from which instances such as he desired might be culled. Nor was he in the least careful as to the accuracy of his interpretations.[75] He had that peculiar faculty of the eighteenth-century mind for seeing only what he believed on *a priori* grounds.[76] He would not admit that he might be wrong, for that would be to give tolerance the name of virtue. So it is that to the modern sense there is something of almost

[75] His treatment of the Spanish Inquisition is a good example of this trait.

[76] Cf. the admirable remarks of M. Faguet, *op. cit.*, p. 66.

unrelieved ugliness in the brutality with which he discusses his opponents. What is above all lacking in his temper is the capacity to understand humanity and, understanding, to forgive. The first necessity, after all, in a statesman, even in a theological statesman, is the readiness to admit error. History, in fact, is strewn with the wrecks of infallible systems and, in the end, De Maistre added but one more to that hapless company.

He mistook the grounds of the Revolution. He misread the character of his age. He seems, indeed, to have hated it too greatly to have made possible that understanding which, politically at least, can be born of sympathy alone. He did not remember, or else he chose to forget, the very obvious fact that no great historic event can come to pass without some justification of equal greatness as its parent. Since the Revolution did not accord with his desires, he chose deliberately to misrepresent its ideals. He would not understand that it had come as a protest against exactly that system of which he urged the reconstruction. He made the capital error of taking no account of the category of time. After all, the events he had regretted were on the book of record, and to ignore them was in nowise to ensure their oblivion. The world that had seen the fall of the Bastile was bound to be a different world. To tilt against its fundamental principles may have been courage; but it was the courage which has been immortalised by the dangerous pen of Cervantes. His plan would perhaps have been admirable in the fifth century after Christ. One recognises then the need of that powerful, even absolute, centralisation for which he contended. But to apply the solution of the problems of the fifth century to the difficulties of the nineteenth was to make too bold a denial of the march of mind. Men had thought too infinitely for his conclusions to be possible. They had known the Papacy too long. They would judge it not by the programme it announced but by the character its actions suggested it to possess. If the Reformation, and its political offspring the Revolution, have any definite beginning, they can be traced back to the era when what most oppressed men was the crimes of Rome. Luther may have been ignorant, fleshly, brutal, but he said boldly what men wanted to hear. It is not enough to proclaim loudly that Rome has never erred when men of genius have occupied themselves with the pregnant examination of her error. It is an inadequate outlook to defame curiosity as sin without attempting to enquire whether it is not in fact as natural as faith itself. Easy it may be to proclaim sovereignty divine, but the real problem comes when its defender is asked to justify the results of its exercise. The brilliance of De Maistre's apologetic does not conceal the viciousness of its determined obscurantism.

But it is of his main tenets that there must be most serious question. He takes his stand upon the splendour of national and religious unity, and his books are in effect a ceaseless hymn to its praise. It is for its preservation that his dogmas are so pitilessly erected. Sovereignty is politically one that thought may cease to be manifold. The Church is a monarchy that the single judge of the content of faith may pronounce his judgment without the fatal dissolvent of argument. To the need for unity are alike sacrificed reason and liberty. We know, of course, the explanation of his attitude, nor can we lack compassion for the suffering he so courageously endured. But a theory which finds no justification in experience is not a theory but a dream. To construct a satisfactory theory of the State we must be equipped with a psychology that is realistic. We must deal with men as they are, and desist from the seductive temptation to deal with men as they would be could they but be induced to appreciate the force of our ideas. For we are given variety and difference as the basis of our political system, and it is a world that takes account of them that we must plan. Race, language, nationality, history, all these are barriers that make us understand how fundamental are the natural limits to unity. And within the State itself it is only upon minute issues that agreement or compromise is possible; upon the basis of conviction, where conscience pricks to the utterance, we are, often despite ourselves, compelled to retain our souls. A system that makes entire abstraction of such facts as these is grounded in falsehood and doomed to dissolution.

Its sovereignty can not remain entire so long as there is disagreement, and the means to unity De Maistre barely sought to discuss. He argued that his papalism would prevent disunion and change but he did not see that this was true only to the point where the system carried conviction. That was the meaning of Hume's caustic saying that even despotisms are built upon consent, and it is only in a world of De Maistres that consent to such a despotism could be possible. The freedom of thought from which the Revolution was born may have been anarchy; we can then but note that its necessity makes it sacred. We can not make a fetich of obedience. To every one there comes a point where to bow the knee is worse than death. It was a realisation which Luther had at the Diet of Worms, which came to Ridley and Latimer in the open square of Oxford, to Dollinger, when, in 1871, he parted with a Church that was dearer to him than life. We who care for truth can not promote unity if its cost be the suppression of such spirits. It may be that such an attitude involves the dangerous exaltation of individuality. Yet this is an interstitial world to be absorbed into which is to lose oneself. A State that is so fundamentally one as never to need the wholesome spur of discontent will doubtless avoid a revolution; but that will only be because its corporate life is dead. The one thing that seems to be historically sure in an uncertain world is the fact that progress is born from disagreement and discussion. We have, then, to organise our State in such fashion as best permits its emergence.

We may, of course, urge as De Maistre would doubtless have argued, that the best of worlds is a static world and that the love of progress is an illusion. That may be true, but the world, after all, is not static, and it is with the given conditions that we must cope. And even De Maistre may be said to have admitted progress when he remarked that every attack on Catholicism has only strengthened it. Development is so certainly the fundamental law of our being that it is therein we must, however difficult be the conception, find our truest identity. And that is to say that we must lay down no immutability of political form. Since each of us lives differently our hopes and thoughts must be different. That, logically, is the negation of the extreme claims of Catholicism. It means that the Pope will not possess the sovereignty of the world, since there are people who do not agree with him. It means that he will be compelled to continuous readjustment not less from within than from without. It was not without reason that Sextus IV and Alexander VI were followed by men like Caraffa and Gregory XIII; that to Pius IX the liberalism of his successor would have been anathema it is difficult indeed to deny. But facts such as these prove the futility of a sovereignty that alone would have satisfied De Maistre.

It is not as a political theorist that he will live

but as the trumpeter of a remarkable reaction. He is the real author of that Ultramontanism by which the nineteenth century Papacy sought the restoration of its prestige. It was upon his argument that it was founded and his book was in reality its watchword. For he gave it cause to hope at a time when the humiliation of the Revolution seemed to have stricken it beyond recovery. He provided logical cause for a hatred that before had been but sullenly instinctive. He created the materials for a new and more terrible Canossa. It was the spirit of De Maistre which barred the way to a united Italy. It was the new hope that he inspired which caused the condemnation of Lamennais. He was the real author of the definition of papal infallibility in 1870. And yet in every victory he suffered a defeat. Cavour built a new Italy upon the ruins of the temporal power. Lamennais is the author of a French reformation that is yet to come. The seed sown at the Vatican Council has yet to produce its harvest. For men have grown in the course of time to love freedom and slavery has become a losing cause. Yet it is impossible to withhold our admiration from a man who battled so earnestly for what he deemed right. Even if he loved a cause we deem mistaken, it is to his honour that he loved it greatly. And it may well prove in the end that he served liberty the more truly because he did not shrink from proclaiming his hate.

V

If in the perspective of history it seems a little grimly ironical to connect the name of Bismarck with the spirit of religion, yet is it none the less certain that his attachment to Christianity was deep and sincere.[77] Though as a young man he had been a sceptic,[78] his friendship with the Blankenberg circle seems to have convinced him of the truth of Christian principles, and he experienced all the typical phenomena of religious conversion.[79] Henceforth he did not doubt the power of God in the direction of the world, and he felt to the full the significance of the need for human redemption from sin.[80] And this new realisation of a vivid faith gave him strength in his political life. It was therein that he found all the sources of his activity. 'If I was not a Christian,' he told Ferrières in the stress of the Franco-Prussian War,[81] 'I could not hold my position for an hour. If I could not count on God's help, I could sacrifice nothing for the sake of earthly masters. If I lost my faith, of what avail would be my fatherland?'

[77] On Bismarck's attitude to religion the most important discussion is that of Baumgarten, *Christliche Welt* (1902), pp. 507-512, 587-591, 626-634. See also Busch, *Our Chancellor,* Vol. I, Chap. II—probably an authoritative statement, and Glaser, *Bismarck's Stellung zum Christentum* (1909).

[78] Glaser, *op. cit.*, p. 14.

[79] *Fürst Bismarcks briefe an seine Braut und Gatlin,* pp. 5-6 (January 4, 1847).

[80] See the most interesting letter to Andrae Roman in Bismarck, *Briefe,* 1836-1873, ed. Kohl, p. 420.

[81] Busch, *Tagenblatter* (1899), I, 249.

Whatever happened in his career he attributed to a divine intervention. If he escaped an accident, it was God who warded off the danger;[82] were the French defeated, God had chosen thus to reward the piety of the German nation.[83] He was, in short, essentially an Evangelical whose religion partook of that curious inwardness which, in Geneva, made of Calvin a tyrant that he might become the parent of resistance to tyranny.

And the political consequences of his attitude were no less apparent than they were logical. Because he came increasingly to emphasise the significance of this inward vision he came also certainly to suspect, perhaps even to deprecate, its expression in religious societies and institutions. Man had only to do his duty and for Bismarck, so the indefatigable Busch informs us,[84] the manner in which his belief found expression was unimportant. It was this religious spirit that he termed 'one of the foundations and bulwarks of justice and the State.'[85] For him the State was essentially based upon the principles of Christianity, and to rob it of that character was to destroy that which gave it its crowning distinction. For it was from this intimate infusion of the Christian spirit that it derived the eternal renewal of its underlying truth.[86]

82 Wilmowski, *Meine Erinnerungen an Bismarck,* p. 186.

83 Bismarck's *Briefe an seine Gatlin aus dem Kriege,* 1870-1871, pp. 70, 76.

84 Busch, *Our Chancellor,* Vol. I, p. 106.

85 Busch, *op. cit.,* I, 115.

86 *Ibid.,* p. 117.

What it is here important to realise is that, like most Evangelical Christians, Bismarck lacked any deep sense of an institutional and organised Church. Indeed, he would probably have denied that religion, as internally grounded, has any need of external form, since, so he would have argued, it finds its most adequate expression in political action. He took no interest in dogmatic problems[87]—even the internal dissensions of the German Evangelical Churches aroused in him no echo of interested response;[88] he had but little confidence in the fortification supplied by religious observances.[89] For him there was but one institution—the State—and it was to that he devoted his energies and, on occasion, sacrificed his convictions.[90] Like the great Stahl, he saw in the State a Church, and his theory of its structure was at bottom theocratic.[91] It was for this reason that he had, in 1847, opposed the emancipation of the Jews; for since the State was Christian in character, its identity would be destroyed by the admission of non-Christian elements into its composition.[92] But the Christian State meant to Bismarck neither the vague socialism of F. D. Maurice and of Kingsley, nor the control of that

87 Whitman, *Reminiscences of Bismarck*, p. 296.

88 Busch, *op. cit.*, I, pp. 154-155.

89 *Aus dem Leben der beiden ersten deutschen Kaiser und ihrer Frauen* (1906), p. 309.

90 Busch, *op. cit.*, I, 121-122.

91 On Stahl, see the admirable essay of Jacobowski, *Der Christliche Staat und seine Zukunft* (1894).

92 Reden, I, 22.

State by a Church. It meant simply the governance of its political conduct by the rules of life which Bismarck, in all sincerity, believed that he received from God. He was thus logically bound to hate all organisations which might embarrass the State, for such embarrassment was the clear proof of an anti-religious spirit. His State was simply the Hegelian conception taken to the plane of action, and *raison d'état* justified everything.[93] What he did for the welfare of the State he could not doubt was for the welfare of his Church since it came directly from his intimate union with God. 'I believe,' he said in 1873,[94] 'that I am serving my God by serving my King,' and it was this which explains his love of unity in political activity. He simply could not understand antagonism to his policy where *raison d'état* was its justification; for it seemed to him not dissimilar to direct antagonism against the divine will.[95] He was thus, perhaps, the most completely Erastian statesman who has ever lived, since his identification of politics with religion is final and absolute. In such a view he would be compelled to regard with vehement hostility the exclusion of any sphere of life from the control of the State; and this surely explains why he seems to have regarded with suspicious dislike the Prussian measure of 1850

[93] Her suspicion of 'raison d'état' was the secret of his antagonism to the Empress Augusta. See the very striking remarks in Bismarck, *Gedanken und Erinnerungen,* I, p. 302.

[94] Busch, *op. cit.,* I, 136.

[95] See the *Bismarck Jahrbuch,* 1895, Vol. II, p. 335.

which had guaranteed autonomy to the Church.[96] He, in fact, deified the State, and in the light of such an identification, the toleration of variety became completely impossible.

It was obvious that in such a mind the Roman Catholic Church would awaken no sympathy. It ran directly counter to all for which he stood; and that the more so in an age when, in its warfare against the Revolution, the Papacy had refurbished the weapons of Ultramontanism. For Rome claimed a sovereignty superior to that of kings. She regarded the Church as a complete and perfect society, determined to brook no interference with her internal affairs. That Church, further, like Bismarck's own State, demanded the undeviating allegiance from its subjects. It was, moreover, an infallible Church, nor did it permit question of its judgments. No organisation was so centralised or so patiently efficient. No organisation was less ready to admit the virtue of change. The Church laid down its fundamental laws and, at the risk of forfeiting their salvation, men were compelled to obey. Clearly in such a view a conflict of sovereignty might arise. The attainment of unity was impossible. If Bismarck could issue commands which the Roman Catholic members of the German empire might refuse, at the papal behest, to obey, the dream of twenty years was a vain and empty thing. A struggle between empire and papacy became again essen-

[96] Reden, VI, p. 269.

tial since the absolutism of Bismarck's sovereignty would not admit the existence of spheres of separate influence. If the Roman Catholic Church differentiated between things which were of Caesar, and those which were of God, Bismarck denied the distinction. Since to him the world meant Germany, within its confines he would permit no division of power. That, to his mind, was the fundamental error of granting ecclesiastical independence. He saw no meaning in that term or, if he did, it was a meaning fraught with danger. If the emperor could not be master in his own house, Bismarck would drive out those who doubted his domination. 'If such a sect as the Ultramontanes,' he declared proudly,[97] 'can not be at one with the ambitions of the State, and even endangers those ambitions, clearly the State can not tolerate their existence.' For it would be the blasphemy of politics to destroy the identity of the ethics of the State. It was the negation of that Hegelian sovereignty the empire was proudly to personify.

VI

Such was the psychological basis of the *Kulturkampf*. That is not to say that it was for the enforcement of these political views that Bismarck embarked upon his most disastrous enterprise. Certainly it was not the definition of papal infalli-

[97] See Wilmowski, *Meine Erinnerungen an Bismarck* (1909), p. 189.

bility which moved him to action; for not only did he very decisively refuse Hohenlohe's suggestion of concerted action against the Vatican Council, but Hohenlohe at one time even suspected that he was the secret ally of the Jesuits.[98] The great canonist Schulte found him unwilling to take action against the infallibilist German bishops.[99] It seems, on the contrary, that with him the Roman policy was the natural result of the method he employed in founding the empire. 'My one ideal,' he said in 1879,[100] 'was the unification of Germany under Prussian leadership. To that everything is accessory.' It was when he discovered that, as he conceived the Catholics of Germany stood in the path of his ambition that he set out to ensure their destruction. That he did not desire war with them is surely evident enough from August Reichensperger's express exoneration of him from hostility in motive to the Church.[101] It was but one of the institutions he felt it incumbent upon him to sacrifice in his pursuit of the Austinian chimera.

It was the unity of the German empire he had set himself to achieve. He had fought Austria as a step towards its achievement, because he

[98] Hohenlohe, *Denkwurtigkeiten*, II, 61-66. It should, however, be noted that, according to Frederic III, Bismarck told the Grand Duke of Baden, on the morrow of Sedan, that he intended to fight infallibility. Kaiser Friedrich's *Tagebucher* (1902), p. 107.

[99] Schulte, *Liebenserinnerungen*, I, 378.

[100] Busch, *Tagenbuchblatter*, II, 547. See the *Life* by Pastor, II, 387.

[101] Pastor, *Ruchensperger*, II, 49.

believed that the new Germany must have a Hohenzollern and not a Hapsburg as its leader. When Sedan gave him victory over France it was possible to state the terms of the new problem, but not, as yet, to solve it. The permanence of the new empire he did not feel wholly assured. Poland was an old danger, and it had by no means proved capable of adequate Germanisation; Poland was notoriously Catholic, and Jesuit influence there was known to be strong. The Roman question puzzled him greatly. He dreamed always of a revanche; and it seemed to him that a Franco-Italian alliance might well serve as its basis;[102] and if he forestalled France, as a Latin and Catholic power she might easily turn to the aid of the stricken Papacy. If the Roman Catholic sympathy for Pius IX was so deep as Bismarck believed, could he feel certain of their loyalty?[103] Bavaria was preponderantly Catholic and Bavaria showed no eagerness to affirm its adherence to the new empire; and when Bismarck had asked for Antonelli's assistance in securing the Catholic vote in the Bavarian Parliament, his request had been politely refused.[104] Alsace-Lorraine, again, was predominantly Catholic in character; and its discontent with its new masters the Papacy was

[102] See Govone, *Mémoires* (French translation), p. 521 *seq.* Boullier, *Victor Emanuel et Mazzini,* p. 251 *seq.*

[103] Hahn, *Fürst Bismarck* (1878), I, 720-723.

[104] Goyau, *Bismarck et Le Kulturkampf,* I, 52. I can not too greatly express my debt to this admirable work—easily the best extant on the subject.

unwilling to alleviate.[105] When he remembered that as a Protestant power, as the victor, moreover, in a conflict with the two greatest Catholic nations, Prussia could hardly inspire affection at Rome, it was not difficult for his mind to consider very seriously if the allegiance German Catholics owed to the Roman see, which he considered essentially a political power,[106] was not at the root of his difficulties. If he could destroy that bond, the obstacle to unity might be removed.

Internal political causes seemed to point in the same direction. The National liberals had been enthusiastic for unification; and they were the theoretical antagonists of clericalism. It was their intellectual leader, Bluntschli, who at Worms in 1869 declared that the success of German liberty depended upon the destruction of Roman influence.[107] They had already urged upon Bismarck the dangers of monasticism[108] and the religious control of schools.[109] Journalists were writing of the French defeat as the prelude to a campaign against Ultramontanism in the party papers.[110] Men of their school were speaking of the great victory as a step forward for Luther's cause.[111] If Germanism was synonymous with Protestant-

[105] Goyau, *op. cit.*, I, p. 53.

[106] Poschinger, *Fürst Bismarck*, I, 68.

[107] Bluntschli, *Denkwurtiges*, III, 232.

[108] *Ibid.*, III, 193.

[109] *Ibid.*, III, 253.

[110] Goyau, *op. cit.*, I, 68.

[111] Goyau, I, 71.

ism, as they did not cease to proclaim, Bismarck would have no doubts as to the requisite policy. 'Not France alone,' wrote the Alsatian Schneegans,[112] 'declared war on Germany; it was Rome which desired a deadly combat with Protestantism.' And Treitschke was proclaiming loudly the import of that religion to Prussia.[113]

If Protestantism thus showed signs of militancy, the Catholics were no less watchful. In the Prussian elections of 1870, some sixty of them were returned to the Chamber, and in men like Windthorst, Savigny, Reichensperger, they had politicians of unusual ability. Their very organisation roused serious anger among the National Liberals, and they were soon charged with having as their object a conspiracy against the State.[114] Bismarck must have noted its formation with some disquiet; for the Ultramontane Bishop Ketteler, urging to him that the German victory over France was too largely interpreted as a Protestant victory with unfortunate results in the pacification of Alsace-Lorraine, had suggested that peace might the sooner come if the Catholics outside Prussia were given the same liberty as within it.[115] Did that mean, as it seemed to imply, that the Catholics were German in a different sense from the Protestants? At any rate he allowed his journalist Blum to announce that the Centre

112 Schneegans, *Memoiren,* p. 54.

113 *Historische und politische Aufsaetze,* III, 610.

114 Majunke, *Geschichte des Culturkampfes,* p. 144.

115 Raich, *Briefe von und an Ketteler,* p. 422.

was hostile to the German State—a sign of growing suspicion.[116] In the imperial elections of 1871 Ketteler's letter became the basis of a definite programme and forty-three Catholics of the centre were elected.[117] To the press the Centre was simply an instrument in the hands of Rome, the tool of Ultramontanism, and thus in its conception anti-national.[118] Its members seemed no less suspicious since Windthorst was an enthusiastic papalist, and Ketteler, as a bishop, might be considered as an official representative of Rome; and Bismarck, at the outset of his career as a deputy, made him understand that between Catholic and layman there was already a grave distinction.[119] It seemed not a little suggestive that the first speeches of these two suspects should be in response to an attempt on the part of the National Liberals to make the ground of conflict one between Rome and Germany.[120] It was, to say the least, menacing that Bismarck, on the eve of the debate, should have given Italy the assurance that he was disposed to be friendly towards it.[121] For friendship with Italy could mean only hostility to the Papacy, and, from such an attitude, it was but a logical road to the Falk Laws. The meaning of

116 Goyau, I, 82.

117 *Ibid.*, I, 95.

118 Holtzendorff, *Das Deutsche Reich und die Constituirung der Christlichen Religionsparteien*, p. 16.

119 Goyau, *op. cit.*, I, 101.

120 Goyau, *op. cit.*, I, 105.

121 Rothan, *L'Allegmane et L'Italie*, II, 380.

his attitude was clear. The old principle of a territorial religion of which the empire should be the divinity had come to be for him the solution of these ecclesiastical complications.

On the first of April, 1871, he made quite apparent the drift of his thought. A Polish member of the Reichstag had denied the voluntary affiliation of Poland with the Empire in the name of his country. It was a direct challenge to Bismarck's conception of the State, and he did not fail to take it up. 'Behind you,' he retorted angrily,[122] 'you have naught save errors and illusions. You think that the Polish nation has elected you to represent it, but, in truth, you have been elected to represent the interests of the Catholic Church, and if you defend them when they are under discussion, you will have fulfilled your electoral function.' It was a notable identification. It could mean only that he had declared war on the Roman Church and the Grand Duke of Weimar regarded it as his first overt attack on Ultramontanism.[123] Windthorst saw clearly the drift of his mind when he declared that it was an attempt to enslave the Church. And it is of interest to note that Treitschke denounced the Roman claim of a free Church within the State as equivalent to a demand for the right to rebellion.[124] It is often difficult to distinguish between

122 Bismarck, *Reden*, V, 16.
123 Busch, *Tagenbuchblatter*, II, 222.
124 Goyau, *op. cit.*, I, 113.

the thought of Treitschke and the practice of his master.

The issue was defined; it was not yet joined. If the Centre was anti-imperial diplomatic negotiations with Rome might bring its members to their senses; and journalistic pressure might make plain to the Pope the danger of embroiling himself with the public opinion of Germany. Tauffkirchen was accordingly despatched to Rome to explain to the Papacy the help given to its enemies by the lamentable aggressions of the Centre;[125] while Busch was commissioned to write articles to the same effect.[126] Antonelli disavowed any attempt at criticism of the Centre,[127] and thus increased the anger of Bismarck who had already found new causes of suspicion in its support of the democrats[128]—for him outside the State—and their opposition to the grant to the successful generals of the recent war.[129] Bismarck appealed in vain to the papal approval of the Versailles ceremony.[130] He began to accuse the Centre of Jesuitism, and to remind the Church that for three hundred years it had failed to conquer the Teutonic genius.[131] But he could obtain nothing satisfactory. Rome pursued its ancient policy of patience; for Ket-

125 Bismarck, *Politische Briefe*, I, 265 ff.
126 Busch, *Tagenbuchblatter*, II, 226.
127 Raich, *op. cit.*, p. 443.
128 Hohenlohe, *Denkwurtigkeiten*, II, 64.
129 *Pastor Reichensperger*, II, p. 30.
130 Bismarck, *Reden*, V, 204.
131 *Reden*, V, 206.

teler had put it on its guard against his accusations.[132] He sent the Prussian minister to dine at the Quirinal.[133] Antonelli's reply was to inform him that 'Rome could not break with the party' he so bitterly hated.[134]

'The members of the Centre,' he said a little later,[135] 'are trying to make us Italians,' and it was of this he had become convinced by his negotiations with Rome. The papal refusal seemed to him evidence that he was dealing with a State within a State, and that reprisals were essential if the sovereignty of the empire was to be maintained. If he sought for means, they were near at hand in an alliance with the National Liberals who as the bitter antagonists of the Papacy were prepared with a policy that might accomplish its destruction. It was the old antagonism of priestcraft and kingcraft.[136] If the Centre treated his government as an enemy it was clearly necessary to treat its master as he had treated Austria and beat him into submission. Rome, as he now saw, was associated everywhere with his enemies. She endeavoured to rule in France, in Bavaria, in Poland; at the Vatican Council, as Dollinger's excommunication seemed to show, she had laid claim once more to the lordship of the world. He would make plain the sovereignty of the State.

[132] Pfulf, *Ketteler,* III, 153.

[133] Favre, *Rome et la République Française,* p. 143-144.

[134] Bismarck, *Politische Briefe,* I, 268.

[135] See Poschinger, *Bismarck und die Parliamentarier,* II, 160.

[136] *Politische Reden,* XII, 348.

VII

It was the ancient contest of Guelf and Ghibelline prolonged into a modern time. What was changed was not so much the manner of the struggle as the roots from which it sprung. As in the medieval time it had been the function of the State to be the police department of the Church, so to Bismarck the Church in the modern age seemed to have a similar part to play.[137] But there was the same attitude of suspicion between the two powers. 'This is a question of Church and State,' said Bismarck at Gastein to Monsignor Vallet,[138] 'as a statesman I hate the Church.' He hated it because it threatened the unity of his State. He conceived of allegiance as one, and it was part of the danger inherent in any ecclesiastical organisation that it undermined that oneness. While, verbally, he admitted the Church's right to absolute freedom in her own domain, he still held that her sphere must be defined by the State and, as the Falk Laws bear witness, controlled by it.[139] The *Kulturkampf* seemed to him 'the primeval fight for supremacy between royalty and priesthood. . . . What we aim at is the protection of the State, the establish-

[137] On the nature of the relation between medieval Church and State the reader can consult Dr. Figgis' brilliant paper, printed as an appendix to his *Churches in the Modern State*.

[138] See the interesting little brochure of Mgr. Vallet, *Le prince de Bismarck à Gastein* (1906), p. 16.

[139] Cf. Busch, *Our Chancellor*, Vol. I, p. 135.

ment of a distinct boundary-line between priestly dominion and Royal rule, defined in such sort that the State may be enabled to abide by it. For, in the kingdom of this world, the State is entitled to power and precedence."[140] But that was virtually to deny the doctrine of a separate sphere for Church and State and to assert the superiority of the latter. He can hardly have hoped for peace when he promulgated such a doctrine against Rome. A remark of Busch's on this attitude perhaps throws light on the Chancellor's mind. 'For Protestant States to achieve peaceful relations with the Church of Rome,' writes that dutiful commentator,[141] 'is—under the most favourable circumstances—a problem like that of squaring the circle, the solution of which one may go very near, but never quite attain.' Such an attitude, added to his fear that the Vatican contemplated a 'gesta Dei per Francos'[142] was sufficient in itself to give him a theory of political action against a foreign and interfering prelate. Regarding the Pope as he did, simply as the head of the Centre party,[143] it is little wonder that difficulties should have arisen. It was not, of course, from theory that he fought. 'It is unworthy of a great State,' he had said in 1850,[144] 'to fight for any question that does not concern its own interests;' and he

140 Bismarck, *Reden,* V, 382.

141 Busch, *op. cit.,* I, 138.

142 *Ibid.,* p. 139.

143 *Ibid.,* p. 147.

144 *Ibid.,* p. 183.

fought Rome as holding in its hand the key to his French and Polish difficulties. He believed, as the National Liberal Bennigsen put it,[145] that the Ultramontanes desired 'not conciliation but domination' and he would strive against that to the end. If the Papacy chose to ally itself with a party which, in attacking him, threatened the unity of the empire, he must vindicate the sovereignty so challenged.[146] It might be, as Krementz stingingly told him, that he was trying to make Prussia play the part of Julian the Apostate;[147] but at any rate Julian had not hesitated to assert the authority of the empire. That was why, as he laboriously explained,[148] he had suppressed the Catholic division in the Ministry of Public Worship, 'for it represented not the rights of the State but rather the rights of the Catholic Church.' They were rather papalists than Germans; and they must go if the integrity of the empire was to be maintained.[149] They destroyed the peculiarly Germanic character he had endeavoured to develop. They were Poles, and they repudiated the German nationality.[150] The Catholic division facilitated the teaching of Polish in Polish schools—a thoroughly anti-German work. And when he remembered that the

145 Oncken, *Bennigsen*, II, 218.

146 See his retrospect of April 21, 1887, in *Reden*, XII, 369 *seq.*

147 Siegfried, *Actenstucke bet. reffend den preussischen Kulturkampf*, p. 46.

148 Bismarck, *Gedanken*, II, 128.

149 *Reden*, VI, 270.

150 See his conversation about Kraezig with Auguste Reichensperger, reported in Poschinger, *Bismarck und die Parliamentarier*, II, 184.

Poles were born rebels, it was not difficult to see a widespread conspiracy.[151] His press continually compared the Ultramontanes to the Poles and the French—the enemies of German nationality.[152] 'Your bishops,' he told Auguste Reichensperger,[153] 'are not safe; Ketteler corresponds with that Pole Kosmian. They only care about ecclesiastical interests. I respect every manner of faith . . . but I can not allow a powerful enemy threatening to Germany to organise itself.' He believed he had proofs of the Polish taint in the Jesuits;[154] later he urged that they were guilty of the almost equal sin of plotting to lead the Social democrats.[155] Hohenlohe explained the true character of the conflict. 'We begin the old medieval conflict again,' he said,[156] 'I am a Ghibelline and I shall always be of that party.' And to consolidate the empire Bismarck, too, would take up the ancient text.

It is thus that we have to interpret the nature of the anti-clerical legislation.[157] The Falk Laws are an attempt to insist on the universal paramountcy of German influences. The expulsion of the Jesuits removed an order which he believed to be concerned with the promotion of Polish

151 Cf. Majunke, *Geschicte des Culturkampfes*, p. 198.

152 Goyau, *op. cit.*, II, 96.

153 Pastor, *Reichensperger*, II, 63.

154 Hohenlohe, *Denkwurtigkeiten*, II, 78.

155 *Reden*, XI, 250-251.

156 Goyau, *op. cit.*, I, 317.

157 M. Goyau has conveniently reprinted the text of the laws in the fourth volume of his excellent work.

interests.[158] The refusal of bishoprics to any save a German who has followed a course of study approved by the government[159] has a clear purport not merely of purging the Catholic episcopate of men not likely to be in sympathy with German ideals, but also of placing their education under a strict governmental supervision. The third clause in the sixteenth article of this law is particularly noteworthy. 'When there exists,' it states,[160] 'against a candidate facts which give grounds for the opinion either that he will not observe the laws of the State and the arrangements made by the authorities within the legal limits of their powers, or that he will disturb the public peace,' his confirmation may be refused. 'Raison d'état,' in fact, will serve as a sufficient excuse for denying an otherwise fit appointment; in this way Germany could rid itself bit by bit of the Ultramontanes. It is important, moreover, to bear in mind both the civil penalties attached to the laws and the establishment of a State Court of Appeal. This was, in implication, the assertion of the superiority of State to Church. The twenty-fourth article[161] went even further and gave the State the right of interference with ecclesiastical functions where it deemed them improperly performed. Against the law of thirteenth of May, 1873, which limited ecclesiastical punishments to those of a

158 This is the Imperial Law of July 4, 1872. Goyau, IV, 225.

159 This is the law of May 11, 1873. Goyau, IV, 227.

160 Goyau, IV, 231.

161 *Ibid.*, IV, 238.

purely spiritual kind,[162] it is difficult to take serious objection; though it is worth remarking that the Church is forbidden to inflict or to threaten pecuniary penalties. The law of the twentieth of May, 1874,[163] virtually handed over the control of vacant bishoprics to the State, thus rendering it difficult to enforce an objectionable appointment. All religious orders, save those of a semi-medical character, were forbidden on Prussian soil.[164] Catholic Churches on Prussian soil were handed over to the old Catholics in such parishes as those in which the majority consisted of their sympathisers, for certain hours of the day;[165] though Bismarck must have known that to the Catholics this was simply the desecration of a sacred edifice. The State charged itself with the surveillance of the fiscal administration of the Church, forbidding it to build or collect funds without permission; a law which of course placed in lay hands half the possibility of church extension.[166] To the lay control of schools, established with a similar object, it is difficult to find grounds of exception. But it is clear that no more thorough-going Erastianism than this has ever been attempted. Every corner of Church policy was swept by the grim hand of the State. While it is possible to admire the relentless thoroughness with which the

162 *Ibid.*, IV, 241.

163 *Ibid.*, IV, 246.

164 Prussian Law of May 31, 1875. Goyau, IV, 256.

165 Law of July 4, 1875. Goyau, IV, 272.

166 Prussian Law of June 7, 1876. Goyau, IV, 274.

legislation is conceived, it is also difficult to deny that such legislation would have annihilated any conception of a Church worthy of the name. It would have turned it into no more than an organ for the propagation of the opinions of an imperious chancellor upon German unity. It would have prevented the Roman Catholic Church from remaining true no less to the letter than to the spirit of its endeavour. It would have made it admit to virtual membership excommunicated members of its own communion. Clearly to antagonism such as this only an unfaltering hostility was possible.

The history of the *Kulturkampf* showed how greatly Bismarck had mistaken the strength of his opponents. He fined, he imprisoned, he inflicted a virtual exile; but the Church replied only with contempt. In the Reichstag itself he found in men like Windthorst and Reichensperger foemen in every way worthy of his own powers. Despite his utmost efforts and unconcealed chagrin the numbers of the Centre grew, and those of the National Liberals diminished until the Catholics were in virtual control of the House. The banished prelates continued, in despite of his laws, to exercise their functions from Rome and Holland, and they found a willing obedience. All his efforts to obtain some compromise with the Centre or with the Vatican met with the utmost diplomatic politeness but also with the completest refusal. Little by little he was compelled to turn from alliance with the National Liberals to his old friendship with the Conservatives—a change which involved also his humiliation. 'If,' he had said in 1874,[167] 'I was stranded on an island where there were only two men, a Catholic and a Scandinavian, I believe I should make friends with the latter.' But in 1879 the same Bismarck was nominating a member of the 'anti-German' Centre, Frankenstein, to the vice-presidency of the Reichstag;[168] on the twenty-ninth of June, 1879, he was dismissing Falk;[169] in 1883 he sent the Crown Prince Frederic to the Vatican;[170] in 1884 he asked for papal mediation in his difficulties with Spain;[171] finally, in 1886 and 1887, came the abrogation of the Falk Laws. It was the 'little Canossa' he had tried vainly to conceal amid his smiles.[172]

VIII

So he learned the meaning of a sovereignty within Germany which yet did not belong to the German State. 'You will never be German citizens,' said the historian Baumgarten to the Catholics in words which might have been Bis-

167 Poschinger, *Stud. bei Bismarck* (1910), p. 159.

168 Goyau, III, 77.

169 On Falk's dismissal and his own interpretation of it, see Fischer, *Falk*, p. 17.

170 Philippson, *Friedrich*, III, p. 367.

171 Goyau, *op. cit.*, IV, 61 f.

172 *Lefebre de Behaine, Léon XIII et Bismarck*, p. 86. The whole of this admirable book, by the French ambassador at Rome during the *Kulturkampf*, must be consulted for Bismarck's tortuous negotiations.

marck's;[173] and if that meant that they were to be faithless to their religion its truth was undeniable. But it was a different Bismarck who, in 1881, acclaimed the German Catholics as his compatriots, and the institutions of their Church, the Papacy included, as part of the great confederation it had been his task to create.[174] It was a different Bismarck from him who, in 1875, had urged that if France submitted to the new Ultramontanism the peace of Europe must be broken;[175] and in the same year had urged the vital necessity of defending the State against an aggressive Catholic Church.[176] In the interval he had learned a mighty lesson.

He had learned that the world, even the Germanic world, is not one and indivisible. He had defined the State to himself as a power which, to maintain itself, must prove its sovereignty over every department of human life. He would have agreed with Calhoun that the division of sovereignty was its destruction. So, in one aspect, he would contend that the *Kulturkampf* was no more than the vindication for the State of rights that were in reality its own. 'We can not,' he said,[177] 'concede to the Church the permanent right of exercising part of the powers of the State; and while the Church is in possession of such a pre-

173 See his amazing *Luther Redivivus* (1878), pp. 254-255.

174 *Reden,* IX, 162.

175 Goyau, II, 109.

176 *Ibid.,* II, 247.

177 Busch, *Tagenbuchblatter,* II, 322.

rogative we must, for the sake of peace, restrain its activities.' But the Falk Laws show clearly that his notion of restraint involved the extension of the powers of the State into a field where no Catholic could admit its exercise and where conflict was bound to result. Doubtless so to derogate from the unity he envisaged as desirable was to lessen the completeness of the sovereignty he pursued; but it was to limit it in the direction of its natural boundaries. It was useless for him to contend that no difficulties would ever have arisen if the Centre had only helped him to complete the unity of the empire.[178] He defined unity in such a manner as to make possible only their opposition. He did not see, as Treitschke so clearly understood, that the sovereignty of a State is simply the power that State has at its disposal;[179] though where the Prussian historian would have found that power in the army, we tend, in the modern State, to find it in the degree of consent a measure can command. Bismarck learned that sovereignty must thus be essentially an illusory concept since its exercise at any moment belongs to the realm not of the certain but of the probable. But his defeat would have taught him also the error in Treitschke's teaching that the State is 'born and dies with the exercise of its sovereignty';[180] for assuredly the German State did not disappear because it was

178 Bismarck, *Gedanken*, II, 150.
179 See Treitschke's *Zehn Jahre Deutscher Kampfe*, II, 238-239.
180 *Op. cit.*

worsted in the *Kulturkampf*. It was simply demonstrated that men belong not to one all-inclusive group, the State, but to a variety of groups, and that, in the last resort, they will follow the demands of their conscience. It was useless for Bismarck to demand its subjugation to the needs of the State, to urge that in making war on the State the Church was usurping one of the State's prerogatives. Such argument was born from the failure to understand that the State is an institution like any other and that rights must find their justification in the support they can command. There may be a divorce between politics and morals, but, in all final questions, we begin to perceive the clear sign of their essential identity. It was Bismarck's difficulty that he failed to understand their union, and was thus unable to resolve his problem into its constituent parts.

IX

Where De Maistre speaks of the Church, Bismarck speaks of the State; where De Maistre discusses the Papacy, Bismarck is discussing the German empire. Otherwise, at bottom, the thought is essentially the same. Nor was their problem different. De Maistre had to confront a world which the Revolution had smashed into an atomic chaos and it was in the world-sovereignty of Rome that he found its new centre of unity. Bismarck found a bewildering congeries of unimportant and fragmentary communities from which a great empire had to be builded and it was in the single hegemony of Prussia that he found his instrument. What De Maistre feared was intellectual opposition; the chief bane of Bismarck was political antagonism. The fundamental faith of each was beyond the sphere of reason—with De Maistre it was the dogmas of Catholicism, with Bismarck the revelations of an evangelical Christianity. Each saw in a world of individualisation the guarantee of disruption and evolved a theory to secure its suppression. Each loved passionately the ideal of unity since that seemed to them both the surest guarantee of survival. Each saw truth as one and therefore doubted the rightness of a sovereignty that was either fallible or divisible; and each in the end came to the realisation that his theories were inconsistent with the facts of life. Each failed to understand that tremendous truth inculcated by Lamennais when he urged that the real unity of doctrine—whether political or religious—can come only from possession of freedom. It is useless to paint truth as one unless preparation is made to carry on the perpetual warfare that will result from disagreement with its nature. That was the fundamental defect in the minds of both. They did not see that however organic be the community in which we live, man is a solitary no less than a social being, and his ideal world is at bottom interstitial. However much he acts in common, he wishes also to act alone; however much he thinks as a member of the herd, he will wish also to think as a lonely wanderer. It is, perhaps, an antinomy; but it is one which no theory of the State dare afford to neglect. For an attitude which makes the boundaries of authority commensurate with the bounds of mind is at war with the instincts most pregnant with human good.

APPENDIX A

A NOTE ON SOVEREIGNTY AND FEDERALISM

HAD he commented with any fullness upon it, the Constitution of the United States would doubtless have provoked the vehement derision of John Austin, for nowhere, either in theory or in practice, has it chosen to erect an instrument of sovereign power. In England, as De Lolme told us a century ago, nature alone has set limits to the omnicompetence of the king in Parliament, and what he so forcibly taught Professor Dicey has reiterated in the most famous of all his books. So that, in some sort, there would seem a theoretical deficiency in American government. We do not know who rules. Certainly the president is not absolute. Neither to Congress nor to the Supreme Court is unlimited power decreed. And, as if to make confusion worse confounded, there cut athwart this dubiousness certain sovereign rights possessed by the States alone.

Professor Dicey would shrug his shoulders and tell us that it is the natural consequence of federalism. It is, he writes, 'the method by which federalism attempts to reconcile the apparently inconsistent claims of national sovereignty and

State sovereignty.' The sarcasm is but thinly veiled. The fathers reconciled these opposites by abolishing altogether any notion of Austinian sovereignty. Federal government, we are therefore told, is notoriously weak government, since in it there is no final arbiter. The legislature of the United States, or of Canada, for the matter of that, is degraded to the level of an English railway company. It is a non-sovereign law-making body. It derives its powers, like the Great Eastern Railway Company, from a written document, which simultaneously limits them. Federalism, Professor Dicey notes further, tends to produce Conservatism. For the Constitution is written and rigid. It acquires a kind of sacrosanct character in the eyes of the people. Change of any kind becomes difficult because it almost seems irreligious. It is condemned before it is attempted. The unitary method of government impresses Professor Dicey as being as far more admirable in conception as it is more efficacious in results.

Any criticism of this well-established doctrine has at least two obvious lines of attack. We might, in the first place, urge that to talk of parliamentary omnicompetence in such downright fashion is to beg the whole question. Theoretically existent, practically Parliamentary sovereignty is, in the technical sense, an absurdity. The British Parliament may be the legal superior of the colonial legislatures; but everyone is well aware that it dare not in fact override them on any fundamental question. When the South African Parliament forbade the admission of Indians to the Transvaal, Great Britain felt that a grave injustice had been inflicted on a meritorious section of its subjects; but Great Britain did not dare, despite the theoretical sovereignty of its legislature, to repair the injustice so inflicted. When Lord Grey tried, in 1849-1850, to turn the Cape of Good Hope into a penal colony, he was compelled, despite the delegation to him of sovereign power, to desist. Lord Brougham caused the Judicial Committee of the Privy Council to be created the supreme tribunal in ecclesiastical cases; but it is notorious that churchmen have refused to accept its decisions as binding in spiritual matters. Sir James Graham, in 1843, took the legally admirable ground that if the courts upheld the right of lay entry into patronage in the Scottish Church he must uphold their decision in Parliament; but that legal rectitude did not prevent Dr. Chalmers and his colleagues disrupting the Church to emphasise their dissent. In a more recent time, when the Welsh miners struck in complete defiance of the provisions of the Munitions Act, it was found simply impossible to enforce its penalties. The American Revolution was, on the English side, an experiment in applied Austinianism. It is surely obvious that a sovereignty so abstract is practically without utility.

The second method of approach is more constructive. It is the result of the view that sovereignty, rightly regarded, ought not to be defined as omnicompetence at all. Sovereignty is, in its exercise, an act of will, whether to do or to refrain from doing. It is an exercise of will behind which there is such power as to make the expectation of obedience reasonable. Now it does not seem valuable to urge that a certain group, the State, can theoretically secure obedience to all its acts, because we know that practically to be absurd. This granted, it is clear that the sovereignty of the State does not in reality differ from the power exercised by a Church or a trade union. The obedience the Church or trade union will secure depends simply on what measure of resistance the command inspires. So that, on this view, when Louis XIV revoked the Edict of Nantes, when a Church issues a new doctrinal order, when a trade union proclaims a strike, all are exercising a power that differs only in degree, not in kind, from that of the State. Analysed into its elements sovereignty is, after all, not such a very formidable thing. It is the obvious accompaniment of personality, and the main characteristic of personality is the power to will. Sometimes wills, whether individual or corporate, conflict, and only submission or trial of strength can decide which is superior. The force of a command from the State is not, therefore, bound to triumph, and no theory is of value which would make it so. When Germany orders its subjects to refrain from the discussion of peace terms it may enforce its rule when only Rosa Luxemburg or Liebknecht is concerned; it could not do so were the Socialists as a whole to rebel.

Aside from the historical accident which has given the constituent States of the American federation a certain sovereignty, at any rate in well-defined spheres, it may well be argued that Hamilton and his coadjutors would have had theoretical justification even if they had not had history to guide them in their determination of the division of constitutional powers. That division is more consonant with political facts than the unitary theory so favoured by the majority of European observers. Certain local groups have a life of their own that is not merely delegated to them by the State. They are capable of directing their own concerns. Their interest in themselves is revivified and inspired by the responsibility for such direction. When New York wants a new Constitution it can apply itself to that manufacture. When Australia needs one, or Canada, they must be made—the phrase is sinister—in Whitehall. The history of Lord Grey's experiments in the direction of colonial self-government makes clear the utter inadequacy of the latter method. If Wisconsin wants an income tax it can obtain one by winning the assent of its citizens. If Manchester wants a ship canal it must persuade Parliament that its needs are more important than the jealousies of Liverpool. There is no more tragic history than that which comes under the rubric 'the decline and fall of the parish.'

Lawyers, for the most part, have tended to believe that the status of a person is something it is in the power of the State alone to confer, and in this view Austin, doubtless, would have most fully concurred. But surely it is abundantly clear that the personality of associations is primary, that it springs from the fact of their existence, and is not conceded to them by the State. This concession theory has, it is true, the authority of great men like Savigny behind it. It was urged, in effect by that subtle lawyer Pope Innocent IV when he argued that the corporate person is sheer fiction. That claim, however, is becoming increasingly impossible of acceptance. Things, for example, like the Disruption in the Church of Scotland, or the failure of the Privy Council as the supreme ecclesiastical tribunal, show that in truth the churches live lives of their own, independent and self-contained, and that they will not tolerate external interference. The State, for good and special reasons, withheld corporateness from trade unions; but the Taff Vale decision showed how real was its existence in despite of statute. The failure of the Sherman Act may be traced to a similar cause. You can not make men compete by Act of Congress. They have wills of their own that the statute does not form. Everywhere we have diversity, plurality. It seems indeed time to admit its existence.

It is really difficult to understand what special merit attaches to unity. Germany points proudly to the complete absence of differences among her citizens. Contempt is openly expressed for a country like the United States where diversity of opinion is most clearly apparent. In Germany, it is moral error to doubt the rightness of her cause. It is certainly dangerous to resist the sovereign mandate to sacrifice all to her need. Yet there is clearly grave danger in her attitude. 'The man,' Lord Acton wrote, 'who prefers his country before every other shows the same spirit as the man who surrenders every right to the State. They both deny that right is superior to authority.'

In fact, there is real moral insufficiency in any theory of the State which impresses upon its members the need for any consistent uniformity of outlook. The fact that no one in Germany doubts her rightness in sinking, for example, the Lusitania, does not morally, or even politically, justify her position in that regard. It is simply evidence that in Germany to-day necessity has exacted the sacrifice of right to authority. Faith there is more urgent than thought. We prefer a country where the sovereignty is distributed, where the richness of the corporate lives is insurance against such sterility of outlook. The Austinian theory of sovereignty, ungenial enough even in its abstract presentation, would as a fact breed simple servility were it capable of practical application. There can be no servility in a State that divides its effective governance. The necessity of balancing interests, the need for combining opinions, results in a wealth of political thought such as no State where the real authority is single can attain. The price of liberty is exactly divergence of opinion on fundamental questions. The well-ordered and neatly arranged products of recent German thought on politics testify to the existence of its opposite. No man, and even more, no State, can ever be so right as not to need doubts of his rightness.

It is probable that even the most extreme supporters of parliamentary authority would sympathise with this view. Certainly Professor Dicey adopted it when he gave his adhesion to the Ulster cause. For he thereby announced his willingness to resist the authority he had declared omnipotent, and he would surely not resist unless he had some hope of success. If the truth of this attitude be admitted, if the State be viewed, in brief, as something more than a delegator of powers, we begin to approach an organisation that in essence is not distinct from a federation even if in name it be different. We begin to see the State as akin to that medieval empire which was above all a community of communities. The sovereign appears as a thing consistently to revere rather than as a thing undeviatingly to obey. It expresses a unity of feeling, not a unity of opinion—the feeling that, as Aristotle pointed out long ago, the object of the State is the good life; while it implies a diversity of opinion as to the means by which that good life may be attained. Federal government may be weak government, but it is weak only as other governments are weak—that is, in the degree to which it commits acts of trespass. Parliamentary government has only remained strong, has only retained the appearance of omnicompetence, by reason of the delicate skill with which its footsteps have been directed.

A last word may be hazarded. One who comes to America from Europe may well crave leave to doubt whether, fundamentally, there is truth in the judgment that federalism is conservative. The forms, it is true, may be preserved, may even seem to be revered as sacred things, but the spirit glows with a life that is ever new and abundant. The one thing that must strike the modern observer of any federal Constitution is the growing impatience with its rigid encasement, the ever insistent demand that the form shall be made equally elastic with the spirit. And in the variety of its group life, the wide distribution of its sovereign powers, he may not unjustly see the surest guarantee of its perennial youth.

APPENDIX B

SOVEREIGNTY AND CENTRALISATION

IT can never be too thoroughly emphasised that the founders of the American Constitution did not intend to create a complete system of government. They took the States for granted, and it was upon their complex foundation that they attempted to build. What they attempted was essentially its supplement, the binding together of certain strands which the withdrawal of British sovereignty had grievously untied. Yet, as the event was to show, it was no easy matter to achieve a working efficiency for the new instrument of sovereign power. If we can say to-day that the interests of the American nation are supreme, and that the old States' rights theory of sovereignty is largely obsolete, we have to remember that a Civil War was needed to give it its death-blow. For the Constitution was doubtfully imposed and regretfully accepted. Men found it difficult to understand that two jurisdictions largely co-ordinate can work towards a similar end. They imagined that co-ordination meant antithesis, and drew a distinction between State and nation. Antagonism not unnaturally resulted; for where men believe there is enmity, its appearance may with certainty be predicted. In the result we may utter our *requiescat* over the grave of localism.

Nationalism, then, is triumphant. The natural question any statute must now raise is not whether Missouri or Alabama will benefit from its enactment, but whether the United States will so benefit. But there is another aspect of this unified sovereignty about which certain doubts may be expressed. It stands for centralisation; that is to say, it changes the whole character of the federal idea. It may be, indeed, that this centralisation is essential to the future of the United States. It may be that until the power of the latter undergoes a further concentration, it can never adequately be exercised. The interests of the whole may so uniquely transcend the interests of the parts as to give their separate claims little or no validity. Yet even an observer handicapped, as I am, by an alien tradition, can not help but realise that there is in America a certain fundamental disunity of circumstance. When I am in Kansas, I know that I am not in New York. The problems, even the thoughts and the desires, are different and affect people differently. Is it wise to make Washington a kind of Hegelian harmonisation of these differences and say that Congress can transcend them in a federal statute? In the result, as every statesman must know, what are called the 'interests of the Republic' in New York will probably be called 'discrimination against the Middle West' in Kansas. And that is intelligible, even if it is rarely praiseworthy. For while action in Kansas would have attempted to cope with the difficulties of the Middle West, action at Washington aims—since a balance of interests must be struck—at their genial evasion. Surely this suggests the existence of a problem which has aroused less attention than it deserves.

The growth of national government, with the consequent strengthening of its sovereign character, leads, as I have urged, to its increasing centralisation. This is true not of America alone. The whole history of England, Maitland once remarked, could be brought under the rubric of the decline and fall of the sheriff. One of the resultant and fundamental problems Great Britain will have to face when its reconstruction comes is precisely this. Its local life will have to be made real. It will undergo revivification. Its units of local government will have to be made real. They will have to receive a sovereignty that is something more than an anaemic reflex of the central power. An interest in local problems will have to be aroused not less keen and vivid than the interest in national problems. Nor is this less true of France. Her local group-life has been sacrificed to the absorptiveness of Paris; with the result that since the fall of Napoleon, France has been striving to regain the local creativeness now stricken with impotence. The vigorous self-government of the modern German city derives from the at any rate partial admission by higher authority that its powers, to be responsible, must be complete. It was there remembered, as in England and France it has been forgotten, that the tissue of the civic parts changes more frequently than the tissue of the national whole. Since in the latter countries an adequate nutrition of final responsibility was not provided, the result has been in a real sense death from starvation.

I know well enough that nothing like this stage has been reached in the United States. Yet the difficulty is ominously near. No kind of working compromise has been reached between the States on the one hand, and the federal government on the other. Each has gone its own way, often almost wilfully duplicating the work of the other. The State, it is assumed, must do what the federal government has not done; the federal government merely acts as the bracket to a series of algebraic symbols. The possibility of a co-operation is not considered. The lines of demarcation are never made plain. It is never adequately realised that both are overcrowded with business, that they can not, with all the good will in the world, waste an ounce of energy in this complex age. Congress, of a certainty, can not give proper attention to local problems. It is, moreover, all the more difficult to obtain a rapprochement with a Constitution uniquely inaccessible to amendment. It may be admitted frankly that the centralisation of the modern federal government has won some tremendous victories. An Englishman needs no convincing that the victory won in 1865 for union, and, implicitly, for centralisation, was a victory for the beneficent forces of the civilised world. He may well stand amazed at the quality no less than the volume of work performed by such centralising agencies as the Interstate Commerce Commission. He has no doubts as to the past. It is about the future that he must feel uncertain.

For there are many able thinkers in the United States who are convinced that where national thought is, generally speaking, superior in quality to State thought, where it is temporally in advance, national, that is to say centralised action should follow. The sovereign, in fact, should show his powers of self-assertion. Where he is in possession of a progressive idea which fails to obtain sanction in a backward state, then he should use his reserve power in compensation for its reactionary character. It is, of course, easy to sneer at people who cling to the ideas of the mid-Victorian age. It is easier still to remember that there is outside the State government a federal power which pays no heed to regional opinion. State government and State opinion must, so the reformer urges, be overridden if progress is to be made.

A typical instance is that of prohibition. Reformers in Maine do not see why they should suffer for the stupid inability of New York to control its liquor traffic. Congress, they say, should legislate for the nation, and prevent either the enactment of anomalies, or the retention of so pathetic an ancestralism as a taste for beer. Now I waive the whole question of whether Maine does in fact benefit from its more acute perception; reputable authority assures me that the contrary is the case. But the real question to which I want an adequate reply—more convincing than rhetorical statements of the case for prohibition—is whether America will not gain more from the slow self-struggle of New York to intelligence, than from the irritating imposition from without of a belief to which it has not been converted. I can not avoid the emphatic opinion that in this, as in other matters, nature is not saltatory. Politically we probably gain more from the slow, and often painful erosion of prejudice by education, than when we attempt its elimination by more drastic methods. It is, of course, annoying for those of us who consider we have found the truth; but if we are to have democratic government we must bear with the inconveniences of democracy.

The traditional separation of powers in American government has been assailed as often as it has been explained. Yet I believe it is in fact a natural division. Of course to lawyers like Professor Dicey, federalism of any kind appears but a step on the road to centralised government; it is, in his own phrase, the union which precedes unification. I am a frank medievalist in this regard. It seems to me admirable that a country which, in certain aspects, is one, should yet adapt its governance to suit the severalty which is no less characteristic of other aspects. In a democracy, the surest guaranty of civic responsibility seems to lie in the gift of genuine functions of government no less to the parts than to the whole. No doubt, on occasion, the dissipation of sovereignty will result in conflict. But even without it there is conflict of a kind far more wasteful, since it in nowise depends upon principle. And anyone who reads the reports of the United States Supreme Court for the last twenty-five years will realise that the national powers have not been extended without opposition and that Washington has not always been victorious. What seems to me dangerous is that the expansion no less than the contraction of the central power should always have been planless and unthinking. It has depended always—witness the recent embarkation upon the governmental regulation of railway wages—upon the haphazard accidents of momentary events, instead of upon a scheme of considered and inherent policy. It has grown without thought of local needs or of local personality. Had the sovereign federation given respectful recognition to those other sovereigns, no less real, which we call the States, there would have resulted no less an impulse to creation than an economy of effort.

It is the fashion to regard federalism as the merest *pis aller* and to hope piously for the time when a more adequate centralisation will render it unnecessary. This seems to me to neglect certain obvious lessons to be drawn from other experience. In education, for example, we have learned that the more pupils per teacher, the less efficient, on the whole, is the instruction. Commercially, Mr. Brandeis has shown that certain business units may become so large as to be physically incapable of successful administration. I would urge that a similar law of diminishing returns applies also to the sphere of government. It becomes more and more obvious that we must recognise certain natural units of political administration, but also see to it that we do not duplicate that power. It is admitted freely that the result will probably derogate from the unique sovereignty of the whole. Yet that is surely but a theoretical derogation from which no practical consequences ensue; and I am pragmatist enough to contend that it is therefore no derogation at all.

I can imagine no more fruitful political thinking than that which should attempt to read for our own day the due lesson of the failure of certain emperors who, because they took the whole world for their field of vision, gave Voltaire the material for the most admirable of his gibes. We seem in genuine danger of going back to an ancient and false worship of unity, to a trust in an undivided sovereignty as the panacea for our ills. Surely the vitality of political life depends rather on the conference of final responsibility where there is the willingness to assume it and the capacity to assume it wisely. Only thus can we prevent

Washington from degenerating into Dublin Castle. In the end, maybe, the ways of attainment will be as difficult as the objects at which they aim; but the good of the universe is manifold and not single. We are as travellers breasting a hill, and we reach its summit by a thousand devious paths.[1]

[1] Cf. Mr. Croly's remarks in the *New Republic,* Vol. IX, p. 170, and the brilliant paper of M. Duguit in the *Revue d' Economie Politique,* 1894, p. 38. Mr. Barker in his *Political Thought from Spencer to Today,* pp. 180-182, has noted the modern attitude to this problem. See also Mr. H. A. L. Fisher's classic lecture on *Political Unions.*

INDEX

INDEX

A

Acton (Lord), on continuity of political thought, 64; on the authority of the State, 121; his theory of liberty, 168 f.; his dislike of W. G. Ward's attitude, 171; condemns the Ultramontanes, 172; journalistic experience, 173; his view of the Catholic situation in England, 174; on papal infallibility, 180; corrects Mr. Gladstone's history, 191.

Allies (T. W.), attacks royal supremacy, 105.

American constitution, sanctity of, 22; based on foundation of States, 277.

American Law, contribution of to theory of Church and State, 119.

Antonelli (Cardinal), attains power, 164-5; urged to withhold syllabus, 178; refuses assistance to Bismarck, 246; supports the German centre, 251-2.

Aquinas (S. Thomas), his attitude to unity, 2.

Aristotle, his theory of the State pragmatist, 18.

Arnold (T.), his theory of a generalised Christianity, 71; difference between him and the Tractarians, 76; his argument against the admission of Jews to Parliament, 89.

Auchterarder case, 35.

Austin (J.), sponsors an omnicompetent State, 68.

B

Baddeley (Serjeant), asks for mandamus against Hampden's appointment, 99.

Barclay (W.), connection of his theory with that of Chalmers, 65.

Baumgarten, quoted, 260.

Bell (T.), his theory of Church powers, 46.

Bellarmine (Cardinal), his federalism, 65.

Bennett (W. J. E.), attacks royal supremacy, 104.

Bennigsen, quoted, 254.

Bentham (J.), desires dissolution of English Church, 69.

Birmingham (Bishop of), limits sovereignty of State to temporal affairs, 112.

Bishops (Catholic), on duty of obedience, 130.

Bismarck (O. von), reasons for kulturkampf, 8; his failure, 29; difference from De Maistre, 212; his religious views, 239-40; his theory of State, 240 f.; lacks sense of institutions, *ibid.;* makes State divine, 242 f.; his antipathy for Rome, 243 f.; source of his struggle with Rome, 245; his troubles with Poland, 246; nervous about empire, *ibid.;* friendship for Italy, 249; attacks the Poles, 250; pressure on Rome, 251; attacks centre, 252; on Church and State, 253 f.; on Polish problem, 255-6; Falk Laws, 257; allies himself with national liberals, 259; makes peace with Rome, 260; learns lesson of Canossa, 261 f.; relation to De Maistre, 263 f.

Bluntschli, quoted, 247.

Boniface VIII, his claims for Church, 2, 28, 50.

Book of Discipline, struggle over, 29-30.

Bowyer (Sir G.), on Wiseman pastoral, 151-2.

Bradley (F. H.), on pluralism as destruction of unity, 1; on pain, 7.

Bramhall (Bishop), attack on Presbyterianism, 49.

Brandeis (L. D.), quoted, 284.

Bright (J.), attacks religious attitude of Russell, 152-3.

Brougham (Lord), connection with Judicial Committee, 81; attacks privilege of Church, 89.

Bruce (A.), attitude to Presbyterian claims, 37.

Bryce (Viscount), quoted, 3.

Burke, argues for Catholic emancipation, 122.

Bull of Pius V, a cause of Catholic persecution, 138.

Burleigh (Lord Balfour of), quoted, 43.

Buchanan (R.), distinguishes Church and State, 47, 56.

Butler (Charles), view of papal power, 128-9, 131; his Gallican tendencies, 133.

C

Camoys (Lord), on Vaticanism, 191.

Canning (G.), advocates Catholic emancipation, 125-6; inserts oath in Grattan's bill, 130.

Capel (Monsignor), answers Mr. Gladstone, 194; his explanation of Vaticanism, 198-9; weakness of, 199-200.

Carlyle (A.), quoted, 162.

Cavour (Count), his ecclesiastical ideal, 164; destroys political foundations of Church, 211.

Catholic revival, place in the 19th century, 211.

Cecil (Lord Hugh), theory of Church and State, 110.

Centre party (German), character of, 248 f.

Chalmers (T.), accepts leadership of Free Church, 29; his theory of Church and State, 38-41; difference between Scottish and English establishments, 42-3.

Chesterton (G. K.), on logic, 23.

Church (R. W.), his account of the reception of Tract 90, 79; his theory of the Church, 87; thinks Church could depose kings, 93; his view of Hampden, 97; attacks Hampden's appointment as bishop, 98; protests against attitude to ritualists, 110.

Cicero, on secret of Roman success, 216.

Civil war (American), effect on theory of States' rights, 277.

Claim of Right summarised, 44, 48.

Clerk (Sir G.), theory of Church claims, 47.

Cockburn (Lord), judgment in Auchterarder case, 53.
Coleridge (S. T.), quoted, 22.
Combes (E.), on separation of Church and State, 8.
Congress, power of, limited, 267.
Cook (Dr.), theory of Church and State, 57-8.

D

Dante, his worship of unity, 1, 164.
Darwin (C.), destroys basis of old dogmas, 211.
Daubeny, foreshadows an Anglican revival, 70.
Dewey (J.), quoted, 20, 23.
Dicey (A. V.), his limitation on theory of Parliamentary sovereignty, 151; on consequences of Federalism, 267 f.; criticism of, 268-9; contradictory views of, 274; views Federalism as a step to unified government, 282.
Disruption, origin of, 34 f.
Dodsworth (W.), reasons for conversion to Rome, 107.
Dollinger (J. von), effect of his 'Pope and Council,' 181; excommunicated, 183; renews his acquaintance with Mr. Gladstone, 184.
Doyle (Bishop), on papal influence, 130; his casuistry, 136.
Drummond (H.), view on position of English Church, 103.

E

Exeter (Bishop of), distinguishes between moral and legal sovereignty of Parliament, 111.

F

Faguet (E.), quoted, 213, 224.
Faithfull (J.), identifies Church and State, 88-9.
Federalism, is weak and conservative, 268; value of, 270 f.; spirit of, 275; regarded as a *pis aller*, 283.
Figgis (J. N.), quoted, 27, 49, 208.
France, attitude to congregations, 63, 67; failure of centralisation in, 279.
Froude (J. A.), quoted, 87.
Froude (R. H.), hates Erastianism, 74; compared to W. G. Ward, 79; nature of his mind, 139.
Fullerton (Lord), dictum in Court of Session, 56.

G

Germany, attitude to State-necessity in, 22; success of local self-government, 279.
Gerson, opposes Ultramontanism, 28.
Gierke (O. von), quoted, 5.
Gillies (Lord), denies possibility of contract between Church and State, 52-3.
Gladstone (W. E.), on Vatican Council, 7; on Newman's conversion, 80; on Gorham decision, 81, 101; on Ecclesiastical Titles Act, 153; repeals it, 155; visit to Dollinger, 184; attack on Syllabus, 185; on meaning of papal infallibility, 186; his deductions from it, 187 f.; their fallacies, 189 f.
Golightly (Rev. W.), urges Newman to attack established church, 95.

Gonsalvi (Cardinal), visits England, 134.
Gorham (G.), connection with Oxford Movement, 81.
Graham (Sir J.), repudiates Presbyterian claims, 37, 58 f.; his theory of Church property, 76.
Grattan (H.), persistent advocacy of Catholic cause, 122.
Gray (J. C.), quoted, 17.
Great Britain, right in American War of Independence on monistic theory of State, 23; failure of centralisation in, 279.
Gregory VII, his theory of Church and State, 2, 28, 50.
Greville (Charles), expects reform of English Church, 71.
Grey (Lord), reforms Irish Church, 72; warns English Church, 88.
Groups, separate life of, 271; personality of primary, 272; differences of valuable, 273.

H

Hallam (A.), on performance of 'King John,' 134.
Hampden (Bishop), appointed Regius Professor of Divinity, 77; revenge for criticism, 79; appointed a bishop, 80; represents broadest latitudinarianism, 97.
Harcourt (Sir W.), his Erastianism, 112.
Harrison (F.), on nature of allegiance, 200.
Hegel (G. W. F.), dominance of his philosophy, 6; his omnicompetent state, 67.
Henry VIII, his imperialism, 2; his thirst for power, 138.
Hickes (Bishop), on non-resistance, 2.
Hobbes (T.), hatred of corporations, 8; of dissension, 25; on Papacy, 137.
Hobhouse (J. C.), his theory of Church property, 77.
Hohenlohe (Prince), against papal infallibility, 181; suspects Bismarck of alliance with Jesuits, 245.
Horsley (Bishop), his protest against Erastianism, 85.
Hume (D.), on public opinion, 163.
Hume (J.), theory of Church as civil institution, 89-90.

I

Inglis (Sir R. H.), the pattern of High Churchmen, 75.
Innes (A. Taylor), answers Manning, 50.
Interstate Commerce Commission, value of, 281.

J

Jacobites, hate Presbyterianism, 33.
James (W.), quoted, 1.
Jeffrey (Lord), judgment in Auchterarder case, 62 f.
Jesuits, their theory like that of Chalmers, 65-6; revived power of, 164-5; may not enter England, 135; uphold papal infallibility, 177; enthusiasm for the dogma, 180; influence in Poland, 246.

K

Keble (J.), his Assize Sermon, 73; unites with Newman, 74; stays in Anglican Church, 80; on Church's right to reform itself, 86; attack on Gorham judgment, 103.
Kinnoull (Lord), relation to Disruption, 35 f., 63.
Knox (J.), his conception of Church power, 30; result of his nationalism, 37; desires to found a theocracy, 49.
Korkunov (N. M.), quoted, 16.

L

Lamartine (A.), quoted, 232.
Law, nature of, 13; sanctions of, 14.
Lecky (W. H.), on extent of Romeward movement, 141.
Leslie (Charles), attacks Presbyterianism, 49.
Liebknecht (K.), different view of State from Kaiser, 21.
Lisle (A. de), on dangers of Vaticanism, 193.
Liverpool (Lord), theory of English government, 124.
Llandaff (Bishop of), opposes Catholic emancipation, 124.
Lloyd (Bishop), complains of impotence of Church, 90.
Lolme (J. de), quoted, 267.
Lotze (H.), argues that pluralism means impenetrability, 6.
Louis XVI, pays penalty for errors of his predecessors, 14.
Luther, his thought related to that of Disruption, 65; his Erastianism, 66.

M

Macaulay (Lord), quoted, 33, 51.
Mackenzie (Lord), opinion in Auchterarder case, 53.
McGill (Professor), quoted, 41.
Mackonochie (Father), pleads for free church, 109.
Maistre (J. de), character, 211; seeming difference from Bismarck, 212; thought of, 213; desires a reconstruction of society, 214; theory of State, 215; value of political mysticism, 216; necessity of authority, 217; opposes variations, 219; hatred of Protestantism, 220-1; criticism of his attitude, 222-4; defence of papalism, 225 f.; of despotism, 227 f.; value of Papacy, 229 f.; his theory of schism, 230; attacks 18th century, 231; examination of his doctrines, 232 f.; author of modern Ultramontanism, 238; comparison with Bismarck, 263 f.
Maitland (F. W.), quoted, 4, 279.
Manning (Cardinal H. E.), erroneous view of Presbyterianism, 50; conversion to Rome, 82; on royal supremacy, 102; on corporate completeness of English Church, 105; view of Mr. Gladstone's compromise, 106; on English Reformation, 107; belief in intellectual captivity, 173; efforts for papal infallibility, 180; answer to Mr. Gladstone, 190; on Vaticanism, 194 f.; weakness of his arguments, 196-7.
Marvell (A.), on pushpin theology, 123.

Maskell (W.), attitude in Gorham case, 102.
Maule (F.), defends Presbyterian Church, 48.
Meadowbank (Lord), theory of Church and State, 54.
Medwyn (Lord), theory of Church and State, 61.
Melville (A.), theory of two kingdoms, 49.
Mill (James), his plan of Church reform, 71.
Milner, sign of revived religious feeling in Anglican Church, 70.
Milner (Bishop), opposes oaths of allegiance, 131-3; is firm Ultramontane, 134.
Mohler, influence of his 'Symbolik,' 140; helps Roman Catholics in England, 156.
Moncrieff (Lord), opposes lay patronage, 35; denies the derivation of Church from State, 42.
Montalembert, his reputation, 139; on 'Church and State,' 178.
Morley (Lord), quoted, 80, 86, 153.

N

Nationalism, dominant political theory in America, 278.
National education, justification for, 18.
Neale (J. M.), attacks Gorham judgment, 104.
Newman (J. H.), attack on Parliamentary sovereignty, 13; his anger against the Liberals, 73; compelled to resist State, *ibid.;* forms association of friends of the Church, 74; notes beginning of Roman problem, 79; is converted to Rome, 80; his hatred of Jerusalem archbishopric, 90-1; feels that State has deserted Church, 96; reproach against Church as merely an establishment, 109; comparison with Chalmers, 113 f.; was fighting a medieval battle, 115-6; his sense of the reality of corporate personality, 117; influence of his visit to Rome, 140; on nature of Church and State, 155 f.; historical relation of his theory to that of the early church, 160-1; his attitude marks the end of the anti-Hildebrandine reaction, 163; his implicit liberalism, 174; wavering views of, 175; hatred of extreme Ultramontanism, 175-6; minimises the Syllabus, 178-9; fears of papal infallibility, 181-2; reply to Mr. Gladstone, 201 f.; theory of sovereignty, 203 f.; on importance of conscience, 205; discussion of his view, 206-7.
North British Review, quoted, 51.
Norwich (Bishop of), on divided allegiance of Catholics, 123.

O

Oakeley (Canon), defends Vaticanism, 193.
O'Connell (D.), on militant agitation, 123; repudiates claim of Pope to temporal allegiance, 129; repudiates oaths, 131; on Catholic democracy, 140.
O'Hanlon (Dr.), on nature of teaching at Maynooth, 129.
Ossory (Bishop of), reason for opposing Catholic emancipation, 124.

P

Palmer (Sir W.), joins Association of Friends of Church, 74; promotes address to Archbishop of Canterbury, 96.
Palmieri, his attitude to sovereignty, 65.
Papacy, change in character after 1846, 164.
Parnell (Sir H.), sums up Catholic case, 122.
'Parmenides,' shows difficulty of problem of unity, 3.
Patronage (lay) abolished, 31; restored, 33; relation to Church freedom, 35.
Peel (Sir R.), opposes Catholic emancipation, 8; repudiates Presbyterian claims, 37; on established churches, 58; on Church property, 77.
Petre (Henry), on Vaticanism, 191.
Philpotts (Bishop) and Gorham case, 81; protests against Church Discipline Bill, 100; renounces communion with Archbishop of Canterbury, 102.
Pius IX, abandons liberalism, 164; imprisons Madeai, 165; promulgates dogma of Immaculate conception, *ibid.;* issues Encyclical *Quanta Cura* and Syllabus, 177; summons General Council, 179; futility of his claims, 190.
Plunkett (Lord), advocates Catholic emancipation, 125, 132; on constitutional principles, 136; quoted, 137.
Pound (Roscoe), on need for pragmatic theory of law, 64.
Privy Council, failure of as Church tribunal, 13.
Pusey (E. B.), suspended from preaching in Oxford, 79; stays in Anglican Church, 80; view of Hampden's appointment, 99; of Gorham case, 101; on ecclesiastical authority, 102.

Q

Queen Victoria, resents Wiseman's Pastoral, 163.

R

Reformation, character of, 27.
Reilly (F.), on Vaticanism, 192.
Religious toleration, justification for, 18.
Richard II, on source of law, 2.
Rickards (H.), on need of Church freedom, 96.
Right, a term with double implication, 20.
Roebuck (J.), answers Russell on hierarchy, 149; on danger of intolerance, 152.
Roman law, influence of its revived study, 162.
Rome, fear of in England, 138.
Rose (H. J.), edits *British Magazine,* 74.
Rosmini, failure of, 164; condemned, 165.
Rossi (Count), murdered, 164.
Rousseau, value of his terminology, 8, 13.
Rutherford (T.), argument to Court of Session, 45-6.
Rutherford, on nature of Church, 45.
Russell (Lord J.), proposes to confiscate Church funds, 72; on

Church as national institution, 76; makes Hampden a bishop, 80; sends envoy to Rome, 145; his Durham letter, 146; his intolerance, 147.

S

Schlegel (F.), converted to Rome, 69; his reputation, 139.
Schneegans (F.), quoted, 248.
Schrader (Father), view on Immaculate Conception, 281.
Session (Court of), its theory of Church and State, 36.
Simeon (C.), as factor in Anglican revival, 70.
Smith (Sidney), refutes case against Catholic Emancipation, 126 f.
South African War, as patriotic test of morality, 22.
South Wales Miners, disobey Act of Parliament, 12, 19.
Spain, its attack on Netherlands justified on monist theory of State, 23.
States, desire to override their opinion in America, 281.
Stuarts, fallacy of their theory of divine right, 2.
Suffragists, oppose State, 12.
Supreme Court of U. S., its limited power, 217.

T

Tablet, quoted, 51.
Talbot (G. J.), attacks Privy Council as Church tribunal, 154.
Tarquini, his theory of sovereignty, 65.
Thirlwall (C.), on Vaticanism, 193.
Tocqueville (A. de), on importance of England for religious freedom, 154.
Tractarianism, relation to romantic movement, 69.
Tracts for the Times, their theory, 83 f.; plead for Church freedom, 94 f.; their living character, 108.
Treitschke (H. von), popularity, 6; quoted, 248, 250; his theory of the State, 262.
Tudors, found a despotism on popular consent, 2.

U

Ulster Unionists, attitude to State, 12.
Union (act of), relation to Church, 32.

V

Vicars, apostolic, declare their loyalty to crown, 128.
Voltaire, on Holy Roman empire, 284.

W

Wade (J.), author of 'Black Book,' 69.
Wallas (G.), quoted, 14, 19.
Ward (W.), on Wiseman's influence, 140.
Ward (W. G.), joins Oxford Movement, 79; converted to Rome, 80; love of papal bulls, 165; his ideal of European organisation, 167; puzzled by Newman, 176; accepts Syllabus as infallible, 179; on value of theocracy, 193.

Welsh (Dr.), action at General Assembly of 1843, 29.
Whately (Archbishop), influence on Newman, 85.
Whitgift (Archbishop), attitude to Presbyterianism, 65 f.
Wilberforce (S.), quoted, 88.
Wilberforce (W.), part in Anglican revival, 70.
William II (of Germany), different view of State from Liebknecht, 21.
Wiseman (Cardinal N.), arrives on mission to England, 78; his social ability, 139; becomes leader of English Catholics, 140; plans hierarchy, 141; attacked for his pastoral, 143 f.; his reply, 145 f.
Worcester (Bishop of), opposes Catholic emancipation, 123.

Y

Young (R.), presented to living of Auchterarder, 35 f., 63.